THE ROOSEVELT YEARS

European Papers in American History
SERIES EDITOR: DAVID K. ADAMS

The Roosevelt Years

New Perspectives on American History, 1933–1945

Edited by Robert A. Garson and Stuart S. Kidd

SERIES EDITOR: DAVID K. ADAMS

E P
A H

Edinburgh University Press

© Respective contributors, 1999

Edinburgh University Press
22 George Square, Edinburgh

Typeset in Janson Text by
Carnegie Publishing, Chatsworth Rd, Lancaster, and
printed and bound in Great Britain by
the University Press, Cambridge

A CIP record for this book is available from the British Library

ISBN 0 7486 1183 5

The right of the contributors to be identified
as authors of this work has been asserted
in accordance with the Copyright, Designs
and Patents Act 1988.

Contents

Notes on Contributors

Anthony J. Badger taught at Newcastle University from 1971 to 1991. Since 1992 he has been Paul Mellon Professor of American History at Cambridge University and a Fellow of Sidney Sussex College. He is the author of *Prosperity Road: The New Deal, Tobacco and North Carolina; North Carolina and the New Deal*; and *The New Deal and the Depression Years*. He is the editor, with Brian Ward, of *The Making of Martin Luther King and the Civil Rights Movement* and, with Walter Edgar and Jason Nordby Gretlund, *Southern Landscapes*.

Patricia Clavin is Senior Lecturer in Modern History in the Department of History at Keele University. She has published widely on the economic and diplomatic relations of western Europe and the USA, including *The Failure of Economic Diplomacy: Britain, France, Germany and the United States, 1931–1936*.

Gareth Davies teaches American politics and history at Lancaster University. His 1996 book, *From Opportunity to Entitlement: The Transformation and Decline of Great Society Liberalism*, was awarded the OAH's Ellis Hawley prize. His most recent publications have appeared in *Political Science Quarterly* and the *Journal of Policy History*. He is now working on a study of American politics during the 1970s.

Robert A. Garson is Head of Department and Director of the David Bruce Centre for American Studies at Keele University. He is the author of *The Democratic Party and the Politics of Sectionalism, 1941–48* and the *US and China Since 1949: A Troubled Affair*.

Leon Gordenker is Professor Emeritus of Politics and Research Associate of the Center of International Studies at Princeton University. He is the author of many books and articles on the United Nations and international organization generally.

Michaela Hönicke is a research and teaching fellow at the Kennedy Institute, Free University of Berlin. She wrote her Ph.D. thesis at the University of North Carolina on '"Know Your Enemy": American Interpretations and Representations of National Socialism, 1933–45'.

Clara Juncker is Associate Professor at Odense University, where she directs the Center for American Studies. She has published widely within the fields of 19th- and 20th-century American literature, African-American studies, southern literature, composition studies and literary theory.

Stuart Kidd is Director of American Studies at Reading University and the author of various essays on the history and culture of the USA during the 1930s. A monograph on the Farm Security Administration photographic project and the South will appear shortly.

S. Jay Kleinberg is Professor and Head of the Department of American Studies and History at Brunel University. She is the author of *The Shadow of the Mills* and *Women in the United States, 1830–1945*. She has written many articles on women, social welfare and families.

Jaap Kooijman is a Ph.D. candidate in American studies at the University of Amsterdam and a former research assistant at the Roosevelt Study Center in Middelburg. His research focuses on the American welfare state and national health insurance.

William E. Leuchtenburg is William Rand Kenan Professor of History at the University of North Carolina at Chapel Hill. His many books on the age of Roosevelt include *The Perils of Prosperity*; *Franklin D. Roosevelt and the New Deal* and *In the Shadow of FDR: From Harry Truman to Bill Clinton*.

Olaf Stieglitz studied history and philosophy at Cologne University and wrote his Ph.D. on the Civilian Conservation Corps. He is currently a teaching assistant in history at the University of Hamburg.

Margaret Walsh is Reader in American Economic and Social History at the University of Nottingham. Her research interests are the history of the long-distance bus industry in the United States, the American West and Women's Labour History.

Introduction

Robert A. Garson and Stuart S. Kidd

The years that enveloped the presidency of Franklin D. Roosevelt were ones of tumult, challenge and change not only in the United States but throughout the world. Franklin D. Roosevelt was inaugurated President of the United States on 4 March 1933. He inherited, at a conservative estimate, 13 million unemployed Americans, which amounted to 25 per cent of the workforce. This was symptomatic of an economy in crisis and one whose production, distribution and financial mechanisms were in disarray. In the international sphere, Roosevelt became president at a point when the international system was beginning to strain beneath the weight of dictatorship, militarism and trade rivalry, and which would eventually collapse into world war in 1939. Eighteen months earlier, in September 1931, Japan had invaded Manchuria, and in the same year that Roosevelt took office, Adolf Hitler assumed power in Germany. Roosevelt would be elected for an unprecedented four terms. None of his twelve years in office was free of either domestic economic problems or international turbulence. As late as 1939, 17 per cent of the American workforce remained unemployed. The war that began in September 1939 would wreak unimaginable misery world-wide and consume nearly 300,000 American lives by the time it had run its course. Although Roosevelt died before the Allied victory was secured, the shape of new orders, both international and domestic, were already clearly discernible in a myriad of forms. A new international system was being forged while war still raged; the American economy had outstripped all previous levels of production, unemployment was virtually eliminated, and a new capitalist order was emerging out of the wartime experience; regulatory and welfare legislation passed by the New Deal remained on the statute books, and the nature and character of institutions such as labour unions, banks and the presidential office itself had changed considerably since FDR had first assumed office in 1933.

The epic contexts of the Roosevelt years, as much as FDR's own responses to them, continue to intrigue historians. In particular, the New Deal retains a currency and a relevance that is compelling for historians who are able to relate past and present through issues such as unemployment, social welfare and federal regulation. Such crossroads between an authorial present and a subject rooted in the past has produced a rich historiography which befits a figure so dominant in his age and a programme so influential. To some degree, historical interpretation has echoed the partisanship expressed in the 1930s. However, it has also been vitalized by new discoveries through archival research, the application of new methodologies and perspectives, and the shifting socio-political and economic contexts in which historians work.

The purpose of the current volume is to reassess selected crucial areas of public policy and culture in the 1930s and to draw readers' attention to some recent developments in historical interpretation and, equally, to some neglected areas of historical research. It represents an international effort to bring together recent scholarship on a number of diverse issues and it is fitting that such a collective endeavour took place at the Roosevelt Study Center in Middelburg, the Netherlands, Europe's leading centre of Roosevelt studies. It is equally appropriate that the colloquium around which these essays revolve was convened by the David Bruce Centre to mark the retirement of one of the pioneers of American Studies in Europe and one of Britain's most persistent and missionary Roosevelt scholars, Professor David Adams.

The range of many essays in the volume is not confined to the 1930s and they alert us to the artificiality or limitations of periodization either in terms of the New Deal or Roosevelt's term of office. Certain ideas related to women, young people, ethnic minorities and the value of work, were well-established before Roosevelt became president, and the New Deal was frequently influenced by them. Similarly, federal regulation and responsibility for social welfare were not new concepts in the 1930s, despite the Roosevelt administration's commitment to them. A corpus of federal legislation and practice had accumulated since the 1880s, especially during the Progressive era, which influenced New Dealers' ideas about political economy in particular. If the New Deal's origins cannot be located solely in the 1930s, neither can its significance be restricted to the Depression decade. As several essays remind us, the New Deal remained influential long after Roosevelt's death. It would have a global impact through the efforts of a 'New Deal elite' responsible for foreign policy formulation in the post-war era, and on the domestic scene it flourished for a time in the unlikeliest of places. It may seem anomalous that two essays in the volume explore the possibility that the white South has acted as a custodian of the New Deal in the second half of the twentieth century. By locating the Roosevelt era within a broader temporal framework it is not the intention to reduce its work to a punctuation mark in the syntax of reform or international relations in twentieth-century America. On the contrary, the long-term perspective enables historians to ascertain with more confidence the very significance of the domestic and foreign policy of Roosevelt's administrations.

Those historians who have described the New Deal as a watershed in twentieth-century American development have proclaimed the Roosevelt administration's commitment to economic management and regulation as marking a break with the prevailing political economy of the United States. However, as Margaret Walsh reminds us, state economic intervention during the 1930s was not clear-cut in either project or purpose. In her exploration of public policy and transport, a much neglected aspect of the New Deal, Walsh finds that a rational policy for transportation was affected by a number of variables which made a holistic approach impossible to achieve. In the short-term, the crises of depression and global war introduced factors into public policy-making which were expedient and which struggled to take account of long-term structural and technological forces involving the emergence of the truck, motor car and aviation modes of transport and the decline of the railroads. Equally, the preoccupations of the Progressive era, particularly with monopoly, continued to engage regulators in the 1930s and served to constrain them. However, as her references to the academic and political advocates of deregulation of the last two decades suggest, the New Deal's idealistic transport planners appeared to some contemporaries as anachronistic as those New Dealers who supported a holistic industrial planning under the National Recovery Administration.

For historians writing about the Depression decade four decades ago, the New Deal and Franklin D. Roosevelt were virtually synonymous. The assumption was that FDR was the inspiration, if not the author, of much of the New Deal, and efforts were made to trace antecedents of the New Deal programme in Roosevelt's experience and background. More recently, the 'great man' theory of history has become unfashionable and historians have become wary of the hagiographical pitfalls of biographical approaches to explain decisive historical developments. The New Deal tends now to be regarded as a product of the collective, if disparate, efforts of administration heads, committed congressmen, agency workers, and private interest groups, or as a stage in the process of capitalist development in which the state's relationships with the economic system and with social formation are of prime importance. In either case, the tendency is to relegate the role of Roosevelt to that of 'broker'; but as the two essays on social insurance remind us, the chief executive's support for legislation was often crucial and FDR played a major role in determining the nature of the New Deal's agenda and its priorities.

Both Jaap Kooijman and Gareth Davies outline the political deftness of Roosevelt and the New Dealers in pursuit of their policy objectives.

Despite differences of emphasis in their interpretations of the signi-ficance of the Roosevelt administration's attitudes to social insurance, both authors assert that the New Dealers had an autonomous agenda and a strong sense of purpose. While both essays stress New Dealers' sensitivity to the opposition which social security provision attracted – whether from the courts, conservative Republicans, private interest groups, or entrenched regional groups – neither writer subscribes to the 'broker politics' thesis.

Kooijman seeks to dispel the widely-held belief that the American Medical Association was instrumental in ensuring that national health insurance was not enacted by the New Deal. He contends that while Roosevelt expediently kept all options open, his preference was to expand medical provision rather than to introduce compulsory health insurance and, ultimately, his actions were determined by what he thought was desirable and feasible. Political manoeuvre and Roosevelt's public ambiguity over health insurance were strategies to ensure flex-ibility for the administration, in case public opinion developed in a contrary direction. Conversely, Gareth Davies' mapping of the political context of the old-age insurance provisions of the Social Security Act of 1935 suggests that the New Dealers employed political manoeuvre to secure their objectives. Davies takes issue with scholars who have claimed that the measure was compromised by caution and bias. The compromises and concessions that New Dealers felt obliged to make were recognitions of the political realities and constitutional uncer-tainties of securing successful passage and implementation of a monumental and innovative liberal proposal. As such, the emphasis of Davies' treatment is that the sponsors' apparent caution is not so much a reflection of their limited ideological or political vision but of their commitment to social security and their determination to overcome powerful obstacles. 'Broker politics' thus became a means to an end, rather than an end in itself, whether to obscure the administration's uncertainty about health insurance or to effect successfully old-age insurance.

The divergent interpretations of Davies and Kooijman to Roosevelt's attitudes to welfare recall the historical disputes of the late 1960s and early 1970s when the significance of the New Deal was contested terrain between the 'liberal establishment' and the 'New Left'. Echoes of both positions are discernible in the volume. William Leuchtenburg's ongoing interest in the Roosevelt legacy is expressed in his analysis of the strength of Roosevelt's influence on the United States' current President, William J. Clinton, and his admiration for the New Deal tradition is evident in his disappointment that the 'shadow' of FDR appears to be fading while it is lengthening with time. Anthony Badger, on the other hand, adds to the New Deal's contemporaneous lustre by identifying a liberal element in the Roosevelt political coalition which is frequently ignored by historians. The Democratic South is often regarded as being at odds with the electoral realignment begun by Al Smith in 1928, and which was consummated by the Depression, the New Deal, and Roosevelt's political appeal. Although the South remained an important element of the Democratic coalition which elected FDR for an unprecedented four terms, white southerners made strange bedfellows with the urban, blue-collar, immigrant and ethnic voters who constituted 'the revolt of the city' which transformed the Democrats into the nation's natural majority party. However, Badger reaches beyond traditional illustrations of the South's role in the bipartisan conservative coalition, which checked the New Deal after 1936, and of the failed 'purge' of 1938, whereby FDR sought to challenge the entrenched conservatism of the region. Rather, he contends that the record of the Roosevelt administration in producing a 'new generation' of liberal southerners is commendable and he argues that the liberal impulse in the South was not suppressed until the 1950s when the race issue began to assume such prominence in southern politics and when the shortcomings of the 'new generation's' views of race relations were truly revealed. Nevertheless, Badger claims, at least one white southerner would not only protect the New Deal's legacy but expand it during his presidential years. That person was Lyndon B. Johnson of Texas.

While the essays of Badger and Leuchtenburg clearly assume that the New Deal is the benchmark of good political practice, others are more sceptical and the contributions of Jay Kleinberg, Clara Juncker, and Olaf Stieglitz may appear to echo the New Left's critique. However, there are crucial differences between the work of these scholars and their counterparts of the 1960s and 1970s. They do not attempt to synthesize the New Deal but focus on a single issue, whether women or youth. As such, their dissenting and critical scholarship may be viewed as refracting the fragmentation of the Left into single issue groups since the 1960s. Neither is it their main purpose to provide a critique of state policy as it applied to their subjects, although Kleinberg clearly indicts the New Deal for its policy towards women and widows. Their points of reference or discourses differ from traditional academic analysis with its focus on the nature and effectiveness of state policy. These authors are more concerned with reconstructing the histories of the constituencies that the New Deal intended to serve and they engage with ideology, value systems, and cultural representation as well as public policy.

Taking issue with Davies' opinion about the momentousness of the Social Security Act, Kleinberg contends that it was based on 'maternalist values' and that it 'gendered' economic participation. By providing widows with assistance rather than work relief, the New Deal applied pre-existing notions of the roles of women in society to this group. The viewpoint is reinforced by Juncker's exploration of representations of women by radical writers in the *Masses* and the *New Masses*. Her essay traverses the historical period from the Progressive era to the New Deal and provides an historical context for an appreciation of the development of female stereotypes by the Left before the 1930s. Not only does Juncker provide evidence that gender stereotyping was deeply engrained in the culture of the period but, alongside Kleinberg, reinforces the view that even the most enlightened intentions could have negative consequences when they were based on *a priori* sexist assumptions. These cultural references also have relevance to African-Americans. Although this group does not form the exclusive subject of a particular essay, the intersection of race and gender had pernicious effects in some of the New Deal's welfare initiatives, as Kleinberg makes clear in her analysis of widows' welfare. An implicit assumption in these essays on women is that, to appreciate the impact of the New Deal on them, one must understand their own lived experiences and the ways in which American culture defined gender roles.

Olaf Stieglitz makes an explicit appeal on behalf of the study of generational history that would move beyond conventional assessments of the impact of New Deal policy on young people. He concludes his survey of the historical literature relating to the Civilian Conservation Corps and the National Youth Administration by calling for historical perspectives that transcend the narrow confines of state policy and that explore the lived experience of youth during the 1930s. His concern is not to valorize the New Deal's programmes for youth so much as to identify how state policy intersected and interacted with the culture of young people during the Depression decade. While teenage gangs, adolescent fashion and youth culture may occupy a less rarified plane than cabinet meetings and congressional committee hearings, they do register lived realities of the Roosevelt era that are as significant, if less traditionally privileged, as those of the policy formulators of the New Deal itself. Stieglitz's concern is to broaden the compass of the consideration of the New Deal and youth and to incorporate discourses about young people that have apparently limited relevance to state policy. As such, his contribution, like those of Kleinberg and Juncker, has an interdisciplinary character.

The nature of the American state during the New Deal period has been of interest to both historians and political scientists since the 1960s. Complex relationships have been charted between the federal government and the business community, labour unions and other private interest groups which throw light on the aims and origins of the New Deal's programmes and the character of the policy-formulation process. Some scholars have utilized the concept of 'state capacity' to understand the *modus operandi* of the New Deal and have explained the success and failure of various programmes in terms of the existence of an adequate administrative and bureaucratic apparatus to implement them successfully. This 'state apparatus' provides the theme for the essays of Stuart Kidd and Leon Gordenker, despite their divergent domestic and international concerns.

Stuart Kidd's study of the administrative politics of one of the New Deal's 'cultural projects' suggests the amount of latitude available to administrators in an era of burgeoning state capacity. Unlike some recent scholarship by cultural historians, he rejects the notion that the Farm Security Administration's photographic project was driven by any grand ideological design or sub-text. Rather it exemplifies how the New Deal provided scope to creative administrators to pursue personal objectives and to aggrandize their own status and spheres of influence. However, as the experience of the Historical Section of the FSA suggests, the latitude available to bureaucrats in the New Deal's information and cultural programmes was proscribed by the political realities of the federal system within which the New Deal administratively operated and by bureaucratic accountability and the need to be seen to serve the socio-economic objectives of parent programmes. While Kidd suggests how a New Deal order was promoted at the very peripheries of agencies responsible for domestic policy, Leon Gordenker focuses on the influence of the New Deal on the upper echelons of international policy-makers. Gordenker contends that in the post-war planning exercise that consumed the attention of the State Department, the architects of a new international order drew on domestic models of governance. Although the planners themselves were inspired by the New Deal, the planning process itself was removed from the hurly-burly of politics and was, essentially, an activity conducted by a small select elite. No criticism is implied by the author of this arrangement. The gist of his essay is that just and productive institutions – indeed, the very globalization of the New Deal order and ethos – could emerge without the pressures of the democratic process.

The planning process described by Michaela Hönicke in her appraisal of the response to Henry Morgenthau Jr.'s programme for Germany after the war's end is of a very different order. The debate is more public and deeply contentious, with governmental departments and their secretaries not only being at odds over Morgenthau's proposals, but indulging in personal vendettas, misrepresentations, distortions, evasions and outright prejudice. Hönicke is sympathetic to Morgenthau and his draconian proposals. She claims that he did not want a Carthaginian peace for its own sake and that his detractors failed to grasp the real meaning of Hitler's war and practically denied the moral enormity of the Holocaust. In one respect she does reinforce Gordenker's argument, for she contends that Morgenthau's plan for post-war Germany followed the New Deal model in both its specific detail – such as the relationship between deindustrialization and trust-busting – and in its general ambition fundamentally to restructure German society so as to make it more democratic. However, she concludes that debate and disagreement had a positive dimension because they allowed pragmatic solutions to prevail over doctrine and, hence, facilitated reconciliation with the enemy. For her, an elite at odds with itself had desirable outcomes in terms of policy-making.

Patricia Clavin's essay examines an earlier period. She does not find a closed policy-making network, dominated by an elite, but a complex process that was sensitive to the fact that the world's leading powers lacked the political will to cooperate in the early throes of the Depression. She moves external affairs to the central stage. While she does not dismiss domestic considerations as a formative element, she suggests that foreign policy is primarily shaped by evaluations of the external world. The external world after 1918 emphasized national, not international, economic obligations. It was in marked contrast to the focus on international institutions that characterized the creation of new political and economic orders after 1945. Roosevelt's famous 'bombshell message', which torpedoed the World Economic Conference in 1933, is not seen as the act of an inward-looking economic vandal, but as a rational response to the nationalistic agendas of the European powers. In Calvin's view, FDR issued a *coup de grace* that was inevitable in the scramble for financial advantage, particularly through resolution of the war debts issue. Domestic recovery strategy was important, but it was not the exclusive concern.

American economic nationalism during the 1930s was celebrated by many contemporaries, including the historian, Charles A. Beard, who called for an 'Open Door at Home'. It has also enabled many of Beard's successors to contrast the American response to economic crisis with those of European states. By counterpointing the conservative and, sometimes, totalitarian responses of European nations to the progressive, democratic and innovative response of the United States, the New Deal became for many American liberals of the 1950s a triumphal symbol of American nationalism in the context of Cold War. However, at the turn of the century, the New Deal does not readily lend itself to such patriotic celebrations in the age of *glasnost* and the global economy.

For historians of the 1950s and the 1960s the New Deal's significance was almost self-evident. The New Deal had endured to become the crucial and inviolate centrepiece of the United States' political economy and welfare system. Most New Deal reforms had survived the death of Roosevelt, the end of the Depression, the distractions of a Cold War context, and the administrations of the Republican, Dwight D. Eisenhower. Moreover, the New Deal's original framework had been supplemented by Roosevelt's liberal, Democratic Party successors, Harry S. Truman, John F. Kennedy and Lyndon B. Johnson, to include aspects such as civil rights, federal aid to education, health insurance and urban planning. However, since the late 1970s the New Deal order has not appeared so secure. Many consider the New Deal no longer relevant to the United States' post-industrial economy and to the solution of economic problems, where high rates of inflation are coupled with high rates of unemployment, and which defy deficit spending, counter-recession strategies. The very expression 'big government' has become a term of opprobrium in many circles. While liberals' commitment to the concept of a strong state was weakened, in particular, by the Vietnam War and the Watergate affair, conservative Americans resented many of the accomplishments of liberal reform during the 1960s and the culture of permissive license with which liberalism appeared to be associated. The emergence of the 'New Right' during the 1970s challenged liberal assumptions about economic management and the 'welfare culture' which the New Deal had spawned, and during the administrations of Ronald R. Reagan the federal government began to dismantle the New Deal order, an unthinkable development for previous generations. This is the point of reference from which William Leuchtenburg writes the volume's concluding essay.

A beneficiary of National Youth Administration assistance during the Depression, Leuchtenburg was to become one of the major figures who shaped historical understanding of the New Deal during the 1960s. Alongside Arthur M. Schlesinger Jr. and Frank Friedel, Leuchtenburg proclaimed the desirability of the activist and compassionate state. In his essay for this volume he is concerned to ascertain the currency of the Roosevelt tradition during the presidency of the first Democrat to occupy the office since 1981 and the only Democrat to be elected for two terms since FDR. He is disappointed by Bill Clinton and finds that his association with Roosevelt is merely symbolic, theatrical and expedient. If neo-liberalism is the progeny of the New Deal, then the child appears to have disavowed its parent. However, in the face of all the rhetorical and cultural reductivism which Leuchtenburg reveals is the lot of FDR's legacy, he still believes that the underlying principles of the programme for which Roosevelt strove, although muted, are not extinct.

The essays in the volume, then, cover a diverse range of aspects and a broad historical period which regards the Roosevelt era as having a broader compass than the years 1933 to 1945. Inevitably, there is much that is missing in the table of contents. The history of labour,

African-Americans, financial and monetary policy, the histories of political institutions, Roosevelt's responses to the 'isolationist impulse' are but a few important topics which are neglected. Such structural absences, of course, signal the scope of the work of the Roosevelt administration which will, in itself, ensure continued scholarly interest regardless of the current political status of Roosevelt's legacy. The purpose of the essays that follow is not to provide a comprehensive appraisal of the Roosevelt's America but to open a few important windows on the era which, we hope, will reveal some of its essence.

2

In Whose Interest? Public Policy and Transport during Depression and War

Margaret Walsh

A curious notion has gained considerable vogue of late. It is that if government officials spend most of their time on any particular subject for a considerable period, their minds become warped or otherwise afflicted, so that they are unable to deal appropriately or adequately with any new subject. The Interstate Commerce Commission in particular has been the victim of this notion. It is charged with being 'railroad-minded', and hence unable to grasp and master the problems of boats, airplanes and motor trucks and buses.[1]

This was the opinion of Joseph B. Eastman, Commissioner of the Interstate Commerce Commission (ICC) and former Federal Coordinator of Transportation, when speaking in 1937 about the Motor Carrier Act (MCA) passed two years earlier. He knew that the origin or first wave of transport regulation, 1887–1917, lay in protection of the public from railroad monopoly and abuse of power.[2] He was, however, also aware that technology in the shape of the automobile, bus, truck, aeroplane, boat and pipeline had created competition. Though notions of monopoly control still loomed large in the American psyche, regulation in the public interest might now have to take cognizance of coordination and cooperation between and within different modes.[3] Yet there was a further complication. The nation was experiencing its worst ever depression and competition was threatening stability. This encouraged government legislators and officials to consider that regulation of competition might create both a fairer and an integrated transport system.

In the 1930s and for a period after the war, the government, its advisers and many outside observers deemed that the second wave of regulation then established was reasonably effective. Yet rising consumer power in the 1950s, further technological advances and then more difficulties in the economy in the 1970s created a context in which this regulation was not merely judged inadequate, but basically flawed. In the 1960s the regulated sectors, of which transport was but one, faced many problems. Shortages, surpluses, inefficiencies, inequalities and even delays in the regulatory process itself aroused political, economic and academic opposition to federal intervention. Consequently a third wave of regulatory legislation emerged, peaking in the late 1970s. For the economy at large these reforms, better known as deregulation, left many markets more competitive, but still partially controlled. In general, since the late 1970s, transport has operated within a framework of minimal intervention where the public or consumer interest was protected by private competition both within and between different modes.[4]

In reassessing public policy towards transport in the 1930s and during World War II, or during the major part of the second wave of regulation, interpretations have varied widely. Writers have approached the subject not only from the perspectives of different generations, but also from a range of disciplines and as specific pressure groups. Two key concepts, the 'public interest' and the 'capture thesis' which have concerned all analysts were highlighted in Tom McCraw's classic survey of the literature.[5] In the ensuing twenty years analysts have paid more attention to the 'capture' image, but the 'public interest' has remained a contested terrain.[6]

Prior to the 1950s the prevailing view in historical writing was that regulation was in the 'public interest'. This concept was capable of multiple meanings. Most interpretations, however, accepted that society must be protected from the evils of monopoly pricing and the abuses of big business. Congress had thus established regulatory agencies which were staffed by experts acting in the common good. Commissioners were detached professionals who investigated problems, heard grievances and took decisions to protect the American people from the intrigues of forceful business groups. This style of regulation may have been weak in purpose, flawed in enforcement and complex in execution, but it was well-intentioned towards protecting the community interest.[7]

Scepticism about the neutrality of government regulators and about the basic structure of this intervention was visible even during the two liberal periods of dynamic regulatory management – Progressivism and the New Deal – but it was not until the 1950s that an alternative viewpoint was coherently developed. Then political scientists proposed private interest theories which, though differing, questioned the motives of both reformers and legislators. Of these theories, the life-cycle approach to regulatory agency was considered the most significant; namely in their youth commissions may well have monitored monopoly and oligopoly, but in their maturity they joined the industrial system. Effectively, the regulators were captured by the regulated groups.[8]

The 'capture thesis' gradually came to dominate academic evaluation. Gabriel Kolko, in particular, argued that both the railroads and big business protected their positions through influencing the passage of government legislation and through membership of regulatory commissions. Here 'capture' was visible not only in the maturity of an agency's life cycle, but throughout its existence.[9] As a conspiracy thesis 'capture' became popular with historians in the 1960s because it confirmed contemporaneous suspicions about government. Indeed, Kolko inspired 'a virtual cottage industry for New Left historians'. The regulation of business was by business, in the interest of business.[10]

The 'capture thesis' not only appealed to the Left. The economist, George Stigler, a member of the Chicago School, boosted the concept in 1971 when he wrote 'that as a rule, regulation is acquired by the industry and is designed and operated for its benefit'.[11] Other economists then placed Stigler's re-formulation of the 'capture thesis' in a broader context by considering both political and social explanations of regulatory policy. Such motivations might include career advancement within the agencies and government, enhanced professional standing and altruism.[12]

Political scientists also recognized the importance of individual incentives and changing preferences within a developing bureaucracy of regulation. There was no 'iron triangle' of influence linking each commission with the relevant congressional committee and an interest group in a firm and predictable pattern. Broadly based coalitions emerged, lobbied and worked with civil servants who in turn had their own agendas. Furthermore, both business and government groups recognized that socio-economic conditions were influenced by technology, prices, cultural values and judicial review.[13]

A more multi-faceted interpretation of regulation, especially in relation to transport, was also being developed by historians. Even before the end of the 1960s Robert Harbeson had sharply criticized Kolko's conspiracy thesis and in the early 1970s Albro Martin basically inverted it to suggest that politicians and commissioners rather than business were in command. Other historians contended that regulation arose from the conflicting demands of assorted groups, including those being subject to that regulation.[14] Pluralism then became the order of the day and case studies the means of establishing a general thesis of diversity.[15]

By the mid-1970s, however, with the American economy faltering after its post-war triumph, motives for regulation became less important than its impact on market operations. Noting serious financial problems in certain industries, particularly in the transport sector, economists claimed that commissions were inefficient. In 'the economist's hour' of the 1970s and 1980s they helped reshape the discussion of regulation in both academic and government circles. Developing the work of the Chicago School of Economics, they argued that a reduction or an elimination of restrictions would create a more efficient use of resources or greater responsiveness to consumer pressures. Deregulation fitted into the national mood of resentment against 'big government' which emerged from the opposition to the Vietnam War and the Watergate scandal. Both Democrats and Republicans increasingly favoured changing regulations and monitoring economic behaviour to allow more competition.[16]

Transport policy has always been a contentious area of government activity. In a nation whose predominant ideology is based on individualism and *laissez-faire* economics, there should be little or no government intervention in the private interest. The implied powers of the Constitution, however, have sanctioned support to assist postal communications and to secure defence and Americans have always been pragmatic enough to allow and to justify public enterprise, provided that the mix remained predominantly private. For example, the debate over 'internal improvements' eventually led to approval of subsidies for roads, waterways and railroads in the nineteenth century. Promotional aid still remained important in the twentieth century for the construction and operation of roads, waterways, airports and airways. By this time, however, regulation had secured a more prominent position. Abuse of power had become a major issue. The establishment and then strengthening of a regulatory commission, the ICC, had resolved several problems. Discrimination was now forbidden, rates were established, government orders were obeyed and regular accounting procedures were followed. Many observers considered that sound government policy in the interests of the shipping and travelling public had been achieved before the United States entered World War I.[17]

But the American economy was not static and the conditions of transport changed considerably in the post-war years. Even before 1917 railroads were offering poor service due to heavy over-capitalization, high competition and restricted earnings. In 1917, when trains failed to deliver an efficient service, the federal government took control of the railroads, enforced cooperation and financed the updating and operating of railroad plant.[18] Following this emergency experiment in management, the government returned the railroads to private ownership, but under different terms. The Transportation Act of 1920 aimed to improve the financial health and adequacy of transport by requiring coordination and cooperation rather than competition. The ICC's rate-making power was also altered to ensure that rates would bring a fair return to the rail industry as a whole. But this new ethos failed to work well. Railroad managers could not forget their older intra-modal competitive behaviour. Increased labour costs further threatened rail profitability.[19] But more importantly, despite a capital improvement programme, managers failed to respond successfully to the new intermodal road competition.

By 1929 there were 23,120,897 cars registered in the United States, providing a degree of geographical mobility for 56 per cent of American families. Not only did these vehicles allow easier and more widespread travel, but they took existing passengers from the trains. So too did motor buses. In the 1920s bus companies grew from pioneering operations linking local communities into regional networks offering both a business and leisure service. By 1930 railroads were carrying only 10.7 per cent of the volume of passenger traffic. They still retained 74.3 per cent of the total freight traffic because as yet trucks were either feeders for the rail network or they served local communities.[20]

The introduction and spread of viable road transport created a new environment for government intervention and management. Privately owned cars were regulated only in respect to safety and payment of licenses. Buses and trucks initially came under similar laws. Faced, however, by the rapid expansion of motor vehicles after World War I many state governments passed new legislation. Any vehicle user now paid a gasoline tax to help finance the construction and maintenance of highways. Vehicles registered as public conveyances were subject to more stringent laws concerned with economic issues such as competition and fares. Entrepreneurs and companies needed a certificate of 'convenience and necessity' to be in business. To gain it, existing operators had to show that they were financially sound enough to run a safe and adequate service throughout the year and that their rates were reasonable. New applicants had further to demonstrate that their service would not duplicate any existing transport service.[21]

By the mid-1920s the railroads, already in serious financial difficulties, expressed concern about the threat of road transport. Some rail companies had cooperated with buses and trucks and had even gone into ownership themselves to provide replacements for revenue-losing train services. Most, however, protested loudly to state governments about unfair competition. These complaints were already filtering upwards to the federal level, not only through lobbying activity and congressional hearings, but also through contested judicial decisions about the right of state governments to regulate inter-state carriers on economic issues such as quality of service and rates. Buses and trucks were no longer a local issue, but were becoming a national concern.[22]

The federal government reacted indecisively. A bill to regulate inter-state commerce by motor vehicles was introduced in 1925. This was the first of a series of forty bills to come before succeeding congresses during the next nine years. The main variations in these bills focused

on the separate regulation of buses and trucks and the designation of
the regulatory agency. On these issues neither Congress nor the ICC
and its officials, nor the various interest groups could agree. It took
the disastrous economic conditions of the 1930s to provide a climate
in which an alliance of strange bedfellows agreed to a pattern of
regulation in which coordination and cooperation was preferable to
ruinous competition.[23] Yet this legislation, important as it was, remained
partial. There would be no federal management of private automobiles
and the fledgling aeroplane was regarded as a separate category. The
critical agenda for transport policy in the 1930s was to bring order
and sense to public land transport.

The severe depression of the 1930s is crucial to an understanding
of transport policy in these years. Economic conditions adversely
affected all modes of transport, but the railroads were in the worst
predicament. The federal government thus initially provided financial
assistance to rail companies. This sectoral help was of no avail without
a full assessment of holistic transport policy, not only because of the
economic crisis, but also because of ongoing changes in motor and
aviation technology. Following debates at a variety of levels, the federal
government eventually attempted a national approach by regulating
all modes of public transport. Nevertheless it retained sectoral bias by
assisting some modes with subsidies. This mixed pattern of intervention
resolved some immediate problems and continued the dual legacy of
federal government promotion and regulation. It failed, however, to
take a long-term view of the transport sector as a whole and to grasp
the issues of coordination and competition. Involvement in World
War II brought yet another set of regulations in which emergencies
and shortages as well as legislation ensured some cooperation. But
neither the federal mediation of the 1930s nor of World War II
produced a transport system that was national and profitable. The war
certainly produced a public transport system which worked, but consumer demand was high and intersectoral competition was modified
by scarcity. When the economic and institutional crises of these years
waned, the United States would subsequently cultivate a dominant
private automobile sector and a partly regulated and partly subsidized
public network which furnished inadequate or expensive transport to
rural sections of the country, minority groups and senior citizens.

The railroads provided the spur to increased government activity
in the 1930s. With the onset of the Depression, their financial condition
rapidly deteriorated. Gross operating revenues fell from $6.3 billion
in 1929 to $3.1 billion in 1933 and the industry's rate of return on
net investment dropped from 5.3 per cent to 1.9 per cent in the same
years. By 1933 75 class I railroads were in the hands of the receivers.[24]
Clearly some action was demanded as the railroads were still regarded

as the backbone of the nation's transport network. The Emergency
Railroad Transportation Act of 16 June 1933, offered both financial
relief and altered operating conditions in the hope of longer-term
solutions. The railroads welcomed economic aid, but disliked its terms.
The Act of 1933 created a Federal Coordinator of Transportation,
who, together with three regional groups of railroad companies, was
required to combine facilities and eliminate duplicated services and
wasteful competitive practices. If the companies refused to cooperate,
the Coordinator, Joseph B. Eastman, might compel action, provided
that this did not lead to further unemployment in the industry.[25]

The lifeline offered to the railroads, like the premise underpinning
the National Industrial Recovery Act (NIRA), signed on the same day,
was industrial self-government. This principle, however, worked poorly.
Railroad managers were determined to retain their independence and
they insisted that any significant economies in operation required job
losses. Neither the railroad unions nor Eastman would accept this
proposition. When the Coordinator suggested other improvements
like a freight car pool, a transportation clearing-house, improved passenger services and a central bureau of scientific research, these were
rejected as impractical or useless. Joseph Eastman could have compelled
some action, but he did not want to create further opposition. He was
in effect hamstrung by pressure politics from both business and government officials.[26] Lacking full support from either bureaucrats or railroad
agencies on a policy of cooperation between the railroads, he turned
his attention to the more general concept of planning coordination
within the transport sector.

Here Eastman was more successful. Favouring cooperation in the
public interest, he used his position as Federal Coordinator to address
the need to blend the activities of newer and older modes of transport.
During his term of office, 1933–6, his four reports collectively suggested
that the nation's public transport network needed to be brought under
government management supervised by the ICC.[27]

The passage of the Motor Carrier Act of 1935 was Joseph Eastman's
'most constructive achievement as Coordinator'.[28] Motor carriers
had already experienced government supervision under the National
Recovery Administration (NRA) codes. Many would have preferred to
retain the NRA principle of self-management, because they distrusted
the ICC which they considered had long been captured by the railroad
interests. When, however, the NIRA was declared unconstitutional
in May 1935 they agreed to support new legislation but under the
auspices of a separate agency. The MCA aimed to prevent wasteful
and destructive competition within both the bus and truck industries
and the transport sector, and to protect the public interest. The ICC,
as supervisory bureau, would achieve these goals through controlling

entry to the industry by certificates of convenience and necessity, through scrutiny of motor carrier operations and by establishing and publishing reasonable rates.[29] Road transport, like rail transport, was now subject to federal regulation.

The industries regulated by the Motor Carrier Bureau (MCB), which was established as a separate section of the ICC, were stronger than they had been ten years earlier when state governments had enacted their motor regulations. They were active lobbyists for their specific but distinctive interests. Buses and trucks had faced serious difficulties during the early 1930s but, unlike the railroads, they recovered and had capacity for expansion.

Under the MCA existing companies were protected and this policy supported larger units which more easily met federal government standards. In the bus industry the Greyhound Corporation already provided a national service and held a virtual monopoly in sections of the country. The MCB was aware of both the potential abuse of monopoly power and of the economies achievable by larger operations. It thus encouraged an amalgamation of independent carriers to form a new nationwide system, National Trailways. Ironically this form of competition, which was encouraged within the bus industry, created a duopoly because most other operators were small companies which did much of their trade in short-haul suburban transport. The for-hire trucking industry had not consolidated to the same extent as the bus carriers. Indeed 82 per cent of firms still operated only one vehicle in 1935. Nevertheless trucking enterprises were also regulated, partly because they offered a cheaper and more flexible means of transport than trains, especially in short-haul business, and partly because larger-scale truckers wanted stability. Federal regulation promoted larger units, as companies merged or were absorbed to meet new and tougher standards of operation. In effect the MCA promoted cartelization in both the truck and bus industry.[30]

The MCB not only supervised business behaviour in the long-distance bus and truck industries; it also scrutinised intermodal relationships. Initial work focused on processing applications for certificates of convenience and necessity, and classifying existing rates and standards. It was virtually impossible to establish national uniform tariffs. Bus rates were still set on the basis of either conditions in local markets or to be lower than existing rail fares. Truck rates were even more problematic, both on account of the variety of commodities carried and the number of small companies, many of which were private rather than public operations. Guidelines generally allowed charges that were similar to or lower than railroad rates.[31]

There would be more competition than coordination between the public modes of ground transport in the late 1930s. Indeed, government administrators still considered that regulation in the 'public interest' required competition. They felt that motor carriers should be competitive within each mode and between modes, regardless of the variety of accessible means of transport. Ironically, the relatively low capital costs of motor transport meant that bus and truck companies would 'naturally' be more likely to compete with each other than to merge into cartels. Their protection under the MCA might bring stability and encourage investment, but it impeded intramodal competition. As for coordination, buses and trucks could provide a short-distance feeder service to the national rail network, especially during the Depression. But motor operators did not wish to be subsidiaries of or become captured by the railroads. They aimed to become long-distance carriers and compete with the trains. Legislation could not create a road transport system that was competitive and that was also coordinated efficiently and effectively.[32]

Buses and trucks were not the only threat to the viability of the railroads. The lines had already lost more passenger traffic to private automobiles than to buses. Car ownership remained high even in the Depression[33] and automobile use was, if anything, encouraged by New Deal spending on highways. Between 1933 and 1942 relief agencies spent $4 billion on roads and streets. Indeed, relief and recovery initiatives accounted for 80 per cent of all federal expenditures for roads and 40 per cent of the total outlay on highways, which, from 1934, included urban sections of primary roads and from 1936, secondary 'feeder' roads. By the end of the decade 80,000 miles of secondary roads, classified as Rural Free Delivery routes, farm-to-market roads or school bus routes, had received federal support. Government subsidies encouraged motor transport, but this frequently had more impact on private than public vehicles.[34]

Subsidies also encouraged air transport, which had moved slowly from the experimental to the commercial stage of development because of high and risky capital investment costs. The federal government assisted flight with payments for airmail, starting in 1926; these continued throughout the 1930s and World War II. The government also promoted air traffic through the establishment of airports, civil airways and navigational aids. A sound and dynamic air system was necessary in the interests of national security. Nevertheless flight was still in its infancy in the 1930s; in 1939 only 276 aircraft serviced the 36,654 miles of domestic airways.[35]

Promotion and regulation of a transport mode were not necessarily incompatible. In the 1930s federal government officials considered the prospect of levelling the grounds for existing and new forms of transport which could both compete with each other and could be integrated into a national structure. Following steps to monitor air operations in the Air Mail Act of 1934 a more comprehensive supervision was attempted with the Civil Aeronautics Act of 1938. A new agency, the Civil Aeronautics Board (CAB), was established. It was modelled on the ICC, but had different goals. CAB was given the 'traditional' regulatory powers over entry, mergers, routes and rates, as well as authority over air-mail payments and subsidies to common carriers. A modification of 1940 to the Act left safety legislation in the hands of CAB but gave enforcement powers to a new agency, the Civil Aeronautics Administration (CAA). Air transport was thus segregated for special treatment using an amalgamation of the 'infant industry' concept, the requirements of national defence, the need for public safety and the resemblance of the industry to other 'natural monopolies'. Whatever common themes had been visible in land transport were in this instance nullified by specific business lobbying as well as by the severity of the Depression.[36]

Yet more complications, uneven treatment and lack of overall coordination emerged from government monitoring of pipeline and water transport. As 'natural' monopolies, oil pipelines had been regulated with the railroads under the Hepburn Act of 1906. They, however, were subject to less control than the railroads. Though the ICC established rates, forbade discrimination and insisted on formal accounting procedures, entry was not restricted, there was no check on pipeline abandonment and no regulation of mergers. Pipelines had less impact on the public because the co-existence of oil production and distribution suggested that shipping oil was their prime, if not only, function.[37]

Like the railroads, domestic shipping had long experienced federal government intervention. Water carriers who jointly hauled freight with the railroads were regulated by the ICC of 1887. Then the Shipping Act of 1916 gave the United States Shipping Board (USSB) authority to promote and regulate deep-water shippers. These carriers, especially the coastal traders, experienced intense competition, excess capacity and declining revenue in the 1930s. Intervention was required if the nation was to retain a healthy commercial fleet. Congress eventually passed the Merchant Marine Act of 1936 creating the Maritime Commission (MC). As with the ICC the MC regulated rates, routes and trade practices and required uniform accounts. Furthermore it continued subsidies and could even authorize government ownership and operation if this would eventually stimulate private commercial shipping.[38] This legislation offered water carriers a chance to develop, but it failed to satisfy the railroads. They wanted water and rail shipping to be jointly supervised by the ICC. Their lobbying paid some dividends. The Transportation Act of 1940 brought domestic water transport partially under the control of the ICC.[39]

Having legislated for all major types of public transport in the 1930s, Congress expressed a national transport policy in the Transportation Act of 1940. Added as a preamble to the Interstate Commerce Act this policy statement recommended that

> Congress ... [should] provide for fair and impartial regulation of all modes of transportation ... so administered as to recognize and preserve the inherent advantages of each; ... [it should] promote safe, adequate, economical and efficient service and foster sound economic conditions in transportation and among several carriers; ... all to the end of developing, coordinating and preserving a national transportation system.[40]

By now the federal government knew that monopoly abuse was no longer a major issue. Competition, while remaining a liberal economic ideal, had also become a serious dilemma. Furthermore the allocation of traffic between modes as well as the distinct problems within each mode were all part of any competent and constructive nationwide strategy. However, although key concerns may have been identified, no guidelines were defined.

The depressed state of the economy had allowed, or perhaps even encouraged serious rethinking about the viability and effectiveness of specific modes of transport. It had also stimulated consideration of a holistic coordinated transport system. But salvage work impeded planning for the future. The outbreak of World War II, defence preparedness and then intervention radically altered transport needs and operations and once again a crisis prevented any systematic planning.

One of the main problems facing transport carriers in the 1930s was their sluggish business. Using an index of 100 for the year 1929, freight tonnage on the railroads fell to a low of 48 in 1932, and only climbed to 67 by 1939. On inland waterways tonnage fell to 60 in 1932, rising back to 100 by 1939. Passenger rail miles fell from 100 in 1929, to a low of 55 in 1933, and struggled to 58 by 1939, while passenger bus miles fell to a low of 84 in 1932, and increased to 128 in 1939.[41] Competition for business took place in a shrinking market, and one in which technology and consumer choice altered the terms of trade. There was much room for improvement and expansion, especially in the rail sector. War brought the expansion, but under stressful circumstances.

The need to move military and civilian freight and to carry both troops and civilian workers, combined with petrol, rubber and parts shortages, forced Americans to use public transport. New records were set for both freight and passenger transport. The volume of freight moved by public carriers in each of the years 1943, 1944 and 1945 was double that of 1939. This increase was achieved primarily by the railroads, which conveyed 70 per cent of the wartime load. The rise in total passenger traffic during the war was relatively small; but because of wartime restrictions on private cars, the impact on public transport was huge. Seats were filled to capacity, with standing room only. Rail passenger miles increased from 26.5 billion in 1941 to 88.1 billion in 1945 and for intercity buses the respective figures were 13.6 billion and 26.9 billion. Railroads that had faced serious difficulties a decade earlier now earned substantial revenue.[42]

Such business was not attained in a free market. A wartime administrative bureau, the Office of Defense Transportation (ODT) was created on 18 December 1941 and it managed traffic flows throughout the war. Headed by Joseph B. Eastman until his death on 15 March 1944, this agency used relatively simple devices like rationing of parts, rubber allocation, speed limits, fuel control and curtailing non-essential services to distribute scarce resources among transport systems. Directives encouraging full use of capacity and rational use of freight and passenger operations stimulated cooperation. Trade associations, like the National Association of Motor Bus Operators (NAMBO) and the Association of American Railroads actively assisted government savings and collaborative campaigns, while the attachment of major businessmen to the ODT strengthened commitment to the war effort.[43]

The ODT, as a civilian control agency, managed the war effort in transport, and the federal government did not need to intervene and run any operations as it had done with the railroads during World War I. This achievement did not stem from any foresight and planning envisaged in the debates, legislation and administrative experience of the 1930s. Although the Merchant Marine Act of 1936, the Civil Aeronautics Act of 1938 and the Transportation Act of 1940 had pointed to the needs of national defence, little had been done to plan an effective, emergency transport system. The ODT, established to 'coordinate the transportation policies of the several federal agencies and private transportation groups' for the successful prosecution of the war, was fortunate. It had the time and the freedom from disruptions of enemy attacks to establish transport priorities. It also managed facilities that were capable of responding to a crisis. Railroads had experienced heavy capital investment in the 1920s. They had also kept abreast of technological advances in motive power and equipment during the Depression. Relief work during the New Deal had improved the highways and the bus industry retained its fleet in operation without significant new additions. The efforts to keep transport moving, however, had long-term effects in terms of deferred maintenance costs, paucity of investment in plant and facilities and a negative image of public transport. These problems, combined with the unresolved issues and inconsistencies created by transport policy of the 1930s, provoked a further reassessment in the 'public interest' during the post-war years.[44]

Individualism and competition have always been central American cultural values. Yet the federal government has also always insisted that there was a 'public interest' in which community took precedence over personal choice. On the argument of security, whether national, economic or social, the federal government has intervened to promote growth or to regulate abuse or competition, using the implied powers of the Constitution. In the transport sector it was thought beneficial to foster national communications both for defence purposes and to ensure an adequate postal service. Some modes of transport, often those with high fixed costs, have accordingly benefited from public investment or promotional subsidies.[45]

The transport sector has also been regulated in the 'public interest'. Initially government commissions, staffed by professionals, administered laws to ensure that rail corporations did not exploit their power. But the domination of railroads over long-distance movement was seriously weakened by the advent of motor vehicles in the first half of the twentieth century. Then the federal government needed to monitor behaviour to ensure both competition and stability in the 'public interest'. The two demands were not easily compatible for either the newer forms of road transport, whose fixed costs were relatively low, or for intermodal relationships. Railroads faced high fixed costs and their stability was threatened by motor competition. Yet many Americans considered that railroads were essential to national security and welfare.

Traditional regulation policy had not foreseen the shape of inter-modal competition. When administrators applied existing practice to roads and air, they weakened some rail and water transport while encouraging road transport. The Depression of the 1930s, in which competition drove prices further downwards, weakened older modes and vulnerable companies. Officials then debated the possibility of intermodal coordination and a national transport policy. Coordination was a viable way of protecting railroads from road competition, especially in a serious depression, but it could also prevent competition between companies within each mode. Coordination also did not offer any answer to the problems of the loss of passengers to private automobiles. The New Deal's approach to regulation was problematic, but any further development was interrupted by the intervention of World War II. Technological changes in motor vehicles and the advent of accessible air transport in the post-war years created a more complex transport economy. Then another approach to defining and ensuring transport policy in the 'public interest' was applied, but again with much debate and without complete satisfaction.

The historiographical debate on public policy and regulation has reflected the politics and views of both the protagonists of federal management and of *laissez-faire*. Substantive issues, ideology and the lobbying of pressure groups are a constant in academic discussion as well as in the American psyche. The situation was no different during the Depression decade and in World War II. Commentators then and since debated political theory, the impact of special interests and consumer preferences. But the circumstances of economic depression and wartime expansion under strained conditions had a decisive impact on regulatory development in their own right. These circumstances became as, if not more, important than the traditional sources of regulation and, as such, add weight to the pluaralistic readings of the nature and sources of the regulatory movement in the United States during the twentieth century.

Notes

1. Joseph B. Eastman, 'The Policy of the Motor Carrier Act', American Transit Association, *Proceedings*, (1937), 288.
2. Naomi R. Lamoreaux discusses three waves of regulatory legislation in 'Regulatory Agencies' in Jack P. Greene (ed.), *Encyclopedia of American Political History*, vol. 3 (New York, 1984), 1107–17. These waves are located in the Progressive period, about 1900 to World War I, as New Deal measures in the 1930s and in the late 1960s and early 1970s. The two earlier waves mainly concerned the economic behaviour of individual industries; the latter used agencies like the Equal Employment Opportunities Commission (EEOC) whose mandate encompassed the economy as a whole. Transport regulation differs in its timing. The first wave dates from 1887 to 1917. Most historians would insist that any consideration of transport legislation must start with the creation of the Interstate Commerce Commission (ICC) in 1887, thereby predating Progressivism. The second wave runs from 1920 to 1940. Though much of the emphasis of this wave falls in the 1930s, the Transportation Act of 1920 had a major impact on the railroads and already in the 1920s Congress was discussing the possibility of regulating motor transport. The third wave of transport regulation, which is specific to transport, is more properly identified as deregulation and is located in the late 1970s and early 1980s. See also the discussion about regulation in Chapter 1 of Richard K. Vietor, *Contrived Competition, Regulation and Deregulation in America* (Cambridge, Mass., 1994), 1–22 and Martin T. Farris, 'Evolution of the Transportation Regulatory Structure of the US', *International Journal of Transport Economics*, 10 (1983), 173–93.
3. For information on Eastman see Claude M. Fuess, *Joseph B. Eastman, Servant of the People* (New York, 1952); Virgil D. Cover 'Joseph Bartlett Eastman's Economic and Social Views on Transportation Problems',

Ph.D. thesis, University of Illinois, 1936 and William R. Childs, *Trucking and the Public Interest. The Emergence of Federal Regulation, 1914–1940* (Knoxille, TN, 1985), 119–41.

4. Vietor, *Contrived Competition*, 1–22, 310–30; Thomas K. McCraw, *Prophets of Regulation* (Cambridge, Mass., 1984), 223–308; Martha Derthick and Paul J. Quirk, *The Politics of Deregulation* (Washington, DC, 1985); Paul W. MacAvoy, *The Regulated Industries and the Economy* (New York, 1979); James Q. Wilson (ed.), *The Politics of Regulation* (New York, 1980).

5. Thomas K. McCraw, 'Regulation in America: A Review Article', *Business History Review*, 49 (1975), 159–83.

6. Lamoreaux, 'Regulatory Agencies', 1107–17; Robert D. Tollison, 'Regulation and Interest Groups' in Jack High (ed.), *Regulation. Economic Theory and History* (Ann Arbor, Mich., 1991), 59–76.

7. McCraw, 'Regulation in America', 160–2; Robert E. Cushman, *The Independent Regulatory Commissions* (New York, 1941); Harold U. Faulkner, *The Decline of Laissez-Faire, 1897–1917* (New York, 1951); Robert H. Weibe, *The Search for Order, 1877–1920* (New York, 1967); Samuel P. Hays, *Conservation and the Gospel of Efficiency* (Cambridge, Mass., 1959).

8. Marver H. Bernstein, *Regulating Business by Independent Commission* (Princeton, NJ, 1955).

9. Gabriel Kolko, *Railroads and Regulation, 1877–1916* (Princeton, NJ, 1965); Gabriel Kolko, *The Triumph of Conservatism: A Reinterpretation of American History, 1900–1916* (New York, 1963).

10. McCraw, 'Regulation in America', 164–6; Lamoreaux, 'Regulatory Agencies', 1109.

11. George J. Stigler, 'The Theory of Economic Regulation', *Bell Journal of Economics and Management*, 2 (1971), 3.

12. Roger B. Noll, 'Economic Perspectives on the Politics of Regulation' in Richard Schmalensee and Robert D. Willig (eds), *Handbook of Industrial Organization* vol. 2 (New York, 1989), 1254–86; Vietor, *Contrived Competition*, 312–13.

13. James Q. Wilson (ed.), *The Politics of Regulation* (New York, 1980); McCraw, *Prophets of Regulation* and Derthick and Quirk, *The Politics of Deregulation*.

14. Robert U. Harbeson, 'Railroads and Regulation, 1877–1916, Conspiracy or Public Interest', *Journal of Economic History*, 27 (1967), 230–42; Albro Martin, *Enterprise Denied: Origins of the Decline of American Railroads, 1897–1917* (New York, 1971); Albro Martin, 'The Troubled Subject of Railroad Regulation in the Gilded Age – A Reappraisal', *Journal of American History*, 59 (1974), 339–71; K. Austin Kerr, *American Railroad Politics, 1914–1920* (Pittsburgh, 1968); George H. Miller, *Railroads and the Granger Laws* (Madison, WI, 1971); Stanley P. Caine, *The Myth of a Progressive Reform: Railroad Regulation in Wisconsin, 1903–1910* (Madison, WI, 1970).

15. Morton Keller, 'The Pluralist State' in Thomas K. McCraw (ed.), *Regulation in Perspective* (Cambridge, Mass., 1981), 78–85; Vietor, *Contrived Competition*, 310–30.

16. McCraw, *Prophets of Regulation*, 222–99; Theodore Kovaleff, 'The Reagan Revolution' in Theodore Kovaleff (ed.), *The Antitrust Impulse. An Economic,*

Historical and Legal Analysis (Armonk, NY, 1994), vol. 1, 209–14; William J. Baumol, John C. Panzer and Robert D. Willig, *Contestable Markets and the Theory of Industry Structure* (Orlando, Fla., rev. ed. 1988), vi–xv, 498–510.

17. For the nineteenth century see George R. Taylor, *The Transportation Revolution, 1815–1860* (New York, 1951); Edward C. Kirkland, *Industry Comes of Age. Business, Labor and Public Policy, 1860–1897* (New York, 1961); Faulkner, *The Decline of Laissez Faire*; and Carter Goodrich, 'Internal Improvements Reconsidered', *Journal of Economic History*, 30 (1970), 289–311. For the twentieth century see Morton Keller, *Regulating A New Economy. Public Policy and Economic Change in America, 1900–1933* (Cambridge, Mass., 1990), 43–51; Roy J. Sampson and Martin T. Farris, *Domestic Transportation. Practice, Theory and Policy* (Boston, 4th ed. 1979); D. Philip Locklin, *Economics of Transportation*, (Homewood, Ill., 7th ed. 1972); Dudley F. Pegrum, *Transportation: Economics and Public Policy* (Homewood, Ill., 1968); and Charles A. Taff, *Commercial Motor Transportation* (Centreville, Md, 6th ed. 1980).

18. For controversial interpretations of the government operation of railroads during the war see George Soule, *Prosperity Decade. From War to Depression, 1917–1929* (New York, 1947), 33–6 and Albro Martin, *Railroads Triumphant. The Growth, Rejection and Rebirth of a Vital American Force* (New York, 1992), 355–6.

19. Sampson and Farris, *Domestic Transportation*, 325–8; John B. Prizer, 'Development of the Regulation of Transportation during the Past Seventy-Five Years', *ICC Practitioners' Journal*, 21 (1953), 206–11; John F. Stover, *American Railroads* (Chicago, 1961), 195–200. For analysts, the most infamous section of the 1920 Transportation Act was the 'recapture' clause whereby stronger rail companies assisted the weaker ones by re-routing excess profits.

20. John B. Rae, *The American Automobile. A Brief History* (Chicago, 1965), 33–104; Margaret Walsh, 'The Early Growth of Long-Distance Bus Transport in the United States' in Theo Barker (ed.), *The Economic and Social Effects of the Spread of Motor Vehicles* (London, 1987), 81–7; Childs, *Trucking and the Public Interest*, 7–24; US Bureau of the Census, *The Statistical History of the United States* (New York, 1976), Series Q1–11, 12–22, 707. Most of the remainder of freight traffic was carried by water.

21. Shan Szto, *Federal and State Regulation of Motor Carrier Rates and Services* (Philadelphia, 1934), 47–113; John J. George *Motor Carrier Regulation in the United States* (Spartenburg, NC), 1–213; Childs, *Trucking and the Public Interest*, 7–24.

22. *Railroad Age* 80–99 (1921–9); ICC, 'Motor Bus and Truck Operation', Docket 18300, *Reports* 140 (1928), Appendix A, 750–3; George *Motor Carrier Regulation*, 214–37; Szto, *Federal and State Regulation*, 193–226; Margaret Walsh, 'Coordination, Cooperation or Competition: The Great Northern Railway and Bus Transportation in the 1920s' in Rondo Cameron (ed.), *Cities and Markets, Studies in the Reorganization of Human Space* (Lanhan, Md, 1997), 163–89; Gregory L. Thompson, *The Passenger Train in the Motor Age. California's Rail and Bus Industries, 1910–1941* (Columbus, Ohio, 1993), 63–90.

23. Margaret Walsh, 'The Motor Carrier Act of 1935. The Origins and Establishment of Federal Regulation on the Interstate Bus Industry in the United States', *Journal of Transport History*, Ser. 3, 8 (1987), 69–70.

24. Robert C. Lieb, *Transportation: The Domestic System* (Reston, Va., 1978), 227.

25. The Act amended the Interstate Commerce Act and affected the powers of the ICC. The 1920 concepts of 'recapture' and establishing an acceptable fair rate value for the industry were abandoned. Now just and reasonable rate-making was to be guided by the need of the carriers for revenues sufficient to provide an adequate transportation service. See Prizer, 'Development of the Regulation', 211–13.

26. Ellis W. Hawley, *The New Deal and the Problem of Monopoly. A Study in Economic Ambivalence* (Princeton, NJ, 1966), 228–31; Merle Fainsod, Lincoln Gordon and Joseph C. Palamatanian Jr., *Government and the American Economy* (New York, 3rd ed. 1959), 286–7; Stover, *American Railroads*, 219.

27. US Senate, *Regulation of Railroads* (73 Cong. 2 Sess., 1934), Doc. 119; US Senate, *Regulation of Transportation Agencies* (73 Cong. 2 Sess., 1934), Doc. 152; US House, *Report of the Federal Coordinator of Transportation, 1934* (74 Cong. 1 Sess., 1935), Doc. 89; US House, *Fourth Report of the Federal Coordinator of Transportation on Transportation Legislation* (74 Cong., 2 Sess., 1936), Doc. 394; Robert E. Cushman, *The Independent Regulatory Commission* (New York, 1972), 393–416; Emory R. Johnson, *Government Regulation of Transportation* (New York, 1938), 163–72 and 339–46; Fuess, *Joseph B. Eastman*, 180–244. There is some discussion whether Eastman was a 'socialist' or a 'Progressive'. Eastman himself considered that he was independent of political affiliation. The term 'socialist', like 'czar', was a pejorative term used by those who did not want government intervention.

28. Fuess, *Joseph B. Eastman*, 231.

29. ICC, *Motor Bus and Truck Operations* 140 (1928); ICC *Coordination of Motor Transportation* 182 (1932); *Report of the Federal Coordination of Transportation* (1934); US Senate, Committee of Interstate Commerce, *Hearings to Amend the Interstate Commerce Act* (74 Cong. 1 Sess., 25 February–6 March 1935); *Public Act No. 255* (74th Cong., 1 Sess., 1935), 1–27; *Bus Transportation* 4–14 (1925–35); Childs, *Trucking and the Public Interest*; James C. Nelson, 'The Motor Carrier Act of 1935', *Journal of Political Economy*, 44 (1936), 464–71.

30. Walsh, 'The Motor Carrier Act', 73–6; Nelson, 'The Motor Carrier Act of 1935', 475–94; Burton B. Crandall, *The Growth of the Intercity Bus Industry* (Syracuse, NY, 1954), 166–220; Childs, *Trucking and the Public Interest*, 119–67; Harold Barger, *The Transportation Industries, 1899–1946. A Study of Output Employment, and Productivity* (New York, 1951), 221–47.

31. US Senate Committee on Commerce, *An Evaluation of the Motor Carrier Act of 1935 on the Thirtieth Anniversary of its Enactment* (89 Cong. 1 Sess., Committee Print, 1 October 1965), 2–3, 9–25; Walsh, 'The Motor Carrier Act', 73–6; Barger, *The Transportation Industries*, 232–47.

32. Walsh, 'The Motor Carrier Act of 1935', 73–6; Walsh, 'Coordination, Cooperation or Competition', 173–80.

33. Car registrations increased from 1,7481,000 in 1925 to 23,034,700 in 1930. They fell to a low of 20,657,200 in 1933, but rose to 27,465,800 by 1940. *The Statistical History of the United States*, 716.

34. American Association of State Highway Officials, *A Story of the Beginning, Purposes, Growth, Activities and Achievements of AASHO* (Washington DC, 1964), 151–3; Charles L. Dearing, *American Highway Policy*, (Washington DC, 1941), 189–205; Charles L. Dearing and Wilfred Owen, *National Transportation Policy* (Washington DC, 1949), 105–20; John B. Rae, *The Road and the Car in American Life* (Cambridge, Mass., 1971), 60–83.

35. Dearing and Owen, *National Transportation Policy*, 17–58; Robert M. Kane and Allan D. Vose, *Air Transportation* (Dubuque, Ia., 4th ed. 1974), 25–34; Fainsod et al., *Government and the American Economy*, 120–1, 301–2.

36. Dearing and Owen, *National Transportation Policy*, 169–73, 178–81; Hawley, *The New Deal and the Problem of Monopoly*, 240–4; Cushman, *The Independent Regulatory Commissions*, 393–416; Fainsod et al., *Government and the American Economy*, 301–3.

37. Pegrum, *Transportation*, 191–2; Lieb, *Transportation*, 79–80; Fainsod et al., *Government and the American Economy*, 639–40.

38. *Regulation of Transportation Agencies*, 10–3; *Fourth Report*, 7–22; Hawley, *The New Deal and the Problem of Monopoly*, 234–9; Fainsod et al, *Government and the American Economy*, 109, 296–7.

39. Truman C. Bingham, 'The Transportation Act of 1940', *The Southern Economic Journal*, 8 (1941), 1–21; George W. Hilton, *The Transportation Act of 1958. A Decade of Experience* (Bloomington, Ind., 1969), 509; Fainsod et al, *Government the American Economy*, 297–301, 304–6; Lieb, *Transportation*, 241–5; Pegrum, *Transportation*, 326–9. The Act sanctioned so many exemptions and miscellaneous arrangements that 90 per cent of domestic water transport was not monitored by federal government. Furthermore that section which was monitored, was governed by 'fair and impartial regulation'.

40. *Public Law No. 785*, (76 Cong. 3 Sess., 1940), 2–3. The Transportation Act of 1940 is alternatively called Title III of the Interstate Commerce Act (1887).

41. *Statistical History of the United States*, 729, 733, 763; Crandall, *The Growth of the Intercity Bus Industry*, 280.

42. Dearing and Owen, *National Transportation Policy*, 139; Margaret Walsh, 'The Intercity Bus and Its Competitors in the United States in the Mid Twentieth Century' in Chris Wrigley and John Shepherd (eds), *On the Move: Essays in Labour and Transport History Presented to Philip Bagwell* (London, 1991), 243.

43. Margaret Walsh, 'Minnesota's "Mr Bus": Edgar F. Zelle and the Jefferson Highway Transportation Company', *Minnesota History*, 52/8 (1991), 318–9; *NAMBO Board of Directors Minutes, 1941–1945*, American Heritage Center, University of Wyoming; Margaret Walsh, 'Missing Connections: The Long Distance Bus Industry in the United States Since 1940', unpublished paper, 2–4; Fainsod et al., *Government and the American Economy*, 840–1; Harold G. Vatter, *The U.S. Economy in World War II* (New York, 1985).

44. Dearing and Owen, *National Transportation Policy*, 138–63; Stover, *American Railroads*, 208; Walsh, 'Missing Connections', 2–5.

45. Maury Klein, *Unfinished Business. The Railroad in American Life* (Hanover, NH, 1994), 122–34 and US Congress, *Intercity Domestic Transportation System for Passengers and Freight* (95 Cong. 1 Sess.) Committee Print, 1977, 5–28.

3

"Just Forget About It": FDR's Ambivalence towards National Health Insurance*

Jaap Kooijman

In January 1935 Morris Fishbein, editor of the *Journal of the American Medical Association*, suggested that the 'socialized medicine' schemes of Franklin D. Roosevelt were based on 'Eleanor advising the President in night conferences', while he was being advised by Secretary of Labor Frances Perkins during the day.[1] The truth is that we only know a little about FDR's personal views on national health insurance. What is known is based either on his public statements or on hearsay. FDR hardly discussed the topic directly with the policy-makers involved, but used mediators such as his personal physician Ross McIntire, surgeon general Thomas Parran, and federal relief administrator, Harry Hopkins. Also, rumour had it that the President's actions were strongly influenced by his friend Harvey Cushing, a highly respected brain surgeon whose daughter Betsey was married to Roosevelt's son James. Other sources have suggested that Roosevelt was either 'cold about health insurance' or favoured such a programme, but recognized the political obstacles.[2]

Historians have assumed that Roosevelt's cautious approach to national health insurance was a direct result of the medical profession's opposition as represented by the American Medical Association (AMA).[3] This was also the view of several of the original participants, including Frances Perkins. She firmly believed that because of the opposition of the AMA, national health insurance 'would have killed the whole Social Security Act if it had been pressed at that time'.[4] Perkins' diagnosis was too clear-cut. Even though the opposition of the AMA was real, the overestimation of its influence reduces the history of national health

* Research for this paper was made possible by a grant provided by the Franklin and Eleanor Roosevelt Institute, Hyde Park, New York, and the generous support, both financially and in kind, of the Roosevelt Study Center, Middelburg, The Netherlands. This paper is based on Jaap Kooijman, 'Soon or Later On: Franklin D. Roosevelt and National Health Insurance, 1933–1945', *Presidential Studies Quarterly*, Spring 1999. The author would like to thank Edward D. Berkowitz, Daniel M. Fox, and Gene Moore for commenting on an earlier draft of this paper.

insurance to a battle between idealistic reformers and medical obstruc-
tionists. In this way, we tend to forget that national health insurance
was not so much a 'lost reform' as an option that was not chosen.

Roosevelt himself was not an enthusiast. His ambivalence towards
national health insurance became apparent in his message to Congress
of 8 June 1934. He announced that the social insurance system he
envisioned would be 'national in scope', to provide 'security against
several of the great disturbing factors of life – especially those which
relate to unemployment and old age'.[5] There was no mention of health
insurance. Three weeks later, Roosevelt appointed the Committee on
Economic Security (CES), chaired by Frances Perkins. Assistant Secretary of Labor Arthur Altmeyer was appointed head of the CES
technical board and Edwin Witte, like Altmeyer a progressive social
economist from Wisconsin, was appointed executive director. The CES
studies of the 'risks to economic security arising out of ill health' were
headed by public health experts Edgar Sydenstricker and I. S. Falk of
the Milbank Memorial Fund. FDR knew the Milbank Fund and its
executive secretary, John Kingsbury, from his time as Governor of
New York. In addition, Kingsbury had been Harry Hopkins' mentor
in the 1910s and the two men had remained good friends ever since.[6]

Even though they saw themselves as objective and scientific, Sydenstricker and Falk were ideologues who genuinely believed in the
righteousness of their objective. Altmeyer and Witte, products of Wisconsin state government, were more pragmatic. While the first two
tried to achieve what was best, the latter limited themselves to what
was possible. As a result, Altmeyer and Witte placed less emphasis on
health insurance as a national objective. Nevertheless, the very presence
of Sydenstricker and Falk led the AMA to assume that the CES would
recommend national health insurance. In the *Journal of the American
Medical Association*, editor Morris Fishbein described Sydenstricker's
views as 'completely antagonistic to the medical point of view'. He
concluded that the medical profession was not 'adequately represented ... if Mr Sydenstricker is the only authority on what constitutes
proper arrangements for medical care'.[7]

In actual fact, the CES cabinet members were far from unified on
the issue. As Sydenstricker soon found out, 'Perkins favors unemployment insurance, Hopkins favors health insurance first, [and] both
Wallace and Morgenthau fear any program that will hurt or scare or
alienate business'.[8] When, in Witte's words, 'telegraphic protests poured
in upon the President' (most of them sent by the state medical societies),
the already weak position of national health insurance was further
undermined.[9] To counter the opposition of the AMA, Sydenstricker
suggested the creation of a Medical Advisory Board. Once the President
had invited prominent physicians such as Harvey Cushing and AMA

President Walter Bierring to express their views, opposition could be expected to cease. Roosevelt liked the idea, and in consultation with Ross McIntire, Sydenstricker and Falk selected the members of the Board.[10]

Yet Witte feared that the strong opposition to national health insurance would make FDR 'feel disgusted with the whole matter', and convince him to abandon social security altogether. But, as Witte was told by Ross McIntire, 'the President knew that the American Medical Association would stir up opposition and ... there is no way of appeasing that crowd'.[11] In other words, unlike Witte, Roosevelt was neither surprised nor intimidated by the strong opposition. Witte finally gave in and told Frances Perkins, 'I certainly believe that we cannot dismiss health insurance at this time without being entirely satisfied that it cannot be put into operation on a compulsory basis in the near future'.[12]

Both Altmeyer and Witte would later claim that it had been their original belief that national health insurance would not be immediately included in the Social Security Act.[13] But the decision to postpone national health insurance was not made until the Conference on Economic Security, held on 14 and 15 November 1935. At the Conference, the Roosevelt administration met with several advisory boards, including the Medical Advisory Board. In his opening speech, Roosevelt promised reformers that national health insurance would someday be enacted. However, almost in the same breath he reassured opponents by suggesting that no drastic action would be taken. Ambiguity dominated Roosevelt's message, prompting one Washington columnist to question 'The Mystery of the President's Speech, or Does the English Language Mean Anything?'[14] That following day, the first meeting of the Medical Advisory Board proved to be a forum of opposition to national health insurance. Witte subsequently concluded that more time was needed to study the plans and win the support of the medical profession. Perkins agreed and extended the deadline to 1 March 1935, meaning that national health insurance would not be included in the Economic Security Bill of January.[15]

By now, Sydenstricker and Falk had accepted that their plan would not be included in the bill. Instead, they pushed for the inclusion of eleven general principles in the CES report to the President, describing a federal-state programme of compulsory health insurance which would be optional for the individual states and maintain the medical profession's autonomy. If these principles were not included, Sydenstricker warned, 'then Fishbein and his crowd will say that they were successful in scotching the President's interest in health insurance'.[16] FDR agreed that the eleven general principles needed to be included and when he presented the Economic Security Bill to Congress in January 1935, again his message was ambiguous: 'I am not at this time recommending the adoption of so-called "health insurance", although groups representing the medical profession are cooperating with the Federal government in the further study of the subject and progress is being made.'[17]

When Harvey Cushing suggested to Roosevelt that an inter-departmental committee for health and welfare activities be created, FDR replied, 'I am glad that again your mind runs along with mine'.[18] Yet the influence of Cushing did not go much further than his participation in the CES Medical Advisory Board. After the second, once again disappointing, meeting of the Board in February 1935, Cushing expressed his grievances to FDR. According to Cushing, the physicians on the Board were 'appointed merely to act as window-dressing', having been 'manoeuvred' into endorsing Sydenstricker's prearranged programme. In addition, Cushing believed that his own membership of the Board placed him 'in the false position before the medical profession of being an advocate of compulsory sickness insurance'.[19]

Cushing's criticism infuriated Sydenstricker. He believed that Cushing was using his access to FDR to undermine the efforts of the Medical Advisory Board. The Roosevelt administration refused to become involved in the sniping. Sydenstricker stated: 'I felt that I was rather left hanging out on a limb unless I could get the facts of the case stated before the Committee as well as before those who deliberately misinterpreted what happened'.[20] FDR also kept clear. He told Cushing that expanding 'the existing machinery' of medical care was 'worthwhile considering', but refused to go into the alleged mistreatment of the physicians. Instead he appeased and distracted. 'Bets was here the other evening – she is an understanding and very wise young lady.'[21] Perhaps he implied that Cushing should follow his daughter's example and be wise enough to drop the subject. Whether true or not, Cushing never wrote Roosevelt on national health insurance again.

At the beginning of the Medical Advisory Board's second meeting, Sydenstricker had reminded Cushing that 'the job that the President and the Cabinet have given us' was 'to find out under what conditions, if and when health insurance does come, it can best be worked out'.[22] Yet Sydenstricker and Falk seemed to forget just that. Roosevelt wanted them to design a possible plan that could be used in the future, not a blueprint for legislation to be enacted on short notice. National health insurance was merely one option to Roosevelt. The extension of medical care was another. No one seemed to doubt, including the physicians and lay reformers, that the subsidizing of medical research and facilities would lead to better medical care.[23]

Meanwhile, the drafting of the CES report on national health insurance continued. After several preliminary versions, Sydenstricker and Falk finally submitted their final draft to the CES staff. Moreover, a National Health Insurance Bill based on their report was being drafted.[24] Roosevelt had told Perkins to file the report in favour of national health insurance, but to refrain from any action until he had decided what to do with it.[25] On 14 August 1935, President Roosevelt signed the Social Security Act, which included the establishment of the Social Security Board. Altmeyer, appointed to the Board, wrote to Roosevelt's secretary Stephen Early, inquiring what needed to be done with the health insurance report. Realizing the 'dynamite' it contained, Altmeyer believed that the report described a 'practical program' which could challenge the opposition. Early ordered his secretary to tell Altmeyer over the phone that it was an 'old report – [and the president] hopes no publicity will be given it. Just forget about it'.[26] The report was never published. Instead, Roosevelt forwarded it to the Social Security Board for further study.[27]

By then, Roosevelt seemed to have come to the conclusion that extending the supply of medical care was preferable to guaranteeing access to it. At the dedication of the Medical Center in Jersey City, partially financed by the federal government, Roosevelt proclaimed that 'we must do more, much more, to help the small-income families in time of sickness'. National health insurance, however, would not be the way to achieve that goal. Speaking before an audience consisting almost entirely of medical professionals, Roosevelt concluded: 'The overwhelming majority of the doctors of the Nation want medicine kept out of politics. On occasions in the past attempts have been made to put medicine into politics. Such attempts have always failed and always will fail.'[28] Either Roosevelt wanted to please his audience on this special occasion, or he had indeed concluded that extending the supply of medical care meant keeping medicine out of politics.

After the enactment of the Social Security Act, Roosevelt decided to leave medical care to the Interdepartmental Committee to Coordinate Health and Welfare Activities and await its recommendations. Since Altmeyer, who by now believed that national health insurance should be added to the Social Security Act, had proposed to make the Social Security Board solely responsible for national health insurance, the Committee was primarily focused on public health, maternal and infant care, hospital construction, and federal aid to blind and crippled children.[29] However, its National Health Program presented at the National Health Conference of July 1938 also recommended a federal-state programme of temporary disability insurance and a federal grants programme to encourage states to develop compulsory health insurance for the indigent. Even though a broad national health insurance programme was not recommended, the proceedings included an outline of Sydenstricker and Falk's original plan, making the reformers believe that its enactment might be feasible in the near future.[30] The AMA, on the other hand, was willing to endorse most of the National Health Program on the condition that the recommendation to provide grants for health insurance programmes be dropped. Yet since the reformers believed that 'a political base had been established for a broad legislative health program', Altmeyer refused to compromise, thereby prolonging the deadlock between the Social Security Board and the AMA.[31]

Despite his initial enthusiasm for the National Health Program, President Roosevelt called for 'careful study' instead of immediate action.[32] When Senator Robert F. Wagner included the programme in his 1939 omnibus bill to supplement the Social Security Act, Roosevelt did not give his endorsement. Once again he preferred the 'improvement of health in those communities that have complete lack of facilities today' over a 'general plan on a nationwide basis'.[33] This time, the intensifying opposition of the AMA may have played a part in his reluctance. 'Franklin says that he does not want to get into any difficulties with the American Medical Association just now when he has so much to contend with', Eleanor Roosevelt told her friend Esther Lape in 1939.[34] By then, with the outbreak of World War II, Roosevelt's main attention had shifted from domestic issues, including national health insurance, to international ones.

Although the President himself ignored medical care in the war years, the Social Security Board continued to push the issue. It was actively involved in the drafting of the Wagner-Murray-Dingell Bill of 1943, which included a new national health insurance plan. Unlike the earlier plan, which would have established a federal-state programme, national health insurance now followed the old-age insurance structure of the Social Security Act. As the bill provided for an exclusively federal programme which guaranteed universal access, it thereby reduced the role of the individual states, thus hurting its political chances in Congress.[35] However, while the Social Security Board and the AMA remained deadlocked, another government agency, the Public Health Service (PHS), formed a coalition with the American Hospital Association (AHA) to advocate federal legislation for medical research and hospital construction. In addition, the wartime policy of the War Labor Board and the Internal Revenue Service encouraged employer-based private health insurance. Meeting little opposition, this new consensus further undermined the cause of national health insurance.[36]

During the war years, Roosevelt's messages on national health insurance remained ambiguous. Even though he publicly called for the extension of social security 'to provide protection against the serious economic hazard of ill health', he merely endorsed a hospital construction bill.[37] Roosevelt never presented his American Plan, which included national health insurance, but did add the 'right to adequate medical care' to his Economic Bill of Rights.[38] 'The only person ... who can explain this medical thing is myself', Roosevelt told his cabinet members. 'The people are unprepared.' Moreover, he did not want to 'go up against the State Medical Societies' without strong support for his domestic reforms in Congress.[39] As far as Roosevelt was concerned, national health insurance had to wait its turn. 'The Chief is ready to go ahead on health insurance', Harry Hopkins told the reformers in 1944, after Roosevelt was re-elected for another term. Subsequently, Falk and Michael M. Davis worked together with Samuel I. Rosenman in drafting a presidential message on national health insurance. However, as Davis would later recall, 'the President's sudden death in April made it a piece of paper'.[40]

If in 1935 Roosevelt had wanted to include national health insurance in the Social Security Act, he could, perhaps, as Wilbur Cohen contended, 'have made a few fireside chats and he could have carried it along'.[41] The AMA leaders were 'playing with fire', admitted Witte: 'If they keep on cutting corners they run the risk that the President may tell the American people what he thinks of them.' [42] But FDR had more to consider than the opposition of the medical profession alone. Opposition to the New Deal was growing in Congress. Roosevelt told his Hyde Park neighbour Gerald Morgan that he doubted if national health insurance would come up in the next session of Congress: 'The latter is exhausted by my suggestions!' [43]

Undoubtedly, national health insurance would have been more politically feasible if it had been supported by a broad popular movement, as was the case with old-age assistance. More important was the lack of support from public interest groups such as labour unions and business. Those public figures who, in March 1935, were sent a draft copy of the health insurance report, showed a polite interest, but concluded that the time had not yet come for such a far-reaching programme.[44] Whether or not, as one historian has said of the American Federation of Labor (AFL), the Social Security Act 'immediately fostered a desire to add insurance protection for those unable to pay for health care', national health insurance was never labour's top priority. Even AFL President William Green, known to be in favour, considered unemployment insurance more important.[45] Progressive businessman Marion Folsom of Eastman Kodak believed that the Social Security Act 'should be enough for a start'. As he would later remember, there were only a few people 'pushing' for national health insurance at that time, really nothing 'for the medical boys to get excited over'.[46]

In addition to the general lack of support, national health insurance could also endanger the fragile compromise between the Roosevelt administration and the southern Democrats. In order to get social security accepted, agricultural workers and domestic servants were excluded from its benefits, so as not to disturb the existing social order in the southern states.[47] Roosevelt was loath to risk fracture of such brittle arrangements. Two notable African-American organizations endorsed national health insurance: the National Medical Association (NMA, the African-American counterpart of the AMA) and the National Association for the Advancement of Colored People (NAACP). By 1934, NAACP Secretary Walter White was already urging Roosevelt 'to stress upon the coming Congress the need of health insurance'.[48] Racial inequality, so carefully circumvented in the Social Security Act, could re-enter the discussion through national health insurance. The risk was too high.

Throughout his presidency, Roosevelt maintained a seemingly ambiguous position on national health insurance. He promised the medical profession that he would keep medicine out of politics, but he never denounced national health insurance altogether. He kept the reformers believing that he was on their side in the battle with the AMA, telling them that the 'same old crowd that has fought us so often is still at it – and only death will mend their ways'.[49] Roosevelt cleverly told each side what it wanted to hear, thereby pacifying the opponents without discouraging the reformers. He neither opposed nor favoured national health insurance in principle, but regarded it as one possible option among others. By remaining uncommitted, he was able to keep all his options open.

Even though the AMA's opposition had convinced the CES cabinet members that national health insurance could endanger the entire Social Security Act, Roosevelt himself was not intimidated by the opposition. Yet he had no compelling reason to deviate from the CES recommendations. Even without the opposition of the AMA, the inclusion of national health insurance would have made the Social Security Act more controversial. Roosevelt had preferred a moderate programme from the start. Moreover, he believed that through incremental reform, national health insurance could be added in the future – after a sound system of social security had been established and after federal investments had extended the medical care for which national health insurance was supposed to pay.

Over the years, the opposition of the AMA became more influential, partly because FDR's own position had weakened. Roosevelt needed all the support he could get for his war effort and could not afford to become involved in a domestic battle. In addition, the AMA's opposition became more organized. In the 1930s the AMA campaign had been targeted at its own rank and file, generated by the editorials of Morris Fishbein in the AMA's *Journal*. However, by the 1940s the AMA had focused its attention on the public debate. The AMA's intensified and extensive campaign further contributed to the myth that the opposition of the AMA was decisive in shaping American health policy.

This brings us back to the AMA's claim that Eleanor Roosevelt was an advocate in disguise. In actual fact, Eleanor Roosevelt shared her husband's preference for the extension of medical care over national health insurance. After FDR's death, she did endorse President Harry S. Truman's national health insurance plan, but continued to stress the importance of federal subsidizing of medical research and education. As she wrote: 'This means not only more medical facilities but more doctors, scientists, dentists, nurses and other specialists.'[50] Like her husband, she recognized that one could not push on all fronts. The Roosevelts understood that delivery was the essence of effective political strategy.

Notes

1. 'Doctors in Debate on Social Medicine', *New York Times*, 3 January 1935, copy in OF 511, Box 1, Franklin D. Roosevelt Library (FDRL).
2. Arthur Altmeyer, *The Formative Years of Social Security* (Madison, 1966), 27; Michael M. Davis, *Medical Care For Tomorrow* (New York, 1955), 280; Michael M. Davis to Odin W. Anderson, 30 April 1958, Falk Papers, Box 1, Folder 23, Yale Library.
3. Daniel S. Hirshfield, *The Lost Reform: The Campaign for Compulsory Health Insurance in the United States from 1932 to 1943* (Cambridge, MA, 1970); Monte M. Poen, *Harry S. Truman Versus the Medical Care Lobby: The Genesis of Medicare* (Columbia, MO, 1979); Paul Starr, *The Social Transformation of American Medicine: The Rise of a Sovereign Profession and the Making of a Vast Industry* (New York, 1982). One exception to this dominant view is Daniel M. Fox, *Health Policies, Health Politics: The British and American Experience, 1911–1965* (Princeton, 1986).
4. Frances Perkins, foreword to Edwin E. Witte, *The Development of the Social Security Act* (Madison, 1963), viii.
5. Franklin D. Roosevelt, 'Message to the Congress Reviewing the Broad Objectives and Accomplishments of the Administration', 8 June 1934, in Samuel I. Rosenman (ed.), *The Public Papers and Addresses of Franklin D. Roosevelt*, 13 vols (New York, 1938–50), vol. 3, 287–93.
6. Paul A. Kurzman, *Harry Hopkins and the New Deal* (Fair Lawn, NJ, 1974), 68, 125.
7. 'The Administration Studies Social Insurance', *Journal of the American Medical Association*, 103 (25 August 1934), 609–10.
8. Sydenstricker to Falk, 3 October 1934, Falk Papers, Box 42, Folder 220, Yale Library.
9. Witte, *Development*, 174. Sydenstricker to Witte, 24 October 1934, Records of the CES, RG 47, Box 16, National Archives (NA).
10. Witte, *Development*, 175–7. Falk to Sydenstricker, 17 September 1934, Falk to Sydenstricker, 18 September 1934, Falk to Sydenstricker, 19 September 1934, Falk Papers, Box 42, Folder 220, Yale Library.

11. Witte to Sydenstricker, 24 October 1934, Records of the CES, RG 47, Box 16, NA.
12. Witte, 'Report on Progress of Work during October [1934]', undated, Working Papers of the CES, RG 47, Box 1, NA. Witte to Perkins, 26 October 1934, as quoted in Hirshfield, *Lost Reform*, 47. I have not been able to locate this letter in the Records of the CES.
13. Altmeyer, *Formative Years*, 27; Witte, *Development*, 174.
14. 'Roosevelt Bars Plans Now For Broad Social Program', *New York Times*, 15 November 1934; Arthur Krock, 'In Washington', *New York Times*, 20 November 1934.
15. Witte, 'Suggestions for a long-time and an immediate program for economic security', 15 November 1934, Records of the CES, RG 47, Box 5, NA. 'Address of Miss Frances Perkins, Secretary of Labor, before the National Conference on Economic Security: The Task That Lies Ahead', 14 November 1934, Records of the CES, RG 47, Box 3, NA. Perkins gave the speech on 15 November 1935.
16. Sydenstricker to Witte, 10 January 1935, Records of the CES, RG 47, Box 16, NA.
17. Roosevelt, 'A Message to the Congress on Social Security', 17 January 1935, *Public Papers*, vol. 4, 45.
18. Hirshfield, *Lost Reform*, 50. Cushing to FDR, 10 November 1934, FDR to Cushing, 13 November 1934, FDR to Perkins, 13 November 1934, OF 103, Box 1, FDRL.
19. Cushing to Witte, 4 February 1935, Records of the CES, RG 47, Box 2, NA. Cushing to FDR, 1 February 1935, PPF 1523, FDRL. Hirshfield suggests that Cushing's actions were prompted by his eagerness to become AMA president. Hirshfield, *Lost Reform*, 55.
20. Sydenstricker to Witte, 21 February 1935, Records of the CES, RG 47, Box 16, NA.
21. Roosevelt to Cushing, 13 February 1935, PPF 1523, FDRL.
22. 'Proceedings: Meeting of the Medical Advisory Board [of the] Committee on Economic Security', 29–30 January 1935, Witte Papers, Box 65, State Historical Society of Wisconsin.
23. Fox, *Health Policies, Health Politics*, 79.
24. Draft enclosed with Falk to Davis, 22 March 1935, Falk Papers, Box 41, Folder 192, Yale Library.
25. Hirshfield, *Lost Reform*, 59; Witte, *Development*, 188.
26. Altmeyer to Stephen Early, 29 August 1935, d.j. [Dorothy Jones] to file, 31 August 1935, OF 1086, FDRL.
27. FDR to John G. Winant, 14 January 1934, OF 1086, FDRL. Additional copy in Arthur J. Altmeyer Papers, Box 2, State Historical Society of Wisconsin.
28. Roosevelt, 'Address at the Dedication of the Medical Center, Jersey City, NJ', 2 October 1936, *Public Papers*, 5, 408–10.
29. 'Minutes of Conference on Medical Care', 29 November 1937, Papers of the President's Interdepartmental Committee to Coordinate Health and Welfare Activities, Box 43, FDRL. Altmeyer, *Formative Years*, 261.
30. Interdepartmental Committee to Coordinate Health and Welfare

Activities, *Proceedings of the National Health Conference*, (Washington, DC: United States Government Printing Office, 1938), 29–32, 55–61. Sydenstricker died in 1936. I. S. Falk became director of the Bureau of Research and Statistics of the Social Security Board, responsible for the studies of national health insurance. For the development of the Social Security Board into an influential bureaucratic power, see Martha Derthick, *Policymaking for Social Security* (Washington, DC: The Brookings Institution, 1979).

31. Davis, *Medical Care for Tomorrow*, 278; Fox, *Health Policies, Health Politics*, 91–2.

32. Roosevelt, 'A Request for Consideration of the Recommendations of the Interdepartmental Committee to Coordinate Health Activities, with Respect to the National Health Program', 23 January 1939, *Public Papers*, vol. 8, 97–9.

33. Roosevelt, 'The Six Hundred and Eighth Press Conference', 22 December 1939, *Public Papers*, vol. 8, 599.

34. ER to Lape, 6 December 1939, Eleanor Roosevelt Papers, Personal Letters, FDRL.

35. Edward D. Berkowitz, *America's Welfare State: From Roosevelt to Reagan* (Baltimore, 1991), 157.

36. Fox, *Health Politics, Health Politics*, 117–20.

37. Roosevelt, 'Statement of the President on the Second Anniversary of the Atlantic Charter', 14 August 1943, *Public Papers*, vol. 12, 351.

38. Poen, *Harry S. Truman*, 40; Roosevelt, 'Message to Congress on the State of the Union', 11 January 1944, *Public Papers*, vol. 13, 41.

39. John Morton Blum, *From the Morgenthau Diaries: Years of War, 1941–1945* (Boston, 1976), 72.

40. Davis, *Medical Care For Tomorrow*, 280.

41. Wilbur J. Cohen, Oral History, 19 August 1966, Columbia University Oral History Collection (microfiche edition, Roosevelt Study Center), 55. Cohen began his career in social security as Witte's assistant during the CES days. He continued to work for the Social Security Administration and became the 'father of Medicare'. See Edward D. Berkowitz, *Mr Social Security: The Life of Wilbur J. Cohen* (Lawrence, KS, 1995).

42. Witte to James D. Bruce, 21 December 1934, Records of the CES, RG 47, Box 2, NA.

43. Morgan to FDR, 21 July 1935, FDR to Morgan, 26 July 1935, PPF 277, FDRL.

44. The report was sent to, among others, Marion B. Folsom (Eastman Kodak), William Green (American Federation of Labor), and Belle Sherwin (National League of Women Voters). See Falk Papers, Box 43, Folder 255, Yale Library.

45. Alan Derickson, 'Health Security for All? Social Unionism and Universal Health Insurance, 1935–1958', *The Journal of American History*, 80 (1994), 1333–56. Green to Altmeyer, 24 March 1935, Falk Papers, Box 43, Folder 255, Yale Library.

46. Folsom to Altmeyer, undated [March 1935], Falk Papers, Box 43, Folder 255, Yale Library. Marion B. Folsom, Oral History, 9 June 1965, Columbia

University Oral History Collection (microfiche edition, Roosevelt Study Center), 44.

47. Jill Quadagno, *The Color of Welfare: How Racism Undermined the War on Poverty* (New York, 1994), 10, 21. Another explanation for the exclusion of farmers and domestic servants is a practical one. 'Unlike large industrial employers, farmers [and housewives], according to a popular prejudice that the Social Security planners did not challenge, kept poor records of their payroll, and in many cases hired live-in help, which meant that part of the laborer's income took the form of room and board.' Berkowitz, *America's Welfare State*, 25.

48. Walter White to FDR, 24 September 1934, OF 121, Box 1, FDRL.

49. FDR to Kingsbury, 6 April 1938, PPF 1031, FDRL.

50. Eleanor Roosevelt, 'My Day', 4 April 1946, in David Emblidge (ed.), *Eleanor Roosevelt's My Day: Her Acclaimed Columns, Volume II: The Post-War Years, 1945–1952* (New York, 1990), 55.

4

New Deal Programmes for Youth: Recent Historiography and Future Research

Olaf Stieglitz

In the 1933 social-issue film, *Wild Boys of the Road*, Eddie, Tommy and Sally, three teenagers from middle-class families, travel on freight trains, make their living with odd jobs, stealing and begging, and end up in a New York City Juvenile Court. Accused of robbery and 'waywardness', the three youngsters are lucky. A compassionate judge, presiding under the sign of the National Recovery Administration's Blue Eagle, 'does his part' by suspending their sentences and promising them local work relief, continued schooling and even jobs for their unemployed fathers. Eddie responds to the prospect of a brighter future, offered by the judge, with a series of flic-flac handsprings on the streets in front of the courthouse.[1]

The film is suggestive. In a recent encyclopaedic essay, the historian Ruth Alexander identifies the developing life styles, behaviours and norms of the new 'youth culture' which emerged in the early twentieth century and registers the numerous reactions of anxious parents and excited experts to these perceived trends. She claims that, 'the Great Depression temporarily interrupted American anxieties about youth'.[2] Her contention is provocative.

Interest in the so-called 'youth problem' continued through the 1930s and *Wild Boys of the Road* is but one example drawn from contemporary popular culture. The film not only registered social trends in the homeless and transient teenagers who were its subjects, but contained both the symbolism and rhetoric of the New Deal. Embedded in the narrative and symbolized by the judge is a confidence and trust in institutionalized authority. This relationship between a motion picture about youth and the New Deal is by no means coincidential. The decade of the 1930s was characterized by a strong and unprecedented commitment by the federal government to the welfare of the United States' young citizens. Their plight, most evident in high unemployment rates, was of direct concern to the New Deal. It prompted Eleanor Roosevelt's well-known remark that 'we may be losing this generation'.[3]

Under the New Deal, two agencies were established which served primarily the interests of youth or, alternatively, what New Dealers perceived were the interests of youth. The Civilian Conservation Corps (CCC), created as President Franklin D. Roosevelt's 'pet programme' in the 'Hundred Days' after his inauguration, employed in its camps almost three million young men over a nine-year period. The National Youth Administration (NYA) was established in 1935 to help students work their way through high school or college. These agencies testify to an ongoing concern about youth in US political culture during the 1930s.

However, historical writing about young people during the Great Depression has tended to reflect Ruth Alexander's interpretation. Partly, this is because the issue of youth in the New Deal era has not benefited from analysis through the 'new social history' as have other periods. The steadily growing literature on the history of childhood and adolescence has largely focused on periods in history when booming economies allowed easy access to those consumable material goods that were necessary to form and to develop a flourishing youth culture. Also, historians of the New Deal who have written about youth have been reluctant to branch out from their field of institutional history to incorporate both the real experiences, attitudes and interests of young men and women and the reactions of the adult generations to them. Often their work is more informative about the New Deal than about youth.

This essay will examine the recent literature related to the New Deal's programmes for youth. It will define 'youth' as comprising young people, roughly between the ages of fifteen and twenty-five, excluding both children and 'young adults' who were already settled in either stable work relations and/or marriage. In its first part, the essay summarizes the findings and perspectives of historical research and interpretation regarding the New Deal's youth agencies and, in particular, the CCC and the NYA. It proceeds to develop a research schedule that encourages historians to incorporate social and cultural elements to the institutional dimension of the New Deal's relationship to young Americans. The aim is to identify and to develop a specific discourse related to the experience of youth during the 1930s which incorporates American traditions, the federal government's commitment and rhetoric, demographic and social trends, and the status of young men and women in, and the representation of them by, popular culture.

The brief references to the NYA in general history textbooks have three characteristics. First, the agency is portrayed as a branch of the larger Works Progress Administration (WPA) which distributed relief money and jobs to students. As such, the NYA is viewed as part of a broader programme in which the WPA provided work relief to adult workers and creative artists. Second, the references indulge in the cult of the celebrity, by focusing on administrators of the programme such as Aubrey Williams, the agency's head, or Lyndon B. Johnson who was responsible for local projects in Texas. Johnson attracts particular interest because he allows historians to speculate about the links between his presidential period and the 1930s and the degree to which the 'Great Society' of the 1960s was inspired by the New Deal. Mary McLeod Bethune's work for the NYA's Division of Negro Affairs is also given prominence especially because it exemplifies a third characteristic of the coverage of the NYA in general textbooks: given the circumstances of the time, it had a remarkable record of racial equality and justice.

Until recently, John Salmond's biography of Aubrey Williams, published in 1983, has been the most authoritative source on the NYA and, effectively, compounded the 'great men/great woman' approach to the agency.[4] This well-researched and written book provides interesting insights into the network of mutual confidence and support among the New Dealers which allowed Williams to engage in his reform efforts despite his inability to compromise with the southern elite on the issue of racial equality. However, because the narrative is focused on the construction of Williams as a 'southern rebel', Salmond is not able to free himself and his readers from the dichotomy between a 'good', liberal southerner and his 'bad', conservative antagonists. The significance of the NYA is presented as a battlefield for Williams' civil rights ideas. Although informative about the NYA, the biography serves to reinforce prevailing textbook notions.[5]

Richard Reiman's *The New Deal and American Youth: Ideas and Ideals in a Depression Decade*, published in 1992, challenged many prevailing views about the NYA and, in particular, the notion that the agency was merely a 'junior WPA'.[6] It fills a void in the historiography on the NYA. The most valuable aspects of Reiman's work are its explorations of the intellectual origins of the NYA, the planning process which led to its creation, and the changing focus of the agency between 1933 and 1943. Drawing on correspondence and agency records, a complex narrative unfolds which links the establishment of the NYA to a popular sentiment about the 'plasticity of young minds'.[7] Deeply embedded in the discourse on adolescence which emerged in the last years of the nineteenth century were assumptions about the necessity of adult supervision and guidance.[8] In the 1930s this notion acquired a strong political meaning. Policymakers feared that the young generation – in effect, the nation's future – was endangered by the appeals of 'totalitarian' or 'un-American' ideologies. According to Reiman, the founders of the NYA were not just engaged in creating another simple relief agency without any broader cultural vision or without a political purpose.

However, the author's emphasis on New Dealers' plans and ambitions sets up a distorted representation of the NYA because it obscures what the agency accomplished in fact. Reiman constructs a conflict between the US Office of Education's plans for the agency to dispense student aid and a group, led by Aubrey Williams, which favoured the provision of vocational and citizenship training. Clearly, Reiman's sympathies are with the Williams faction, and he pays much attention to the creation of rural residential centres, which placed out-of-school youths in group-living arrangements where they would receive both vocational and citizenship training.[9] While Reiman isolates the mostly unfulfilled – or, alternatively, partially realized – visions and plans of the NYA's leadership cadre, he does not throw much light on the mainstream NYA programmes. The large majority of the NYA's funding was assigned to student aid and work relief. Furthermore, while Reiman demonstrates how much the New Deal's policy for young Americans was influenced by and contributed to contemporaneous social discourses, he fails to develop the meaning of concepts like 'citizenship' or 'work' in the NYA's context. Clearly they are central to the social discourses he delineates and, as such, crucial to his most salient point about the significance of the NYA transcending its status as a relief agency.

Much recent historical writing has focused on Texas and on the role of Lyndon B. Johnson as the agency's state director. This literature tends to reinforce the prevailing understanding in two respects: it stresses the importance of leadership and confirms the NYA's efforts on behalf of ethnic minorities and women.[10] Carol Weisenberger, in her study of 1994, *Dollars and Dreams: The National Youth Administration in Texas*, skilfully examines the difficult task of translating national guidelines into the practical necessities of a southern state and places Lyndon Johnson at the forefront of the process.[11] Determined to achieve the policy goals formulated by Williams and Bethune and inspired by the rhetoric of Eleanor Roosevelt, Johnson, and his successor Jesse Kellam, were 'blazing new trails' which required considerable finesse in political tactics.[12] Weisenberger utilizes archival sources and the testimony of almost 200 former NYA members to show that Johnson used his position to build a state-wide political network which promoted the agency's operational effectiveness while serving LBJ's political interests. In the process, both the idealism of the enterprise and the crucial role of leadership are confirmed by the Texas example. Research into the NYA at state level reveals the mechanism of policy implementation and the compromises that policy-makers were obliged to make to adapt to local circumstances. However, the perspective of the young clients of the NYA remains largely ignored. A social historian interested in the lives and experiences of adolescent Americans would not find much in the recent historical scholarship about the NYA to arouse his or her attention.

The neglect is less glaring in historians' analyses of the Civilian Conservation Corps and scholarly interest is unflagging. The CCC holds a much fonder place in the national memory. Ranking among the most popular of all the New Deal's agencies, the abiding image of the tanned, healthy and optimistic young man performing a meaningful and valuable job in the Triple-C's reforestation camps belongs to those vignettes recalled as 'bright spots' in a mostly dark decade. Furthermore, the CCC continues to have relevance because of current youth unemployment and the social problems of inner-cities in the United States and other nations which have reinvigorated conscious concerns about the need to support young people and to maintain social stability. Political scientists and journalists frequently employ the CCC as a historical citation and even offer it as a blueprint for an operational and effective future youth policy. Indeed, some local, state or federal programmes, established in the United States during the last thirty years on behalf of the underprivileged or to re-socialise criminal youth, contain, if not the actual shape of the Three C's, at least its spirit.[13] The reputation of the CCC as one of the great successes of the New Deal is the point of reference with which every historian writing about the subject has to engage.

Two different 'genres' of historical literature form the backbone of historical writing about the CCC. The first comprises the personal memories of former members, both from the ranks of common enrolees and by the CCC staff. Often, these accounts are highly subjective, but they do contain valuable information on the policy, the structure, and the daily life of the Corps. First-person testimony corroborates and develops our understanding of the typical routines of the CCC, the nature of the work projects and the accompanying educational programmes. Work experience receives particular emphasis in the texts written by former Corps members, and eight hours of physical labour daily shapes the reminiscences of many. Detailed statements like the one following are typical:

> The planting bar was used in a definite step pattern. It was first driven into the ground, pulled back toward you, then pushed away from you, leaving a slot in the ground of about one half inch wide, 2 inches across, and 4 to 5 inches deep. The seedlings were then dropped into the slot and the bar was driven into the ground in back of the seedling, again pulling it toward you to tighten up the soil on the seedling, then aways from you to tighten the top soil around the plant. Then it was heeled-in where the planting bar was last placed. This sounds like a lot of monkey business but the foresters came

along in back of the crew to spot-check and make sure we were planting the trees right.[14]

Such information is an important addition to other work-related data on the CCC as can be found in the statistics of Annual Reports and other official records. From a methodological standpoint, first-person testimony is a problematic kind of source, for it often lacks historical rigour and a distanced perspective. But on the grounds that it was an aim of the CCC to form the personalities and characters of its members, long-time memory as articulated in those texts is important for the historian. The paragraph quoted above not only contains insights about the manual nature of many of the Corp's work projects and its 'frontier' spirit, but it also demonstrates how 'scientific' work had to be performed, how much it was rationalized economically, and, last but not least, how much it was controlled.[15]

Regional studies comprise the second, and more influential, source of information and interpretation on the Civilian Conservation Corps.[16] During the last decade a number of studies have been published that trace the history of a single CCC camp or chart the accomplishments of one of the Corps' districts. What differentiates these regional studies from the personal memoirs is their scholarly standard. The authors have conducted intensive research in local and regional records, thereby utilising the enormous amount of material available in archives and other public facilities of historical interest, and thus produce more objective and balanced results. Some scholars restrict their findings to the presentation of detailed lists of changing staff members or compute the laboured men-days on the projects, but the most important of these contributions scrutinise the agency's relationships with local and regional power structures. This approach, which corresponds to a general trend of historical writing on the New Deal, has produced important findings, especially with regard to the CCC's policy towards African-Americans[17] and, more recently, towards Spanish-speaking enrolees.[18] Moreover, there is growing interest in locating the CCC within a network of different welfare organisa-tions.[19] The pragmatic idea of organizing the enrolment policy of the Corps on the basis of already existing welfare agencies proved to be a significant disadvantage for ethnic minorities, especially for African-Americans in the South. Local prejudices, though, played an important role in integrating the Triple-C in a regional network of assistance, and the agency showed only a modest intention to confront them. Although historians are aware of this discriminatory aspect, the gist of their interpretative emphasis is that the CCC was a successful means of federal youth welfare policy which has relevance to conditions today.

Eric Gorham is a scholar who has adopted a much more critical perspective on the CCC. A political scientist by training, Gorham first negotiated the agency in relation to the debate on national service.[20] *National Service, Citizenship, and Political Education*, published in 1992, is primarily concerned with more recent examples of organization, established to promote political socialization, but he dedicates a chapter to the Corps which provides historical context and a yardstick for recent plans to create a national service agency. His main emphasis is on the Corps' concept of citizenship and its programme of training, and Gorham concludes that it did not fulfil the standards of a truly democratic and liberal education. He argues that this is due to structural factors. The Corps produced citizens of 'unpolitical nature' because the process of political socialization in the agency took place in an hierarchical formation that systematically discouraged 'critical thinking' and which promoted one model of political government as a stable, almost natural 'fact' without considering possible alternatives.[21] In Gorham's opinion, the 'totalitarian danger' registered by Richard Reiman as a leitmotif in the establishment of the National Youth Administration, underpinned the CCC's efforts to educate young men.[22] Gorham's critique resembles and re-formulates the contemporaneous protests of liberals and radicals who resented the Army's role and its prioritization of efficient work over education.

Of greater significance is Gorham's theoretical and methodological awareness. In an article he published in *Social History* he applied the theories of Michel Foucault specifically to the policy of the Civilian Conservation Corps. In conceptual terms, his analysis is grounded in Foucault's *Discipline and Punish*, the French philosopher's study of criminal justice, the development of the prison system and its role in producing what he calls 'docile bodies'.[23] Gorham draws attention to the strict timetables of the CCC, its formal work classifications, its bureaucracy and first of all its language to demonstrate that 'the pro-gramme modernised the young man, teaching him attitudes and behavior that reflected a more modern subjectivity'.[24] As such, Gorham traces the micro-structures of power found in modern democratic societies. It is an approach long overdue; not only because the work of Foucault has aroused interest in a growing number of historians, but because of the congruence between the organisation of the CCC and those institutions of discipline upon which Foucault focused. Gor-ham's work may be criticized for slavishly and mechanically adopting the concepts and language of *Discipline and Punish* and for its 'ahistoric' tendency, because it takes no account of the relationship of the agency to discourses on youth that date back to the late nineteenth century, fails to show how the agency developed during the 1930s, and neglects the conflicting interests of groups and departments which had a vested interest in the Corps. However, it does suggest possibilities about how to enliven an entrenched discourse by examining the functionality of language in situations of value transmission, a central aspect of both the NYA and the CCC. If Gorham has neglected important archival sources essential to the working historian, he does provide a framework with which the research-historian can work. Moreover, integrating the research on New Deal agencies into what has become known as the 'New Cultural History' keeps historians' debates in close touch with discussions in other fields within the humanities and promises to broaden our view on the 1930s in general.

The work of Gorham and Reiman, in particular, may serve as points of departure to develop a fuller sense of the lives and interests of young Americans during the Depression decade and the ways in which they related to the ideology and policy of the New Deal state. Together, they suggest that, to a large extent, both the CCC and the NYA drew on prevailing concepts and discourses, transforming them to suit the specific interests of each agency and thus producing new formulations of ideological social meaning. However, to appreciate fully the experience of youth in these agencies the analytical terrain perhaps needs to be broadened to include other discourses about, for example, work, sexuality and citizenship.

During the early twentieth century the relationship between concepts of 'work' and 'time' was a contentious issue in industrial relations, a preoccupation of social reform movements and an aspect of American popular culture.[25] All the New Deal's work relief agencies were embedded in this discourse on the value, significance and the content of the concept of 'work' and all of them, in formulating their own definitions of 'work', excluded some aspects in favour of others. The CCC, for instance, as an agency for young, working-class unemployed persons placed no value on creativity in the work process, but instead stressed the educative value of physical labour and traditional virtues of industry, honesty and responsibility in strong relation to the aspect of time. Those enrolees called 'gold-brickers', 'clockwatchers', or 'slackers', 'those who do just enough to get by but not serious enough to get a discharge', risked stiff sanctions from Camp officers.[26] The usual punishment was to deduct a certain amount of money from the boys' monthly pay, thus stressing the relationship between the 'honest workday' and the chance to participate in expensive leisure-time activities. Despite the promotion of the interests of unionized labour by the New Deal, unionisation or collective bargaining were not considered relevant to juveniles. Strikes were a common practice among the enrolees. But although most strikes were unpolitical in character and were organized spontaneously in order to achieve improved camp conditions, Army leaders tended to judge such 'refusal to work' as a clear sign of a prevailing left-wing radical spirit in the Corps. Some Officers linked such actions to the 'un-American' character of recent immigrants among the enrolees in that 'gaining objectives through the medium of 'striking' may be part of their past training'.[27]

Similarly, the CCC also participated in the discourse on gender. The demographic composition of a Triple-C camp created an all-male atmosphere which in one way or another had to respond to the 'masculinity crisis' of the late nineteenth and early twentieth century and, in particular, to the so-called 'sexual revolution' experienced by young Americans during the 1920s.[28] The Corps celebrated the strong male body and its economic, moral and eugenic value. According to the Director's Annual Report of 1940: 'The tanned, healthy, well-muscled men who are discharged from the Corps at the end of their enrolment are in marked contrast to the pale, oft-times stoop-shouldered, undernourished youths who replace them in camp.'[29] The consequence of the Corps' emphasis on the male body was to stabilize gender roles perceived as endangered. To achieve this objective, traditional working-class notions of masculinity like physical activity and aggressive competition had to be underscored on a basic level, but were 'channelled' with the help of ideals rooted in the Victorian understanding of an inward-oriented 'manhood'. 'Men like that,' the CCC's newspaper informed its readers, '...will make forests grow. They will build nations.'[30]

Such statements indicate that the aspect of 'citizenship' constitutes another important field of investigation.[31] In fact, all those prevailing discourses of class, race, gender, youth and work became incorporated under the umbrella of that concept, furnishing all of them with specific meanings in the CCC as well as in the NYA. In the Triple-C, officially formulated theories of citizenship included all different groups of enrolees – Anglos, African-Americans, Spanish-speaking Americans – as completely equal in terms of rights and duties, although the CCC was usually made up of segregated companies.[32] According to the accepted leitmotif of 'separate but equal' treatment, 'successful' African-American enrolees, for example, were attributed the same characteristics as their white comrades: industry, honesty, respectability and patriotism. Moreover, African-Americans profited enormously by the Corps' medical and educational programmes. These are undoubtedly positive achievements of the agency, yet they hide significant discrimination. The numbers of African-American members in the CCC were never close to reaching the official quotas: they lived and worked in segregated camps under the command of white officers, and the establishment of such camps was almost impossible in the South and provoked constant racism in northern states. Nevertheless, in the words of one African-American corpsman, the double standard could have a beneficial effect:

But I found out that my officers and companions stretched points in my favor ... perhaps because they were reluctant to have it said that they were prejudiced because of my color ... Whenever inspectors or dignitaries visited camp, it was my work they singled out for praise. And all encouraged me in my singing by telling me that my voice was made for classical songs ... Had I been white I would have been just another enrollee.[33]

Talking about young people should never be a social control discourse only, and historical research should include more than just adults' published opinions on the young generation. In order to appreciate the relationship between the New Deal's youth agencies and its juvenile clients, it is necessary to accept young men and women as historical agents in their own right and to evaluate the subjective experience of adolescents. Did they really appreciate the agencies because they were supposedly designed to benefit them, or were the New Deal's alphabetical agencies considered a threat to teenage autonomy? What motivated individuals in their decision to enrol in one or the other organisation? Clearly, powerful forces must have been at work to prompt a seventeen-year-old who lived in a small town to join the Civilian Conservation Corps and leave his familiar environment. Limited employment opportunities, probably reinforced by the rest of his family being on relief, were the most significant factors. However, the individual situation is likely to have been much more complex and would vary from one individual to another. Parental influence and peer-group pressure must have been major considerations. The history of those rejected is another dimension that deserves historical scrutiny: young probationers or parolees, for instance, considered the CCC to be a medium for social re-integration, but their enrolment was officially restricted. Others were excluded because of medical reasons. Most of the 'mental defections', to use the language of the Corps, that physicians diagnosed at inspections, were probably completely unknown to rural people. How they lived on with their 'new illness' would be an interesting question, but to answer this and other not strictly institutional ones require new historical perspectives.

Further historical examination is especially urgent with regard to young women. Residential programmes for female youth during the New Deal, first under the Federal Emergency Relief Administration and later under the NYA, were small in both number and scale.[34] In offering a redefinition of domesticity as a 'women's career', these programmes not only reflected a gendered approach to welfare policy in general, but also a clear response to trends of the 1920s. As path-breaking studies by Glen Elder and John Modell show, in their efforts to analyse life-courses along institutionalized stages of adolescent behaviour like dating, first job experience or engagement for example, the Great Depression heavily cut the amount of disposable income and re-established close family ties and values.[35] For young women of the post-flapper generation, this created other and probably larger problems than for their male friends. The New Deal and its youth programmes, in either excluding women completely (the CCC) or patronizing them (as did some projects of the NYA, although others offered real material help), added to the disappearance of the 'public woman' of the 1920s.

However, even in the 1930s youth cultures in both their male and female designs remained concerned with aspects of consumerism and material goods like clothes, music, magazines and other fashion accessories, and there were gangs and secret societies at schools as well as colleges with highly coded rules of conduct. These cultures were very diverse according to class, gender and ethnicity and also varied according to regional circumstances. Traces of these cultures are to be found not only in the scholarly literature of the Depression decade but also in autobiographies, fiction and films designed for the youth market. Not only do they articulate the interests of young Americans more clearly and precisely than the adults who claimed to represent and understand them, but these very material artefacts of American popular culture were utilized by young people to construct a distinctive identity. Such issues may seem to be far removed from either the institutional histories of federal agencies or the theoretical analysis of hegemonic ideologies. However, historical scrutiny of these aspects promises to provide a fuller appreciation of America's young people during the 1930s which will, in turn, add to our understanding of the significance of the New Deal's welfare policy towards them.

Notes

1. *Wild Boys of the Road*, 1933, produced by Warner Brothers and directed by William A. Wellman. Cast: Frankie Darro, Dorothy Coonan, Edwin Phillips, Rochelle Hudson. Sally, the girl in the gang, remains a 'wild boy' as long as she lives as a tramp. To earn herself the return fare home, the judge wants her to work as a domestic servant, thus re-establishing traditional gender-roles.

2. Ruth M. Alexander, 'Adolescence' in Mary Kupiec Cayton, Elliott J. Gorn and Peter W. Williams (eds), *Encyclopedia of American Social History*, vol. 3 (New York, 1993), 2046.

3. Joseph P. Lash, *Eleanor and Franklin: The Story of Their Relationship*, (New York, 1971), 536–7.

4. John Salmond, *A Southern Rebel: The Life and Times of Aubrey Willis Williams, 1890–1965* (Chapel Hill, 1983).

5. It is interesting that the Civilian Conservation Corps was also headed by a southerner: Until his death on New Year's Eve 1939, Robert Fechner was responsible for a much worse record concerning nondiscriminatory activity.

6. Richard A. Reiman, *The New Deal and American Youth: Ideals and Ideas in a Depression Decade* (Athens, Ga., 1992).

7. Ibid., 6.

8. Joseph F. Kett, *Rites of Passage: Adolescents in America, 1790 to the Present* (New York, 1977), 243ff.

9. Reiman, *New Deal and American Youth*, Chapter 7. See also Michael G. Wade, '"Farm Dorm Boys": The Origins of the NYA Resident Training Program', *Louisiana History* 27 (no. 2, 1986), 117–32.

10. Christie L. Bourgeois, 'Stepping over Lines: Lyndon B. Johnson, Black Texans, and the National Youth Administration, 1935–1937', *Southwestern Historical Quarterly* 91 (no. 2, 1987), 149–72; Ronald M. James and Michelle McFadden, 'Remnants of the National Youth Administration in Nevada', *Nevada Historical Society Quarterly* 34 (no. 3, 1991), 415–20; Olen Cole Jr., 'Black Youth in the National Youth Administration in California, 1935–1943', *Southern California Quarterly* 73 (no. 4, 1991), 385–402; Florence F. Corley, 'The National Youth Administration in Georgia: A New Deal for Young Blacks and Women', *Georgia Historical Quarterly* 77 (no. 4, 1993), 728–56.

11. Carol A. Weisenberger, *Dollars and Dreams: The National Youth Administration in Texas* (New York, 1994). See also her 'Operating the Texas National Youth Administration by the Book – More than Relief', *Locus* 2 (no. 1, 1989), 49–67.

12. 'Blazing New Trails' is the title of Weisenberger's fifth chapter. Dealing with the First Lady, see Mildred W. Abramowitz, 'Eleanor Roosevelt and the National Youth Administration 1935–1943 – An Extension of the Presidency', *Presidential Studies Quarterly* 14 (no. 4, 1984), 569–80; on the head of the Division of Negro Affairs refer to Elaine M. Smith, 'Mary McLeod Bethune and the National Youth Administration' in Mabel E. Deutrich and Virginia C. Purdy (eds), *Clio Was a Woman: Studies in the History of American Women*, (Washington, DC, 1980), 149–77.

13. Besides some book-length accounts by political scientists or sociologists dealing with this aspect, contributions to the American debate published in popular magazines include: 'National Service: Reinventing the Wheel', *The Economist* (13 June 1992), 29; Bob Cohn, 'Doing Something Meaningful: A National-Service Program Helps Urban Youths', *Newsweek*, 114 (no. 9, 28 July 1989), 38. For a similar discussion in Great Britain see Ann Thedford, 'Roosevelt's New Deal Program for Unemployed Youth – A Model for Today' in *Contemporary Review*, 241 (no. 1399, 1982), 93–7. In the summer of 1996 the German weekly magazine *Die Zeit* published a series of articles discussing the problem of youth unemployment with regard to a national service agency and some of them used the CCC as a positive frame of reference.

14. Charles A. Symon, *We Can Do It! A History of the Civilian Conservation Corps in Michigan, 1933–1942* (Escabana, Mich., 1982), 111. The best

among the more recently published memoirs is Edwin G. Hill, *In the Shadow of the Mountain: The Spirit of the CCC* (Pullman, WA, 1990). See also Charles E. Humberger, 'The Civilian Conservation Corps in Nebraska: Memoirs of Company 762', *Nebraska History* 75 (no. 4, 1994), 292–300; David D. Draves, *Builder of Men: Life in the C.C.C. Camps of New Hampshire* (Portsmouth, NH, 1992); Robert E. Ermentrout, *Forgotten Men: The Civilian Conservation Corps* (Smithtown, NY, 1982).

15. For this kind of analysis see Eric B. Gorham, 'The Ambiguous Practices of the Civilian Conservation Corps', *Social History* 17 (no. 2, 1992), 229–49, here p. 237. Gorham's approach to the CCC is discussed below.

16. Some recent publications are: Kenneth E. Hendrickson Jr., 'Relief for Youth: The Civilian Conservation Corps and the National Youth Administration in North Dakota', *North Dakota History* 48 (no. 4, 1981), 17–27; Roger L. Rosentreter, 'Roosevelt's Tree Army: The Civilian Conservation Corps in Michigan', *Michigan History* 70 (no. 3, 1988), 205–16; Peter M. Booth, 'The Civilian Conservation Corps in Arizona, 1933–1942' (MA thesis, University of Arizona, 1991); Suzanne H. Schrems, 'A Lasting New Deal Legacy: The Civilian Conservation Corps, the National Park Service, and the Development of the Oklahoma State Park System', *Chronicles of Oklahoma* 72 (no. 4, 1994–5), 368–95; Frank Knox, 'The CCC: Shaper of Destinies', *Pacific Northwesterner* 36 (no. 2, 1992), 17–26; Matthew A. Redinger, 'The Civilian Conservation Corps and the Development of Glacier and Yellowstone Parks, 1933–1942', *Pacific Northwest Forum* 4 (no. 2, 1991), 3–17; Billy G. Hinson, 'The Civilian Conservation Corps in Mobile County, Alabama', *Alabama Review* 45 (no. 4, 1992), 243–56.

17. Ann Burkly, 'Blacks in the Civilian Conservation Corps: Successful Despite Discrimination', *Proceedings and Papers of the Georgia Association of Historians* 14 (1993), 37–45; Olen Cole, Jr., 'African-American Youth in the Program of the Civilian Conservation Corps in California, 1933–42: An Ambivalent Legacy', *Forest and Conservation History* 35 (no. 3, 1991), 121–7.

18. María E. Montoya, 'The Roots of Economic and Ethnic Divisions in Northern New Mexico: The Case of the Civilian Conservation Corps', *Western Historical Quarterly* 26 (no. 1, 1995), 14–34.

19. Successful in integrating the CCC into the network of New Deal agencies on a state level is Douglas C. Adams, *Conservative Constraints: North Carolina and the New Deal* (Jackson, Miss., 1992).

20. Eric B. Gorham, *National Service, Citizenship, and Political Education* (New York, 1992).

21. Ibid., 129.

22. 'If the New Deal really intended to control youth's behavior and mold their minds (which it did not), it selected in the NYA an instrument singularly ill-equipped for their task', states Reiman in *The New Deal and American Youth*, 6–7. That may be true, but it certainly employed another concept of political socialization in the CCC with regard to another segment youth that originated mostly from a heterogeneous working class.

23. See Michel Foucault, *Surveiller et punir: La naissance de la prison* (Paris, 1975).

24. Gorham, 'Ambiguous Practices', 230.

25. A valuable overview of this debate is Gary Cross, *Time and Money: The Making of Consumer Culture* (London and New York, 1993); for an informative discussion of developing discourses in turn-of-the-century America, see Alun Munslow, *Discourse and Culture: The Creation of America, 1870–1920* (London and New York, 1992).

26. Minutes of the Advisory Council to the Director, 5 February 1934 RG 35, Entry 10, National Archives. The minutes continue: 'Mr Fechner says that in his opinion malingering is just as bad or worse than refusal to work ...'. See also Olaf Stieglitz, '*100 Percent American Boys': Disziplinierungsdiskurse und Ideologie im Civilian Conservation Corps, 1933–1942* (Stuttgart, 1998).

27. See the report of Camp Investigator A. W. Stockman, Camp PNM–2-A, Co. No. 3342, Adamana, AZ, 28/29 October 1938, RG 35, Entry 114, Box 11, National Archives.

28. The 'masculinity crisis' and the historiography dealing with it is discussed in Gail Bederman, *Manliness and Civilization: A Cultural History of Gender and Race in the United States, 1880–1917* (Chicago and London, 1995).

29. Civilian Conservation Corps, *Annual Report of the Director of the Civilian Conservation Corps, 1940*, (Washington, DC, 1940), 8.

30. *Happy Days. Authorized Newspaper of the CCC*, 1 (no. 9, 15 July 1933), RG 35, Entry 18, National Archives.

31. For a broader discussion of this topic see Olaf Stieglitz, '" ... very much an American life": The Concept of "Citizenship" in the Civilian Conservation Corps, 1933–1942', in Knud Krakau (ed.), *The American Nation – National Identity – Nationalism*, (Münster 1997), 185–95.

32. The most elaborate theory of citizenship for the CCC is Kenneth Holland and Frank E. Hill, *Youth in the CCC. Prepared for the American Youth Commission. Ed. by the American Council on Education*, (Washington, DC, 1942).

33. From a letter to the editors, *Happy Days*, 5 (no. 30, 12 December 1937), 7.

34. Susan Wladaver-Morgan, 'Young Women and the New Deal: Camps and Resident Centers, 1933–1943', dissertation, Indiana University, 1982. Reiman, *New Deal and American Youth*, 143ff.

35. Glen H. Elder Jr., *Children of the Great Depression: Social Change in Life Experience* (Chicago, 1974); John Modell, *Into One's Own: From Youth to Adulthood in the United States, 1920–1975* (Berkeley, 1989), especially Chapter 4.

5

The Unsuspected Radicalism of the Social Security Act*

Gareth Davies

Writing in the mid-1980s, the historian Clarke Chambers made the following comment on the historiography of the Social Security Act of 1935: 'I know of no development in social policy more extensively and critically recorded by so many movers and shakers than the story of social security. Here is a body of literature weighty enough to give even the most sanguine of scholars pause.'[1] Over a decade on, the task is still more daunting, for recent years have seen an explosion of writing on the subject. With important exceptions that are referred to below, much of this literature has emphasized the essential conservatism of the arrangements that the New Dealers set in place. These criticisms have concerned both the needs-based public assistance, or 'welfare' titles of the Social Security Act, and its contributory, social insurance programmes. Taken together, and at the risk of over-generalizing, critics argue that the Roosevelt administration perpetuated old distinctions between the 'deserving' and the 'undeserving' poor, that it left too much power with the states and localities, and that its programmes discriminated against African-Americans and women. And as with so much other recent writing on the 1930s and 1940s, these overwhelmingly left-leaning scholars mourn the road not taken, contending in some cases that the New Dealers missed an historic opportunity to build a more social democratic state.[2]

My purpose here is to suggest that, at least in the case of social security, such criticisms overstate the amount of freedom that the administration enjoyed, and understate its achievement in the face of formidable constraints. In the case of Old Age Insurance (OAI), which was the only federally administered title, and which provides the focus for this essay, it would be hard to deny that the Social Security Act represented a momentous breakthrough in United States social policy. Even Mimi Abramovitz, who is generally critical of the Act, acknowledges that OAI was 'an historic milestone in terms of the role

---

* The author would like to acknowledge his debt to Mertha Derthick, without whose criticisms and advice this essay could not have been written.

of the state'.[3] And Linda Gordon, whilst contending that much more could have been done, observes that 'Social Security was a major achievement ... and a historic transformation in the role of the federal government'.[4]

Nevertheless, OAI is presented by these and other scholars as having been a conservative and overly cautious measure. Its payroll tax has been criticized as regressive and – in the context of the Depression – deflationary, while many experts both then and since have regretted the decision to rely exclusively on employer and employee contributions (the alternative would have been for the federal government to make some contribution to the fund[5]). Rather than ape the lexicon and practices of the private insurance industry, critics argue, the Roosevelt administration should have recognized that equitable old-age security required a decisive break with tradition. Such critics follow in the footsteps of Barton Bernstein, who alleged a quarter of a century ago that 'the government, by making workers contribute to their old-age insurance, denied its financial responsibility for the elderly'.[6] One book that makes many of these criticisms is Jerry Cates's cleverly titled *Insuring Inequality*. Sharply critical of OAI's 'antiredistributional approach', Cates writes of the 'astonishing conservatism of the 1935 Act's provisions in the face of the great need among the Depression-era aged'.[7]

More recent works have criticized OAI from different standpoints. Gwendolyn Mink is one of a number of scholars who finds gender-biases in the contributory programmes. Focusing on the exclusion from coverage of retail, clerical, hospital, domestic, seasonal and 'casual' workers, and pointing to the high proportion of women employed in these categories, she concludes that occupational exemptions 'rendered working women invisible as productive citizens, unprotected against interruptions to their work lives, and unequal in old age and death'. 'To the extent that the "welfare state breakthrough" of the New Deal hangs on the development of national social insurance', she tells us, 'we can say that the modern U.S. welfare state was crafted (mostly) by men – for men, capitalism, and democracy.'[8] Other scholars see OAI as having been racially discriminatory, noting that millions of African-Americans were barred from coverage when agricultural and domestic workers were exempted from coverage. Robert Lieberman believes that 'the systematic exclusion of blacks through occupational classifications was crucial to the passage of the act'.[9] Connecting to the two bases for exclusion, Gwendolyn Mink tells us that the New Deal welfare state 'tilled the soil of a racialised gender politics of dependency'.[10]

Not all recent work on the Social Security Act takes this line, of course. Edward Berkowitz, Blanche Coll, and Sheryl Tynes, while sensitive to the limits of OAI, pay far greater attention to the radicalism of its break with the past than do the aforementioned scholars.[11] In the same spirit, this essay will seek to recapture the policy-making environment of 1935, focusing on how new social insurance was to America, how dramatically and controversially it burst upon the political scene, and how formidable were the obstacles to its enactment.

It is highly unusual in the American experience for so momentous a national experiment as OAI to have been launched without something similar having been tried before at the state level. But, as the chairman of the Social Security Board remarked in 1938: 'Social insurance in the United States remained, up to the time the Social Security Act began to develop, an almost wholly untried programme with the single exception of our workmen's compensation legislation.'[12] It is true that the principle of social insurance had been of consuming interest to an influential group of academics and reformers during the earlier part of the twentieth century (one thinks of John B. Andrews, John Commons, and Isaac Rubinow), and that policy-makers of the New Deal era benefited from their years of advocacy and research. But if one looks at the substantive record, it is one of repudiation and ultimate disillusionment: state-level campaigns for health insurance and old-age insurance came to nothing during the 1910s, and the following decade saw dispirited reformers withdrawing from the fray.[13] With that partial and now largely discredited exception of workmen's compensation, the first glimmer of light came in 1932 with the passage of Wisconsin's unemployment compensation law.[14] But this had yet to be implemented, and supporters of social insurance disagreed passionately about its merits. What of lessons from the private sector? Here, some welfare capitalists had introduced old-age insurance for their employees, while private insurance practices more generally offered some guide to federal policy-makers baffled by the mysterious business of calculating premiums and projecting claims: Marion B. Folsom, Gerard Swope and Walter Teagle were among the private sector executives who provided useful assistance to the Committee on Economic Security (CES), the body that President Roosevelt set up in the summer of 1934 to put a bill together.[15]

But on the whole, the small group that put OAI together during the second half of 1934 felt it was working in the dark. Should the emphasis be on stimulating state programmes, or on devising a fully national scheme? Should benefits be flat-level, or contribution-related? What level of contributions would be necessary, and how should long-range calculations about demands on the fund be made? Should the government contribute to the fund? How should payments be collected? How should data be stored and payments made? Should all workers be included? What about their survivors? What should be done about those companies that already had private old-age insurance plans? What should happen to older workers who retired in the next few years without having made sufficient contributions to have 'earned' a living benefit?

Faced with these and other complex questions, senior figures associated with the CES seemed to have little interest in OAI. J. Douglas Brown, the Princeton economist who headed the OAI working group (assisted by Barbara Armstrong, Otto Richter, and Murray Latimer [16]), discovered early that Frances Perkins, Chairman of the CES, and Edwin Witte, the Committee's Executive Director, were much more interested in unemployment compensation. Although it involved many of the same complexities as OAI, 'unemployment insurance had in some way become an "American" idea'. In contrast, 'old age insurance was still a foreign and, therefore, a questionable concept'.[17] Insofar as they showed any interest in OAI, Witte and Perkins tended to favour state programmes, despite their impracticability. Brown recalls that convincing them otherwise 'required awesome descriptions of the complexities of forty-eight separate old age insurance systems'.[18]

In addition to being fraught with complexity, it was improbable that a federally administered retirement scheme based on compulsory contributions would enjoy much political support. Not everybody appreciated the difficulty. One of the architects of OAI remembers that by 1934 'the insecurity of the aged was becoming a distinct and persistent theme within the general clamour for action against mounting hardship'.[19] But OAI would do little or nothing to ease that clamour, for an insurance-based scheme could only make payments on the basis of contributions, and once a fund had been built up.[20] By contrast, the notion of immediate non-contributory pensions enjoyed tremendous popularity, as was illustrated by the advent of Dr Francis Townsend's utopian 'revolving pension' movement. Described by Berkowitz and McQuaid as 'bizarre economics' but 'good politics', this scheme promised all elderly Americans a pension of $200 per month, on the one condition, scarcely onerous, that they must spend it all.[21] The plan was unveiled in California in 1934, and dominated some of the year's western congressional contests.[22] Whether legislators were attracted by it, or (as tended to be the case) wished to defuse its appeal, they were unlikely to see OAI as a suitable alternative, and far more likely to support non-contributory 'welfare' measures for the dependent aged.

In the face of all of these factors, it is not surprising that the administration was tempted to omit OAI from the Economic Security Bill. Just two months before the CES submitted its proposals to the President, this seemed the most likely outcome. Addressing a national conference on economic security in November 1934, Roosevelt concentrated almost entirely on unemployment compensation, and confessed 'I do not know whether this is the time for any federal legislation on old age security'.[23] Hitherto, Douglas Brown and Barbara Armstrong had quite welcomed the freedom that CES disinterest permitted their working group, but now it was a serious problem. Writing some forty years later, Brown recalled that the 'staff group was so distressed by this setback that we took desperate measures', secretly fanning a media campaign that criticized Roosevelt for ignoring OAI.[24] This seems to have been an important turning-point, for a stung FDR reacted by putting Edwin Witte under pressure to defuse the issue (Witte, together with Frances Perkins, had written his recent speech). 'From then on', Brown recalls, 'the President seemed to take a greater interest in old age insurance.'[25]

In fact, Roosevelt had a long-standing interest in old-age insurance, having indicated his preference for it even as he signed New York's non-contributory Old Age Assistance law in 1930.[26] It is unlikely that he would have lost interest in it during 1934, as Brown suggests. More likely, it was his very enthusiasm for the contributory approach that made him wary of going ahead with an undeveloped version that might discredit the whole principle of social insurance. He might also have feared that its likely unpopularity would threaten other – less controversial – aspects of his programme. These fears certainly existed elsewhere in the administration, and they persisted throughout the legislative battle of 1935, as is vividly recalled in the recent memoir of the late Thomas H. Eliot, legislative draftsman of the Social Security Act: 'At times ... I wondered whether Congress was ready to pass any bill that provided for social insurance. Few of the influential members of the House and Senate were keen about social insurance, and many hated and feared it.'[27]

In the light of all this, the decision to go ahead with old-age insurance was quite a bold one. Having made it, the administration now had to decide what form it should take, and how it should be presented. Here, constitutional qualms, as well as the broader question of social insurance's political unpopularity, came to the fore. From numerous published accounts, and from the archival record, it is clear that the framers of social security were very worried about the Supreme Court. Frances Perkins, Secretary of Labor and Chairman of the CES, would later recall that 'the problems of constitutional law seemed almost insuperable'.[28] Arthur Altmeyer, Assistant Secretary of Labor and Chairman of the CES technical board, remembers that the Court's prior record 'furnished no clue as to how the Supreme Court might feel about a nationwide social insurance system financed 100 per cent by specific federal payroll taxes'.[29] And Thomas Eliot, while he was waiting for 'something definite to draft, ... thought mostly about the omnipresent question of constitutionality'. He could conceive of success in the case of unemployment compensation, and assume it in the case of the matching grant programmes, 'but what in the world could be devised to carry out the president's wish for a contributory old age insurance programme that would pass judicial muster?'[30]

This apprehension had a number of sources. First was the simple fact that nothing like OAI had ever been attempted before; accordingly, the Court had never been asked to make a ruling in a comparable case. In Altmeyer's opinion, the most relevant legal precedent was the Court's ruling in *Hammer* v. *Dagenhart* (1918), which had overturned the federal Child Labor Act. Based primarily on its understanding of the commerce clause, but also taking a narrow view of the federal government's taxation power (the constitutional basis for OAI), this ruling had 'created considerable doubt as to how far the Constitution of the United States permitted the federal government to go in enacting social legislation'.[31] As the CES went about its work, the highest court had yet to rule on any of the New Deal's early measures, but the portents were not good, in at least three respects.

First, there seemed so many bases upon which OAI might be overturned. Did the general welfare clause of the Constitution allow the federal government to levy taxes for purposes that were not enumerated in Article I? If it did, then how should the general welfare be defined, and who should do the defining? Did the payroll tax deprive employers and workers of their property without due process of law? And might it not be argued that by entering the insurance business the federal government invaded the reserved powers of the states and citizens under the Tenth Amendment? The answers were by no means certain, but it is notable that even Thomas Eliot doubted the constitutionality of OAI, as did many other CES staffers.[32] Second, aside from issues of constitutional fragility, there was an intense suspicion of the Supreme Court, even before the rulings of 1935 that destroyed the early New Deal. In Roosevelt's opinion, the Court was not just judicially conservative, but thoroughly politicised.[33] Given that, as Richard Maidment has observed, much of the early New Deal 'rested in the constitutional equivalent of a twilight zone', it seemed probable that the Court's majority would find ample opportunity to exercise what the administration saw as its political bias.[34]

The third basis for pessimism seemed to confirm the other two: implementation of a whole series of New Deal measures was being blocked by lower federal-court injunctions. In part, these rulings were based on the sloppy draftsmanship of statutes, and could be blamed on poor legal advice from Justice Department lawyers. But Michael Parrish tells us that another factor was also at work: successive Republican presidents had 'packed the federal courts with jurists who normally cast a sceptical eye on legislation that touched the rights of property and contract or that appeared to upset the traditional balance between federal and state jurisdiction'.[35] Either way, the judicial context was deeply worrying for the framers of social security.

In response to the legal problem, the administration had a number of options. First, it could attempt to put together a proposal able to withstand constitutional scrutiny. Douglas Brown and Barbara Armstrong did at one stage try to devise such a scheme, but the former recalls that it 'was so cumbersome, ineffective, and actuarially unsound that no further attempt was made to produce a jerry-built scheme in order to avoid a head-on constitutional test of a truly workable system'.[36] The second option, implicit within Brown's statement, was simply to bite the bullet, putting forward a bold OAI scheme, and awaiting the verdict of the Congress and the courts.

In the event, the administration took a third course. On the one hand, it did put forward a bold scheme of compulsory, national old-age insurance that the CES regarded as 'workable' and actuarially sound. Nowhere was its boldness more apparent than in the decision to include agricultural and domestic workers in OAI, despite actuarial and administrative problems that had led many experts to advocate their exclusion. But on the other hand, it also made a number of substantive and presentational decisions that were calculated to facilitate the progress of old-age insurance through the legislature and the courts. For example, Eliot insisted that Title I of the Economic Security Bill must be the popular and uncontroversial Old Age Assistance (OAA) title, which provided matching grants to approved state programmes for the aged: 'It wasn't a new or strange idea; it wasn't a great enhancement of federal power at the expense of the states; it was desperately needed; and it was undoubtedly constitutional.'[37] Additionally, the administration insisted on a single omnibus bill, hoping that support for the other titles would allow OAI to survive, despite its likely unpopularity with Congress. (The danger, of course, was that the reverse would happen: that the unpopularity of OAI would sink the whole bill.) A further presentational decision was the one that located the OAI payroll tax in a separate title (Title VIII) to the remainder of the proposal (Title II). It was thought that this would give OAI a better chance of surviving judicial scrutiny.[38]

The other way in which the administration tried to boost the prospects of OAI was to emphasize that it was a thoroughly 'American' plan, based on the same actuarial principles as private insurance, encouraging thrift and rewarding work. Martha Derthick comments that: 'In the mythic construction begun in 1935 and elaborated thereafter on the basis of the payroll tax, social security was a vast enterprise of self-help in which government participation was almost incidental.'[39] During the legislative campaign of 1935, the construction took various forms. Most significantly, in terms of substance, Franklin Roosevelt overrode the almost unanimous entreaties of his advisers (Henry Morgenthau Jr., the Treasury Secretary, appears to have been his only ally), and insisted that social security be funded entirely by contributions.[40] As part of the same campaign to demonstrate that OAI and unemployment compensation were actuarially sound and administratively feasible, the administration withdrew agricultural and domestic workers from coverage during committee hearings, together with a number of other groups.[41] (This decision had a disproportionate impact on African-Americans and women, as has been suggested, but neither race nor gender lay at the heart of the administration's decision.[42]) And in testimony to both the House Ways and Means Committee and the Senate Finance Committee, administration witnesses celebrated the insurance principle in the most eulogistic terms. With the benefit of hindsight, we can see this as the beginning of the long process by which the political standing of social security was converted from 'cruel hoax' to 'sacred entitlement'.[43]

But none of these manoeuvrings could alter the fact that social insurance was unpopular, and a liability to the bill. In the House, OAI attracted little attention or interest relative to Old Age Assistance, but when it was debated, conservatives and Republicans characterized it variously as un-American, tyrannical, invasive, experimental, socialistic, economically damaging and unconstitutional.[44] Stunned by all the criticism, Edwin Witte told one correspondent 'that we have all been taking it too much for granted that the economic security legislation will be passed in some form just because it is an Administration bill'.[45] He felt that the biggest single problem for the administration was the extraordinary popularity of the Townsend Plan. By 1935, its appeal was nationwide: 500,000 elderly Americans had joined Townsend clubs and a twenty million-name petition had been delivered to Congress, demanding the plan's enactment. Witte told one academic colleague that 'all members of Congress are afraid of the Townsend people', who had 'a host of lobbyists' and 'letters … pouring in in a greater volume than ever'. Although they did 'not want to vote on the Townsend plan', with its obvious impracticability, they were 'afraid' of opposing it.[46]

A second problem, according to some friends of the bill, was the President's hands-off approach. Witte felt that 'unless the President definitely tells the House leaders that he wants the bill passed quickly, and in its present form, the probability is that weeks will be consumed before the House finishes with the bill'.[47] But the President seemed reluctant to get involved. As Witte told Frank Graham, 'the President very evidently does not intend to bring any pressure to bear upon Congress for any of the bills he has recommended, taking the position that if public opinion does not demand the legislation, it probably should not be enacted'.[48] Confiding in Grace Abbott at the end of March, days before the House committee completed its executive sessions, Witte referred to the 'grave danger that entire sections may be eliminated from the bill'.[49] At one stage, according to Arthur Altmeyer, senior committee members approached FDR to discover 'whether he wanted the omnibus character of the bill kept intact and to tell him that the opposition to the old age insurance proposal was so great that it would not be possible to get a favourable vote on this feature of the bill'.[50]

Roosevelt insisted on keeping the bill intact, and OAI survived the Ways and Means Committee. But on the House floor in April it came under renewed attack, with the Republican minority voting to delete it from the bill. John Taber (Republican, New York) solemnly warned colleagues that 'never in the history of the world has any measure been brought here so insidiously designed as to prevent business recovery, to enslave workers and to prevent any possibility of the employers providing work for the people'. Meanwhile, his New York colleague, Daniel Reed, imagined 'the lash of the dictator', while James W. Wadsworth, also from the Empire State, warned of 'the entrance into the political field of a power so vast, so powerful as to threaten the integrity of our institutions and to pull the temple down upon the heads of our descendants'.[51] Meanwhile, the Senate Finance Committee, which had completed its public hearings in February, was waiting for the completion of proceedings in the House before marking up the bill.

Hostility to OAI appears to have been if anything more intense in the Senate. Even at the height of its problems in the House, Witte remarked that he had 'taken for granted that our hardest fight will be in the Senate' where there was 'a much stronger committee' and 'a still more conservative one'.[52] This sombre evaluation was confirmed by the course of the Finance Committee's executive sessions in early May, not least because they coincided with the Supreme Court's overturning of the compulsory pension scheme set up by the Railroad Retirement Act, a ruling that sent shock waves throughout the administration. The direct legal relevance of this decision to OAI was limited (although Eliot considered that 'language used in this decision seemed to apply to … OAI'[53]), but Owen Roberts' impassioned defence of private economic freedom augured ill for social security, and provided legislators already suspicious of OAI with another basis for defying the administration. More pessimistic now than ever, Witte told Raymond Moley that conservative senators 'may defeat the entire bill or leave only the Federal grants-in-aid to the states for old-age assistance'. Although he was also worried about unemployment compensation, he felt that 'the real fight will probably come over the compulsory old-age insurance system'. In his view, only support from the top would save it. Reminding Moley that FDR 'has been very peculiarly interested' in OAI, Witte observed that 'without the President's support the social security legislation would certainly not have gotten to first base in the present Congress'. Clearly hoping that Moley would use his influence with Roosevelt, Witte concluded that 'the President's support is needed more at this stage than ever before'.[54]

In the event it seems to have been Witte's masterful testimony that helped OAI to survive the committee stage.[55] But on the Senate floor the bill suffered a fresh blow as legislators, by a 51–35 margin, passed the Clark amendment. This exempted from OAI employers who set up their own private insurance arrangements. In the opinion of the administration, it would enormously complicate the government's actuarial calculations, leaving it with the worst risks, while leaving millions of workers in covered occupations unprotected against old-age dependency (employers could have fired their workers before retirement age, depriving them of their pension rights). The conference committee only agreed to withdraw the Clark amendment when the President insisted that he would not sign a bill that contained it.

Congress duly approved the conference bill in August, and OAI had therefore survived the legislative battle. But in the meantime, during the months leading up to the signing of the act, the Supreme Court had started to overturn some of the New Deal's most significant measures, including the National Industrial Recovery Act and the Emergency Farm Mortgage Act.[56] Moreover, the degree of opposition to OAI remained deeply dispiriting for New Dealers, even as they celebrated the final passage of the bill. Eliot remembers his shock that 'nearly every Republican representative had voted to kill old age insurance, and a majority of senators had been willing to gouge and distort that programme. I felt that a great number of hostile critics were just waiting, ready to pounce if the [Social Security B]oard made a single mistake'.[57]

The hostility did not dissipate, but rather intensified, as the administration attempted the enormous task of implementing the Social Security Act. The three-member Social Security Board (SSB), headed first by John B. Winant, then by Altmeyer, had to staff and administer a bureaucracy whose intimidating task it was to process 38,000,000 applications for social security numbers. Altmeyer remarked in 1938 that 'this old-age insurance programme probably involves the largest record-keeping job ever undertaken by any private or public organisation'.[58] A celebrated expert went so far as to tell him that the administrative problem was insuperable.[59] The administration's political enemies took full advantage of its seeming vulnerability: Alf Landon's 1936 presidential campaign featured a strong attack on social security, which he branded 'unjust, unworkable, stupidly drafted and wastefully financed'.[60]

Landon's attack fizzled, and the SSB seems to have accomplished its daunting tasks with extraordinary efficiency. But the biggest hurdle remained, in the shape of the Supreme Court. In early 1936, with *U.S. v. Butler*, a 6–3 majority had overturned the Agricultural Adjustment Act's processing tax, and this represented the most direct threat yet to the survival of social security. Thomas Eliot remembers that 'the applicability of its decision to our old age benefit programme was obvious'.[61] Such was the administration's despair regarding the future of both Social Security and the National Labor Relations Act, *inter alia*, that it conceived its rash court-packing plan. But in April 1937, the latter measure was upheld in the landmark *Jones and Laughlin* case. And then the following month, as part of the same 'switch in time that saved nine', the Court upheld OAI in *Helvering* v. *Davis* (301 US 619), one of three simultaneous rulings that sustained the Social Security Act.[62]

Together, these cases from 1937 represented a historic milestone in the development of constitutional law and practice. Whereas the *Jones and Laughlin* ruling had centred on the scope of the commerce clause, the particular importance of *Helvering* lay in the expansive view that the Court's majority took of the federal spending power: although it was limited by the general welfare clause, it was for Congress and not the courts to determine when the bounds of the clause were exceeded.[63] Wilbur J. Cohen, a young SSB staffer at the time when Benjamin Cardozo handed down the Court's historic decision, claimed some four decades later that he could 'still remember many of the words he spoke because they were like poetry'. He recalled 'walking down the steps of the Supreme Court building in a glow of ecstasy with Mr Winant and Mr Altmeyer. We had hoped and prayed for this day, and yet when it occurred it was still unbelievable to us'.[64]

It was the end of a long road, a road fraught with anxiety and uncertainty, but one whose drama and contingency seems lost to many recent scholars of social security.[65] Jerry Cates and Linda Gordon, among others, have tended to see the drama in terms of pressures from the Left that might have allowed the New Dealers to accomplish social reforms far more sweeping than those of the Social Security Act.[66] I have tried to illustrate that pressures from the right were at least as formidable. The central question of 1935 was whether the United States government was constitutionally entitled to have any social policy at all, independent of the state governments. In the light of this fundamental uncertainty, together with the various other barriers to innovation that have been described above, the Social Security Act represented a radical development in American social provision.

Notes

1. Clarke Chambers, 'Social Security: The Welfare Consensus of the New Deal' in Wilbur J. Cohen (ed.), *The Roosevelt New Deal: A Programme Assessment Fifty Years After* (Austin, 1986), 146.
2. With respect to this wider tendency, I refer in particular to the various contributors in Steve Fraser and Gary Gerstle (eds), *The Rise and Fall of the New Deal Order, 1930–1980* (Princeton, NJ, 1989); Alan Brinkley, *The End of Reform: New Deal Liberalism in Recession and War* (New York, 1995); Edwin Amenta and Theda Skocpol, 'Redefining the New Deal: World War II and the Development of Social Provision in the United States', in Margaret Weir, Ann Shola Orloff, and Skocpol (eds), *The Politics of Social Policy in the United States* (Princeton, NJ, 1988), 81–122. Exponents of the 'social democratic moment betrayed' school include Nelson Lichtenstein, 'From Corporatism to Collective Bargaining: Organized Labour and the Eclipse of Social Democracy in the Postwar Era' in Fraser and Gerstle, *Rise and Fall of the New Deal Order*, 122–52; and Ira Katznelson, 'Was the Great Society a Missed Opportunity' in ibid., 185–211. In terms of the Social Security Act, devotees of the latter school include Jerry Cates, *Insuring Inequality: Administrative Leadership in Social Security, 1935–54* (Ann Arbor, Mich., 1984) and Linda Gordon, *Pitied But Not Entitled: Single Mothers and the History of Welfare* (New York, 1994).
3. Mimi Abramovitz, *Regulating the Lives of Women: Social Welfare Policy from Colonial Times to the Present* (Boston, 1988), 251.
4. Gordon, *Pitied But Not Entitled*, 4.
5. This would have meant lower payroll taxes on workers and employers, and could have been funded from the progressive income tax. It would also have signalled a frank break with the pretence that OAI was just another actuarially based insurance scheme.
6. Barton J. Bernstein, 'The New Deal: The Conservative Achievements of Liberal Reform' in Bernstein (ed.), *Towards a New Past: Dissenting Essays in American History* (London, 1970), 274.
7. Jerry Cates, *Insuring Inequality*, 24. Cates distinguishes between the victorious 'conservative social insurance' advocated by the 'Wisconsin school' (whose most important representative was Edwin Witte, executive director of the Committee on Economic Security), and the 'liberal social insurance' of the 'Ohio school', whose representatives included Isaac Rubinow and Abraham Epstein. For a lucid explication of the differences between the two approaches, see Chapter 5 of Edward D. Berkowitz and Kim McQuaid, *Creating the Welfare State: The Political Economy of 20th-Century Reform* (Lawrence, KS, 2nd ed. 1988).
8. Gwendolyn Mink, *The Wages of Motherhood: Inequality in the Welfare State, 1917–1942* (Ithaca, NY, 1994), 127–30.
9. Robert C. Lieberman, 'Race, Institutions, and the Administration of Social Policy', *Social Science History* 19 (Winter, 1995), 511–42.
10. Mink, *Wages of Motherhood*, 127.

11. Edward D. Berkowitz, *America's Welfare State: From Roosevelt to Reagan* (Baltimore, 1990); Blanche Coll, *Safety Net: Social Security and Welfare, 1929–1979* (New Brunswick, NJ, 1994); Sheryl R. Tynes, *Turning Points in Social Security: From 'Cruel Hoax' to 'Sacred Entitlement'* (Stanford, Calif., 1996).

12. Arthur J. Altmeyer, 'Social Security: Insurance Against Economic Hazards' in American Council on Public Affairs, *The Federal Government Today: A Survey of Recent Innovations and Renovations* (New York, 1938), 32. Confirming this claim, Edward Berkowitz has noted that in the 1930s 'no one knew a great deal about social insurance in America, because with very few exceptions it had never been tried in this country'. Edward D. Berkowitz, *Mr Social Security: The Life of Wilbur J. Cohen* (Lawrence, KS, 1995), 27.

13. The best account of this process remains Roy Lubove, *The Struggle for Social Security, 1900–1935* (Cambridge, Mass., 1968).

14. For the discrediting of workers' compensation, see Edward D. Berkowitz, *Disabled Policy: America's Programs for the Handicapped* (New York, 1987).

15. According to one CES participant, J. Douglas Brown, it was the support of 'progressive industrial executives' that helped him to overcome the doubts that many cabinet members nourished about old age insurance. See J. Douglas Brown, *An American Philosophy of Social Security: Evolution and Issues* (Princeton, NJ, 1972), 21–2.

16. Armstrong was a California law professor with a long-standing interest in labour legislation, while Latimer was an economist with a particular interest in industrial pension plans, who went on to chair the Railroad Retirement Board. Richter was an actuary with the American Telephone and Telegraph Company.

17. Brown, *An American Philosophy of Social Security*, 8.

18. Ibid., 14. That Witte et al. could have contemplated state OAI programmes demonstrates to Brown's satisfaction their lack of interest in the question, as well as their loyalty to the Wisconsin unemployment insurance plan. For a long list of reasons why state schemes would not have worked, see ibid., 14–15.

19. Ibid., 6.

20. Additionally, objections were raised on constitutional, administrative and economic grounds.

21. Berkowitz and McQuaid, *Creating the Welfare State*, 114. For the Townsend plan and its political impact, see Berkowitz, *America's Welfare State*, 18–27; Gordon, *Pitied But Not Entitled*, 225–34; Martha Derthick, *Policymaking for Social Security* (Washington, DC, 1978), 193–6, 218–24.

22. Rep. John McGroarty (D-Calif.) attributed his victory over the GOP entirely to his advocacy of the Townsend Plan, and warned fellow legislators that they too would go down to defeat unless they followed his example. *Congressional Record* 16 April 1935, 5792–4.

23. *New York Times*, 15 November 1935, 1.

24. Brown, *American Philosophy of Social Security*, 16.

25. Ibid., 17.

26. Arthur J. Altmeyer, *The Formative Years of Social Security* (Madison, 1968), 4.
27. Thomas H. Eliot, *Recollections of the New Deal: When the People Mattered* (Boston, 1992), 111.
28. Frances Perkins, *The Roosevelt I Knew* (New York, 1946), 286.
29. Altmeyer, *Formative Years of Social Security*, 15.
30. Eliot, *Recollections of the New Deal*, 95–6.
31. Altmeyer, *Formative Years of Social Security*, 14–15.
32. Eliot, *Recollections of the New Deal*, 112, 118; Brown, *American Philosophy of Social Security*, 12.
33. FDR remarked during the 1932 campaign that the early years of the Hoover presidency had seen 'the Republican party ... in complete control of all branches of the Federal Government – the Executive, the Senate, the House of Representatives and, I might add for good measure, the Supreme Court as well'. Cited by Carl Brent Swisher, 'The Supreme Court in Transition', *Journal of Politics* 1 (November 1939), 349.
34. Richard A. Maidment, *The Judicial Response to the New Deal: The U.S. Supreme Court and Economic Regulation, 1934–1936* (Manchester, 1991), 56.
35. Parrish, *Anxious Decades: America in Prosperity and Depression, 1920–41* (New York and London, 1992), 333.
36. Brown, *American Philosophy of Social Security*, 11.
37. Eliot, *Recollections of the New Deal*, 111–12.
38. OAI's claim to constitutionality rested on the power of the federal government to levy taxes for the general welfare. It was felt that the Court would view with disfavour a payroll tax whose revenues were explicitly directed to a particular group of citizens. Separating the tax mechanism was seen as disguising the link. Commenting on an incongruous situation, Jane Perry Clark remarked that 'by a somewhat anomalous train of judicial reasoning, it has been indicated that if a tax bears shining on its face the purpose for which its funds are to be spent, it may not stand on constitutional legs'. Clark, *The Rise of A New Federalism: Federal-State Cooperation in the United States* (New York, 1938), 289.
39. Derthick, *Policymaking for Social Security*, 231–2.
40. European social insurance schemes were invariably funded in part from the government's general revenues. In the US case, this would have made social security more 'progressive', would have meant a lower payroll tax, and would have obviated some of the problems associated with maintaining a large reserve. As well as wanting OAI to appear as a 'true' insurance measure, FDR did not want to mandate expenditures on future generations.
41. This decision is treated in greater detail in Gareth Davies and Martha Derthick, 'Race and the Social Security Act of 1935', *Political Science Quarterly* 112 (Summer 1997). Collecting contributions from these groups was thought to be difficult, and perhaps impossible. Abraham Epstein, Director of the American Association for Old Age Security, and a passionate believer in social insurance, had warned legislators that the problem was 'terrifically difficult', and that 'you are not going to collect

it'. He feared 'an administrative problem which will become a fizzle and therefore react ultimately against the whole plan'. *Economic Security Act, Hearings Before the Senate Committee on Finance* (74 Cong. 1 Sess. 1935), 514–15.

42. Moreover, we should bear in mind that inclusion in this unpopular new scheme of compulsory taxation was not necessarily seen as a great privilege by OAI's prospective 'beneficiaries'. Witte recalls the impassioned insistence of some representatives of churches, hospitals, and educational institutions that their workers not be compelled to participate. See Edwin E. Witte, *The Development of the Social Security Act* (Madison, 1963), 153–7.

43. Tynes, *Turning Points in Social Security: From 'Cruel Hoax' to 'Sacred Entitlement'*.

44. For the preoccupation of the House with OAA, see Witte, *Development of the Social Security Act*, 143.

45. Letter, Witte to Frank Graham, 1 March 1935, CES Files, Box 16.

46. Letter, Witte to Prof. Mary B. Gilson (an economist from the University of Chicago), 11 April 1935, CES Files, Box 15, National Archives.

47. Ibid.

48. Witte to Graham, 1 March 1935. Graham was President of the University of North Carolina, and had worked on the CES.

49. Letter, Witte to Abbott, 28 March 1935, CES Files, Box 16.

50. Altmeyer, *Formative Years of Social Security*, 34.

51. All cited in ibid., 37–8.

52. Witte to Gilson, 11 April 1935.

53. Eliot, *Recollections of the New Deal*, 114.

54. Letter, Witte to Moley, 10 May 1935, CES Files, Box 15.

55. Joseph P. Harris, assistant to Witte, told Grace Abbott that 'Mr Witte made a wonderful statement on Friday just before final action was taken and undoubtedly swung several votes'. Letter, Harris, to Abbott, 20 May 1935, CES Files, Box 13. Reflecting her relief, Miss Abbott's letter of 18 May had spoken of her 'delight' at the outcome. In reply, Harris was similarly pleased, telling her that 'we are all feeling very good'.

56. See Swisher, 'Supreme Court in Transition', 352–5.

57. Ibid., 126–7.

58. Altmeyer, 'Social Security', in *Federal Government Today*, 35.

59. Altmeyer, *Formative Years of Social Security*, 71.

60. Berkowitz, *America's Welfare State*, 41.

61. Eliot, *Recollections of the New Deal*, 141.

62. The other two cases were *Carmichael* v. *Southern Coal and Coke Company* (301 US 495), and *Steward Machine Company* v. *Davis* (301 US 548).

63. Kermit L. Hall (ed.), *The Oxford Companion to the Supreme Court of the United States* (New York, 1992), 861. In the earlier *Butler* decision, the Court had acknowledged that the spending power of Congress under the general welfare clause exceeded the specific powers enumerated in Article I, Section 8 of the Constitution, but had reserved for itself the power to determine what constituted the general welfare.

64. *Congressional Record*, 16 September 1975, 28874. Cohen became a ubiquitous figure in the politics of social security, his long career culminating

in 1968 when Lyndon Johnson made him Secretary of Health, Education, and Welfare.

65. It was the end of the constitutional road, but OAI remained politically vulnerable until 1950. Its standing strengthened markedly following the amendments of 1939 to the Social Security Act.

66. Gordon devotes Chapter 8 of *Pitied But Not Entitled* to describing a wide range of radical voices and left-leaning coalitions who were part of the economic security debate, and implies that their social democratic prescriptions were by no means unrealistic. And Cates, struck by the 'policy competition' of the period, warns of the danger of assuming that nothing more than a limited compromise measure was possible in 1935. In his view 'very little was predetermined ... Political unrest demanded social policy response, but the nature of the response appeared to be up for grabs'. Cates, *Insuring Inequality*, 22–5.

6

Widows' Welfare in the Great Depression

S. Jay Kleinberg

The twentieth-century welfare state incorporated maternalist values designed to put children first and to emphasize the importance of mother-centred child-rearing to society, which New Deal programmes reinforced. The stress on the maternal role in children's and society's well-being, also seen in the earlier ideologies of 'Republican Mother-hood' and the 'Cult of True Womanhood', lauded women's role in the education of their children, recognized the importance of their household labour, and ensconced women firmly within the domestic sphere. Progressive and New Deal reformers subscribed to a vision of motherhood that constrained even as it enabled, largely ignoring women except as the mothers of dependent children. By assuming that married women were and should be their husbands' financial dependents, social policy as it developed in the early twentieth century restricted women's legitimate endeavours to the home and its socio-political, but not economic, projections. Progressives and New Dealers alike believed that the good mother stayed at home to look after her children, and resisted wage-earning for mothers.[1]

Yet a growing proportion of women and mothers from diverse backgrounds became economically active for at least some portion of their adult lives, especially if they were widowed.[2] Concentrating on the employment and welfare prospects of widows during the Great Depression, this essay examines the effectiveness of New Deal social policy in solving the problems of young and old widows. The Great Depression and the New Deal's responses to it simultaneously improved widows' likelihood of receiving assistance and restricted their economic strategies to dependency. The New Deal replaced widows' previous tactics of combining wage earning, charity and child labour with the status of wards of the state. The widespread use of emergency assistance, rather than work relief, and Aid to Dependent Children (ADC), rather than employment, defined widows and other single mothers as econ-omically inactive. Maternalist policies supported such mothers at subsistence levels while disapproving of waged employment, especially for white women.[3]

The spread of state-funded widows' pensions in the 1910s and 1920s attested to the widespread belief that the mothers of young children should be outside the labour force, yet low levels of funding meant that many widows and most other single mothers had jobs. Despite pensions, which went primarily to white widows, the proportion of employed widows grew slightly from 30 to 34 per cent between 1910 and 1930, only declining after the Social Security Act provided Aid to Dependent Children to young widows and Old Age Assistance and Old Age Insurance Pensions to older ones. These social welfare policies bolstered the family wage ideology by limiting legitimacy in the labour force to certain age/social groups. The New Deal 'aged' and 'gendered' economic participation, condemning the labour of children and that of older people (although arguably for different reasons) and devaluing that of women. During the Depression the proportion of households headed by women rose by as much as one-quarter in some cities, so that public policy decisions on employment and welfare affected a growing proportion of families.[4]

Antagonism toward women workers grew, especially if they were married and (it was assumed) had a husband to support them. Surveys of public attitudes towards married women's employment during the Depression elicited overwhelmingly negative responses, as economic necessity forced single and married women into competition for scarce jobs. Unmarried women carried placards declaring 'fire married women: hire needy single women' while rumours that married women were being fired led them to conceal their marital status from employers.[5] The widespread belief that maternal employment caused 'truancy, in- corrigibility, robbery, teenage tantrums, and difficulty in managing children' impugned mothers' ability to work and care for a family simultaneously. State laws prohibiting the public employment of mar- ried women, and private companies' discrimination, challenged the legitimacy of all women's place in the labour market.[6]

The iconography and popular culture of the Depression featured the forgotten man and unemployed labourer striving to support his family in the face of a hostile, failing economic system. Labour union newspapers depicted out-of-work men as plutocrats' victims. If included at all, women were plutocrats, the women's auxiliary, or aproned house- wives. Both cartoons and posters depicted work as a male prerogative. Brawny male limbs figured in posters to 'protect your hands', and stalwart men held the tools to 'promote confidence' in Works Progress Administration posters.[7]

Depression-era cinema touted marriage as the solution to female employment problems. *Golddiggers* (Busby Berkeley, 1933), a film about unemployed actresses, concludes with 'Remember My Forgotten Man', a powerful musical depiction of unemployment in which the breadlines consist of downcast men in tattered overcoats with war medals pinned inside. The unemployed actresses marry wealthy men, while the real unemployed, the forgotten men, shuffle along receiving handouts. This prevalent representation of unemployment led to an emphasis on re-employment for men and the neglect of women's employment problems.[8]

Farm Security and Resettlement Administration photographs such as those by Dorothea Lange captured maternal despair and rural poverty. The 'Migrant Mother' pictures a mother sitting alone with three children in a pea-pickers' camp in California, equating motherhood with helplessness. Like most women in FSA photographs, the mother's gaze is averted in misery, not confronting the camera directly. Many FSA photographs posed women in family groups, holding children or leaning on a door-frame for support; more often men worked or lounged with other men. Designed to obtain support for the FSA, these images embodied class, racial, and gender dynamics which the New Deal did little to alter.[9]

Yet popular culture also depicted widows and married women as stalwart figures keeping their families together despite the hardships. Ma Joad in *The Grapes of Wrath* bolstered morale and sustained the family as her men weakened and despaired during the hardships of their trek west.[10] *Ma Perkins*, the radio serial sponsored by soap manufacturers Procter & Gamble in 1933, also featured a universal mother, in this case a widow who re-opened her late husband's lumber yard in the first episode. She was a mother figure who gave her listeners hope as she grappled with the basic problems of survival for herself, her three children, and her employees, with whom she had a quasi-maternal role relationship.[11] Styling these very different leading characters as 'Ma' firmly placed them within the domestic orbit.

Ma Perkins was a statistical rarity. Few widows owned their own businesses during the Depression and their continued concentration in a limited range of jobs made them economically vulnerable. Widows comprised 17 per cent of the female labour force in 1930, but 32 per cent of all female agricultural workers and 28 per cent of domestic servants, contrasted with only 6 per cent of clerical workers.[12] Disproportionately concentrated in service occupations, widows and other lone mothers suffered high levels of unemployment and occupational displacement during the Great Depression. A Women's Bureau study of the effects of the Depression on wage earners' families in South Bend, Indiana, in 1935 concluded that 'married women and those who had been married fared worse than single women during this time of unemployment'. It found that not quite one-tenth of single women, compared with one-quarter of the widowed, separated or divorced, and one-third of married women had been out of work for an entire year.[13]

The intersecting dynamics of race, gender and politics reinforced the economic vulnerability of women of colour. African-American widows, twice as likely as native-born white widows to be in the labour force and to work in service or agricultural jobs, fared badly in the Depression as the federal Agricultural Adjustment Act payments enabled landowners to mechanize production and evict tenant farmers and sharecroppers, using crop subsidies to shed workers. The proportion of African-American women with farm jobs decreased from 27 per cent in 1930 to 16 per cent in 1940. The number of impoverished female-headed African-American families increased throughout the cotton belt while rural white widows also fared badly in the eastern cotton belt, the Ozarks, and Appalachia.[14]

Limited employment opportunities and the scarcity of relief meant that rural widows and their children suffered great hardship during the Depression. Widows with young children were over-represented on rural relief rolls, with many of them contributing to the support of aged parents as well as to their own young children. In a strategy replicated in rural and urban districts across the nation, rural widows returned to their parents' home, compounding the poverty across the generations. Female-headed rural relief families lived on meagre incomes. In 1935 less than one-fifth of rural widows on relief found jobs, with wages averaging $13 per week, compared with two-fifths of the male householders obtaining work at an average weekly income of $26.[15]

The collapse of agriculture drove many rural women into the cities in search of employment as domestic servants, overcrowding the domestic labour market and exacerbating urban women's employment problems. Studies of the urban relief population showed consistent over-representation of servants in relief cases and 'evidence of a serious depression in domestic service, complicated by the racial factor, low wages, and the relative ease with which such service can be dispensed with by the household which has met economic adversity'.[16]

As a result, employment conditions for servants deteriorated during the Depression. Employers across the nation took advantage of surplus labour to lower wages by 50 to 75 per cent, frequently hiring white workers to replace women of colour in their kitchens. As unemployed white women 'traded down' to less socially desirable employments, such as private household service, African-American women's unemployment rates sky-rocketed. Three-fifths of the female relief applicants in Pittsburgh came from the African-American community, although they comprised only 6 per cent of the adult population. While two-thirds of Baltimore nursemaids were African-American in 1928, only one in ten was by 1934. In New York 'slave markets' flourished where African-American women, desperate for work to support themselves and their families, stood on street corners hoping for an employer to drive by offering a day's work. As late as 1939, African-American women comprised nearly one-fifth of unemployed females nationwide, with servants still having particularly high unemployment levels.[17]

Displacement affected women in other urban occupations as industrial relocations exacerbated unemployment and reduced wage levels in the textile industry. Female factory operatives comprised 23 per cent of women workers, but 35 per cent of unemployed women in 1937.[18] As the mills moved from New England to low wage states in the South, northern women's and children's employment opportunities declined, further exacerbating widows' economic problems since they relied upon child labour to make ends meet. The mills transferred some male overseers and superintendents south, but not female operatives. Widows who previously combined wage earning with mothers' pensions became more dependent upon the state, since neither they nor their children could find work. The southward flight of capital did not even benefit southern widows as employers took advantage of low regional wage levels to cut labour costs. Southern textile workers' low pay undercut rates in other industries that employed large numbers of women, such as tobacco, and further depressed wage scales.[19]

The Depression also curtailed widows' use of their children as wage earners. Sending children into the labour force, which had been commonplace in the late nineteenth and early twentieth centuries, became more difficult by the time of the Depression itself. The New Deal eliminated child labour in key manufacturing and service sectors. As a result, the number of working fourteen and fifteen year-olds fell by about two-fifths between 1930 and 1940. The proportion of older children in the labour force also declined, although not as sharply, and the nature of child labour altered during the Depression. While many teenagers held jobs, they worked part-time for pocket money rather than full-time to purchase basic necessities.[20]

Before the Depression widows and dependent children were the main clients of outdoor (non-institutional) assistance. In 1929, 92 per cent of public assistance was spent on mother's aid. A small amount went to blind people (nearly 8 per cent) and less than 0.5 per cent went to the elderly, since only two cities granted old-age pensions. By 1935, the actual amount cities and states spent on special allowances had trebled, and the balance of recipients shifted in favour of the elderly. Old-age assistance accounted for 52 per cent of the Special Entitlement spending; mothers' pensions for only 41 per cent, while the blind received 7 per cent. By 1935, three-fifths of all cities had old age assistance programmes, although few South Atlantic and South Central Divisions expended any money on old-age assistance through 1935.[21]

Although women and children were no longer the primary recipients of assistance, their actual numbers among the relief population still increased. There were strong regional biases in public assistance. Eight northern and western states accounted for nearly 70 per cent of the expenditure on mothers' pensions in the early 1930s, while the former Confederate states and the District of Columbia sustained a mere 4 per cent of mothers' aid families. Southern states granted few pensions to African-American mothers and had fewer places for African-American children in public institutions.[22] In 1932, New Orleans (among other cities) stopped accepting relief applications from African-Americans. Private charities felt unable to bridge the gap because of their own financial situation, so 'Negro families are said to be suffering greatly', a situation which also applied to the large portions of the Hispanic population in the South-west.[23]

Even border cities that assisted African-American widows practised discrimination. Baltimore provided mothers' aid to African-American widows in approximate proportion to their numbers in the population, but given blacks' relative poverty this still meant that they were less well served than whites. Such widespread discrimination led southern welfare workers to conclude that 'the Negro is bearing the brunt of the depression in the South'.[24] Discrimination against poor blacks was not limited to the South, however. Across the nation a smaller proportion of impoverished blacks and other widows of colour obtained assistance from public or private authorities.[25]

Single African-American mothers survived by taking in washing when they could get it, begging, picking over trash cans and dumps for discarded vegetables and fruit, and their neighbours' generosity.[26] The dreadful economic conditions and an inability to get assistance to tide them over the hard times accelerated their migration out of rural areas and out of the South. This disrupted families as poor widows left their children behind in order to obtain work in the cities.[27] The Depression-inspired migration dismayed northern social workers who already experienced great difficulties providing for the local poor. W. A. Hill, an African-American social worker in Chicago, hoped that widows' home communities could be persuaded to assist them, which would be 'a much more satisfactory arrangement for them' and would also relieve Chicago of the responsibility for their welfare.[28]

Mothers who could not afford to feed themselves and their children faced stark choices. Between 1910 and 1930 the number of children in institutions had declined as a percentage of the population, but with the coming of the Depression, it started to increase as unemployed widows and other single mothers used these institutions to resolve their child-care and wage-earning dilemmas.[29] In New York City the proportion of children placed in orphanages and children's homes trebled between 1925 and 1932, 'largely due to the breaking up of homes of destitute families', according to the City Budget Office.[30]

By 1932 rumours circulated that falling tax collections would curtail pensions in some areas and force more mothers to put their children in institutions. Most jurisdictions maintained relief payments, but delays brought dreadful hardship into the lives of widows and their children when states and cities took 'pension holidays' pending the receipt of tax revenues. Pennsylvania passed the Talbot Relief Act which retro-actively cut mothers' assistance appropriations, but later rescinded it. Counties in Idaho, Arkansas, and Nebraska discontinued widows' pension payments in 1932 and 1933.[31]

The private sector, which had bridged the gap between barest subsistence and reasonable survival before the Great Depression, could do little to aid widows who encountered more competition for diminishing private charity funds. In city after city charitable fund-raising efforts failed as the Depression bit harder into middle- and upper-class life styles. Charities responded by closing their books to new cases, cutting clients from their caseload, and switching from cash relief to commodity distribution.[32] With private sources of aid curtailed, widows relied more heavily on governmental agencies, particularly the federal government, for assistance.

Widows and other single mothers epitomized the problems women encountered during the Depression. Like all women, they suffered because of the perception that unemployment was primarily a man's problem. Government programmes viewed men as workers and women as dependents. Harry Hopkins, in charge of the Federal Emergency Relief Administration, believed that relief demoralized recipients and undermined the independence of their families. 'Give a man a dole, and you save his body and destroy his spirit. Give him a job and pay him an assured wage and you save both the body and the spirit.' Hopkins did not mean 'man' in the generic sense. He admitted that 'we haven't been particularly successful in work for women'. [33] Women wanted work relief for the same reasons men did: it paid better than welfare and enabled recipients to maintain their self-respect. Mothers' pensions, as has been well-documented, required behavioural conformity, which most jobs did not.

Women found it difficult to get emergency or work relief when they were eligible for mothers' assistance. In a common strategy, the Temporary Emergency Relief Administration in New York 'adopted the policy of allowing no grants from the emergency funds for cases eligible for mothers' aid'.[34] Instead, female household heads were routinely shunted on to emergency aid programmes while male household heads got jobs. Men benefited from Emergency Relief Administration jobs while women received distributions of government clothing, cloth, flour and blankets. Early New Deal efforts such as the Civilian Conservation Corps also aided young men but ignored young women.

Most of the initial work relief found work for men on construction projects with few jobs for women.[35]

Widows and other single mothers were not treated like other heads of households for purposes of financial assistance. To reverse the common saying, they got hand-outs, not hand-ups. The proportion of single mothers receiving government assistance increased sharply during the Depression because states shifted the support of mothers and children on to federal welfare funds, providing for mothers and children who might otherwise have languished on city or state waiting lists or been ruled ineligible under mothers' pension laws. Cities contained their welfare costs while the federal government subsidized relief expenditure.[36]

Widows became increasingly dependent upon relief because the nature of the family economy shifted in these years. Few younger children worked, older ones suffered unemployment, and fewer relatives could spare the funds to help out. In 1926 widows' pension families earned three-fifths of their income, while charities and the state provided the rest. During the Depression, this ratio reversed: family efforts accounted for 39 per cent; 45 per cent came from mothers' assistance funds and 11 per cent from the Emergency Relief Board, Works Progress Administration, National Youth Administration and Civilian Conservation Corps. The median income of families reliant solely upon mothers' assistance was about half that of a family with at least one working member.[37]

Few widows got public work. Female New Dealers strove to get women included in job programmes, but their employment only numbered in the thousands. The Civilian Conservation Corps employed 2.5 million young men, but the female counterpart employed 8,000 women, did not pay a salary, and was eliminated by a budget cut in 1937. The Civil Works Administration paid real wages, but emphasized construction projects and provided only marginal employment for women – painting murals and teaching adult literacy. In Pennsylvania, for example, just 3 per cent of CWA workers in 1934 were women.[38]

Between 8 and 12 per cent of Federal Emergency Relief Administration jobs went to women in 1934–5. Its successor, the Works Progress Administration (WPA), also hired few women although it employed millions of men building bridges, libraries, post offices and roads. While stipulating that women should be employed, local WPA officials limited them to between 12 and 18 per cent of the WPA labour force. Women headed about 25 per cent of the households on Baltimore's relief rolls, but obtained only 10 per cent of the WPA jobs.[39] Country widows also had little chance of obtaining work; 11 per cent of the female heads of household got public jobs 'since most work projects in rural areas were designed for male workers'.[40] By 1937 only 14 per cent of the heads of families employed on WPA projects were women.[41]

Federal relief administrators ordered state programmes that employed women in large numbers to cut them from the rolls in order to mute criticisms. When Harry Hopkins discovered that Colorado's WPA register was 27 per cent female in 1936, he ordered the numbers be slashed back to the national average of 16 per cent.[42] African-American and Hispanic women suffered even more than white female household heads since they received lower wages and were frequently forced off the work relief rolls into poorly paid domestic and agricultural labour. The consequences of this routine discrimination were stark: white men constituted over 74 per cent of those employed on WPA projects in 1938; African-American men made up 12 per cent; white women were 11 per cent and African-American women were a mere 2 per cent.[43]

The emphasis on construction projects throughout the Depression marginalized women workers, with little imagination demonstrated in the jobs found for them. There were canning and mattress-stuffing projects, sewing rooms, and housekeeping services, but government officials did not value female skills, especially those of women who had either been out of the labour force altogether or worked at domestic jobs. As widows, women had less trouble than married women in getting certified as heads of households, but relief workers frequently dismissed their applications because there were few appropriate work projects.[44]

Sewing shops employed over half the women on WPA projects in 1936. Less than one-fifth of women employed by WPA undertook clerical, technical, or educational projects, while about one-tenth were on various home economics projects. In some states the proportion doing sewing climbed higher. Eighty-seven per cent of the women on WPA projects in Massachusetts sat in the sewing rooms. Southern states maintained racially segregated projects that had proportionately fewer openings for African-American women than their numbers in the relief population warranted. Baltimore provided three racially segregated sewing projects for women, two for whites and one for African-Americans. These ran on a commercial basis with employees being dismissed if they did not meet production quotas. The WPA project rigidly reinforced the garment industry's gender stereotyping: men did the cutting, women the sewing, which prevented them from upgrading their skills.[45] Thus WPA projects provided little expansion of the female skill-base, even within the narrow confines of the work women obtained through it.

WPA housekeeping programmes typified the agency's attitudes toward women workers. Women in a number of cities received training to act as housekeepers for poor, motherless households. St Louis, Missouri, established a 'Widowers' Department' at the start of the New Deal which provided older (frequently widowed) housekeepers for men bringing up children on their own. The housekeeper service enabled the family to stay together, since the alternative was to disperse the children to relatives or institutions in order to care for them while the father worked. This was one of the very few public acknowledgements of the problems faced by widowed men with young children. At the same time, this programme located jobs for women whose primary expertise was in child care and household management. As such it provided employment for middle-aged widows who had raised their own families but had little but domestic skills to offer in the marketplace.[46]

Similar programmes in other cities employed a few hundred or, at most, a few thousand workers and recognized the social importance of motherhood by replacing absent mothers with paid substitutes. Despite the small numbers, these programmes prevented the disintegration of poor families, replacing the deceased or ailing mother in families that otherwise would have been unable to purchase household help.[47] The programmes reduced the need for institutional care, as did the expansion of mothers' pensions in jurisdictions that had previously been unable or unwilling to meet the needs of lone mothers and their children. In Pittsburgh, for example, the occupancy of children's institutions fell steadily from 84 per cent in 1931 to 66 per cent by 1937. In the same interval the number of widows and other single mothers granted mothers' assistance rose from 2,812 children a month to 6,277. The declining birth rate (from 22 per thousand in 1930 to 17.5 in 1938) also contributed to the decrease in the institutional population, as older children were more likely to be retained by their mothers.[48]

While housekeeper programmes provided social support to vulnerable families, they demonstrated the potential of maternalist social programmes to political interference. The St Louis programme lasted only two years before 'the use of public funds for the service of housekeepers was questioned'.[49] This programme served the needs of single-parent households where the father was the single parent, but fell foul of politicians who had a narrow model of family life. The social security programme also had a constricted view of which types of elderly and single parent families should be supported by the state. Like the housekeeper programmes, the Social Security Act indicated that when maternalists and politicians clashed, the politicians prevailed.

The Social Security Act made explicit assumptions about class, work, social authority and gender. It assumed a particular model of family roles in which women stayed at home and men supported their wives, providing relatively well for individuals it defined as worthy workers but relegating others to poorly funded and locally controlled welfare programmes.[50] The original programme served industrial workers, but not domestic servants, farm labourers, or public employees, excluding about half the working population, nearly three-fifths of female workers, and more than nine-tenths of African-Americans.[51]

The Social Security Act deprived women, especially from minority groups, of equal protection. Widows and dependent children obtained lower levels of federal funding than other social security recipients. The federal government contributed one-third of the cost of Aid to Dependent Children (ADC) but half of the pensions for the blind and aged. Dr Abraham Epstein, Executive Secretary of the American Association for Social Security and a long-time campaigner for old-age pensions, believed this unfair situation arose because 'while we watched for the aged and the blind watched for themselves, nobody watched for the poor widows and orphans and they got stuck'.[52] Since ADC had been conceived as a child-welfare measure, it provided no direct support for the mothers who looked after children, but still expected them to stay at home. It incorporated gendered patterns into law and treated women and men inequitably.[53]

African-American organizations protested at perceived racial biases in the Act and sought unsuccessfully to have an anti-discrimination clause included. 'Widespread and continued discrimination on account of race or color' meant that 'Negro men, women, and children did not share equitably and fairly in the distribution of benefits accruing from the expenditure' of federal funds under the New Deal. The National Association for the Advancement of Colored People believed the bill deliberately excluded farm and service workers precisely because so many were black.[54]

There were great regional variations in pension levels. Southern states took longer to submit plans for ADC and resisted the establishment of minimum standards. Aid per family averaged about $32 per month nationally in 1938, ranging from $65 per month in Massachusetts to less than $10 in the South. Southern states also kept African-American women off ADC rolls by adopting rules that disqualified them. The 'employable mother' regulation prevented mothers with school-age children from receiving assistance. African-Americans comprised 14 to 17 per cent of all ADC recipients between 1937 and 1940, but despite higher levels of poverty and female-headed households, they were a smaller proportion of the ADC rolls than even their relative numbers warranted.[55]

States were more proactive in obtaining aid for the elderly than the young. Three times more elderly received social security assistance than did young people initially, although the number of needy was about the same in both groups.[56] In the long term, however, ADC resulted in growing numbers of women and children on the welfare rolls. Welfare authorities used social security to remove mothers from work projects and placed them on the cheaper ADC. Once the federal government shared the cost, states permitted the number of recipients to rise. In Fall River, Massachusetts, the number of assisted mothers quadrupled in the first year of ADC and rose six-fold by 1939. The demographic characteristics of ADC also changed. In the early 1930s about four-fifths of all mothers' aid recipients were widows, but this proportion dropped to three-fifths by 1939.[57] ADC mothers came from modest backgrounds, most were recent widows, and few (less than 10 per cent) had been employed while their husbands were alive. ADC thus expanded the number of poor women who received help to bring up their children, and in the process, it side-lined them from economic participation.[58]

In 1939 the Social Security Act was amended to include widowed and orphaned survivors of men in covered occupations. It strengthened the family wage economy by basing elderly widows' pensions upon their late husband's contributions and ignoring their own earnings. According to the Chairman of the Social Security Board the new benefits were 'a family concept. You just cannot think of these people as individuals. You have to think of them in their family relationships'.[59] Married women who worked in pensionable occupations gained little from the amended act because of the maximum limits set upon a couple's pension income, while widows lost their benefits if they re-married.

In order to keep costs down, the pension earned by a female worker would be subsumed into the old-age pension she got through her husband. She received nothing extra based on her own earnings. This was done to appease business leaders such as Eastman Kodak's Marion B. Folsom who objected to pensions for aged wives and widows because they would 'cut down on the benefits which must be paid to the single man'.[60] With more women working in their early or middle years (but not collecting pensions on their own account) their contributions would finance wives' allowances because married women received no extra retirement pension on their own account.[61] Working wives subsidized those who did not hold jobs and who, therefore, made no direct contribution to the pension system.

The pension model simply ignored the rising number of women breadwinners and heads of families. Despite increased levels of female employment, the social security legislation assumed women depended upon men for support, but not vice versa. Elderly widows received smaller pensions than single women or men. A male retiree received all of the pension to which he was entitled. He was credited with 50 per cent more for his wife once she reached retirement age, whether she had worked outside the home or not. When he died, she received a widow's pension of half the combined amount. Put slightly differently, a man on his own got 100 per cent, but a widow only received 75 per cent. Unless a husband depended entirely upon his wife for support, he could not obtain a pension based on her earning record.

Congress and the Social Security Board assumed that women married men for venal reasons. To prevent women entrapping foolish old men in wedlock to get their social security benefits, the amended Act stipulated that the supplementary wife's pension would be paid only if the marriage had occurred before the husband reached the age of sixty. Divorced and separated women were excluded from retirement benefits through their husbands' social security contribution, which exacerbated the displaced homemaker syndrome as divorce levels rose in the late 1930s and during and after World War II.[62]

Young orphaned children of men in covered occupations received survivors' benefits under the terms of the revised Social Security Act and their mothers also received a pension, unless they remarried. This differentiated between two groups of mothers and children with drastic consequences. The first group contained the widows and orphans of men covered under the provisions of social security retirement clauses (survivors' benefits) while the second consisted of impoverished lone mothers and dependent children receiving benefits on ADC. Survivors' benefits were higher than those paid under ADC, privileging widows and orphans whose husbands and fathers were within the social security system, while further disadvantaging those outside it. The removal of these widows from the ADC roster under the Social Security Act amendments of 1939 stigmatized the programme by deleting the supposedly worthy poor and morally acceptable.[63] The amended Act disadvantaged women of colour, whose late husbands were largely outside the covered occupations or who had not married; they received the lower ADC payments.

Social security, like other forms of widows' pensions, simply ignored fathers who looked after their children following their wives' decease. They could not get a widowers' pension, nor did their wives' earnings accumulate credits for their children's upbringing. Not until *Weinburger* v. *Wiesenfeld* (1974) did the Supreme Court decide that men and widowers' children were entitled to survivors' benefits on the same basis as women and widows' offspring.

The legacy of the Great Depression and New Deal for widows, then, was one of heightened gender differentiation, but increased public provision. In this social and economic emergency, men got work, women got dole. Men were workers, women were mothers. The amended Social Security Act provided assistance for widows only while they had young children or if they and their husbands had reached retirement age. It stranded many women between motherhood and old age as displaced homemakers, with no pension, no job, and nowhere to turn. The social security system demanded the same payments from women and men, but provided lower returns to working women on their retirement contributions. The lack of coverage for occupations in the service and agricultural sectors left African-Americans and Hispanics particularly vulnerable. They received neither retirement pensions nor survivors' benefits, which doubly disadvantaged them.

Despite these limitations, the Social Security Act did transfer some resources to older widows through survivors' benefits. As a result, many turned their backs on the extended families that had nurtured their counterparts before 1939. In 1940 over half of all older widows resided with their children (either as household heads or dependents), by 1970 about one-quarter did so.[64]

Regional discrepancies remained as the social security system embedded existing racial and gendered hierarchies and reinforced their rigidity in law. It viewed women as men's dependents, keeping down the costs of social welfare policy by providing for them only as mothers and relicts while ignoring their claims to equity in their own right. For all the legislative gains made by some groups, notably organized labour and despite some women achieving positions of power, public policy relating to widows, lone mothers and, indeed, women in general, continued to regard them in terms of their role in the family rather than as individuals. Gender and marital status defined women as much, if not more, at the end of the Depression than at the beginning. The New Deal incorporated earlier understandings of race, gender and marital status and made them the broad planks upon which its welfare policy rested. The inability to perceive women except in their family context meant that the reality of women's economic situation remained hidden and subsumed under assumptions about family roles and relationships that did not reflect many women's actual situation.

In a time of economic crisis, the New Deal returned to Progressive era understandings about the family economy, gender and race rather than forging a new path. Viewed from that perspective it was an old deal, now sanctioned by federal law. Serious and detrimental regional differences continued to discriminate between the experiences of widowed women, indeed all women, on racial and occupational grounds. This deal built prejudices into law. A few widows received favoured treatment as the wives of men in preferred occupations and the mothers of their children. The majority of younger mothers bringing up children on their own received a meagre hand-out, subject to prevailing local customs. Most female heads of households received a less favorable deal than men, simply because they were women.

Notes

1. See the essays in Linda K. Kerber, Alice Kessler-Harris, Kathryn Kish Sklar, *US History as Women's History: New Feminist Essays* (Chapel Hill, 1995); Seth Koven and Sonya Michel (eds), *Mothers of a New World: Maternalist Politics and the Origins of Welfare States* (London, 1993); and Louise A. Tilly and Patricia Gurin (eds), *Women, Politics and Change* (New York, 1992). Also Theda Skocpol, *Protecting Soldiers and Mothers. The Political Origins of Social Policy in the United States* (Cambridge, Mass., 1992); Linda Gordon, *Pitied But Not Entitled: Single Mothers and the History of Welfare* (New York, 1994); Gwendolyn Mink, *The Wages of Motherhood: Inequality in the Welfare State, 1917–1942* (Ithaca, NY, 1995).

2. These comments also apply to divorced and deserted women who were largely excluded from public programmes in this era.

3. S. J. Kleinberg, 'The Economic Origins of the Welfare State, 1870–1939' in Hans Bak, Frits van Holthoon and Hans Krabbendam (eds), *Social and Secure? Politics and the Culture of the Welfare State: a Comparative Inquiry* (Amsterdam, 1996), 94–116.

4. Joanne L. Goodwin, *Gender and the Politics of Welfare Reform* (Chicago, 1997); US Department of Commerce, Bureau of the Census, *Historical Statistics of the United States, Colonial Times to 1970*, vol. 1 (Washington, DC, 1975), 133. Between 1930 and 1940, the proportion of employed widows returned to 30 per cent while that of wives rose from 12 to 16 per cent.

5. Valerie Kincaid Oppenheimer, *The Female Labor Force in the United States: Demographic and Economic Factors Governing Its Growth and Changing Composition* (Berkeley, 1970), 44–6; US Department of Labor, Women's Bureau, *A Survey of Laundries and Their Women Workers in 23 Cities*, Bulletin number 78 (Washington, DC, 1930), 90.

6. T. H. Watkins, *The Great Depression: America in the 1930s* (Boston, 1993), 220. Marion Elderton, 'Unemployment Consequences on the Home', *Annals of the American Academy of Social and Political Science* 154 (1931), 62.

7. Elizabeth Faue, *Community of Suffering and Struggle: Women, Men, and the Labor Movement in Minneapolis, 1915–1945* (Chapel Hill, 1991), 69–99 discusses the iconography of the labour movement. Examples of New Deal posters can be found in Watkins, *The Great Depression*, 183, 243.

8. Notable exceptions to this gendering of employment include Meridel LeSueur, 'I was marching' in Elaine Hedges (ed.), *Ripening: Selected Work, Meridel LeSuer* (New York, 2nd ed. 1990)

9. Julie Boddy, 'Photographing Women: The Farm Security Administration Work of Marion Post Wolcott' in Lois Scharf and Joan M. Jensen, *Decades of Discontent: The Women's Movement, 1920–1940* (Boston, 1987), 153–76.

10. John Steinbeck, *The Grapes of Wrath* (London, 1990, orig. 1939).

11. Jeanne Westin, *Making Do. How Women Survived the '30s* (Chicago, 1976), 235–7.

12. US Department of Commerce, Bureau of the Census, Fifteenth Census, *Population*, vol. V, *General Report of Occupations* (Washington, DC, 1933), 378; A. J. Badger, *The New Deal: The Depression Years, 1933–1940* (Basingstoke, 1989), 23–9; Lois Rita Helmbold, 'Beyond the Family Economy: Black and White Working-Class Women during the Great Depression' in Melvin Dubofsky and Stephen Burwood (eds), *The Great Depression and the New Deal* (New York, 1990), 234–5.

13. US Department of Labor, Women's Bureau, *The Effects of the Depression on Wage Earners' Families. A Second Survey of South Bend* by Harriet A. Byrne, Bulletin 108 (Washington, DC, 1936), 17.

14. Federal Emergency Relief Administration Bulletin 5054 in Women's Bureau papers (WB), RG 86, Box 6, National Archives.

15. Margaret Hagood, *Mothers of the South: Portraiture of the White Tenant Farm Woman* (New York, 1977, orig. 1939), 168; Typescript, 'Women Who Are Heads of Families on Relief, July, 1935', WB, RG 86, Box 6, National Archives.

16. FERA Release no 6572 'Women in the Urban Relief Population, October, 1935', WB, RG 86, Box 6, National Archives.

17. US Department of Labor, Women's Bureau, *The Negro Woman Worker* by Jean Collier Brown (Washington, DC, 1938), 3; Jo Ann E. Argersinger, *Toward a New Deal in Baltimore. People and Government in the Great Depression* (Chapel Hill, 1988); Brenda Clegg Gray, *Black Female Domestics during the Depression in New York City, 1930–1940* (New York, 1993); US Department of Labor, Women's Bureau, *The Woman Wage Earner. Her Situation Today* by Elisabeth D. Benham, Bulletin 172 (Washington, DC, 1939) 48.

18. US Department of Labor, Women's Bureau, *The Woman Wage Earner*, 49.

19. US Department of Labor, Women's Bureau, *The Effect of Migrating Industries Upon Women's Opportunities for Employment*, WB, RG 86, Box 6, National Archives.

20. US Department of Labor, Children's Bureau, *White House Conference on Children, 1941* (Washington, DC, 1941), 226–7; Walter I. Tratter, *Crusade for the Children: A History of the National Child Labor Committee and Child Labor Reform in America* (Chicago, 1970), 216; US Department of Commerce, Bureau of the Census, *Historical Statistics of the United States, Colonial Times to 1970*, vol. 1 (Washington, DC, 1975), 132; Glen Elder Jr., *Children of the Great Depression: Social Change in Life Experience* (Chicago, 1974), 65.

21. US Department of Labor, Children's Bureau, *Trends in Different Types of Public and Private Relief in Urban Areas, 1929–1935* by Emma A. Winslow, Bureau Publication No. 237 (Washington, DC, 1937), 10–11.

22. United States Congress, House of Representatives, *Economic Security Act Hearings before the Committee on Ways and Means* (74 Cong. 1 Sess., 1935) 80.

23. Margaret Wead, Family Welfare Association of New York, 18 February 1932, in Children's Bureau files (CB), Box 441, National Archives.

24. Florence W. Hutsinpillar to Frances A. Griggs, Executive Secretary,

Mothers' Pension Commission, Wilmington, Delaware, 11 August 1932, CB Box 546, National Archives.

25. Bertha Keiningham, 'The Traditional History of Mothers' Relief' (unpublished typescript, Maryland Room, Enoch Pratt Free Library, Baltimore); Cheryl Lynn Greenberg, *Or Does It Explode? Black Harlem in the Great Depression* (New York, 1991), 145.

26. A White Case Worker, 'The Southern Negro and Depression' *The Churchman* (10 September 1932), clipping in CB Box 546, National Archives.

27. Darlene Clark Hine, 'Black Migration to the Urban Midwest. The Gender Dimension, 1915–1945' in Joe William Trotter Jr. (ed.), *The Great Migration in Historical Perspective. New Dimensions of Race, Class, and Gender* (Bloomington, 1991), 132–3.

28. W. A. Hill to Alida Bowler, 16 September 1932, CB Box 418, National Archives.

29. Lawrence K. Frank, 'Childhood and Youth' in President's Research Committee on Recent Social Trends, *Recent Social Trends in the United States*, vol. 2, (Westport, Conn., 1970, orig. 1933), 771.

30. Quoted in Greenberg, *Or Does It Explode?* 43.

31. *New York Times*, 1 December 1932. Agnes K. Hanna to Caroline Degener, 22 December 1932, CB Box 403, National Archives.

32. Family Welfare Association, *Scrapbook, 1929–1939*. Family Service Association of Fall River, 'History' (typescript in possession of Family Service Association); Charles H. Trout, *Boston: The Great Depression and the New Deal* (New York, 1977), 88.

33. Quoted in James Patterson, *America's Struggle Against Poverty, 1900–1980* (Cambridge, Mass., 1981), 59, and Argersinger, *Toward a New Deal*, 64.

34. Mary Ruth Colby to Florence Hutsinpillar, 22 September 1932, CB Box 404, National Archives.

35. Fall River Family Welfare Association 'Highlights, 1934' (typescript, Family Welfare Association, 1934).

36. Gene D. L. Jones, 'The Chicago Catholic Charities, the Great Depression, and Public Moneys', *Illinois Historical Journal* 83 (1990), 13–30; Ralph Carr Fletcher and Katherine A. Biehl, 'Trends in Direct Relief Expenditures in Allegheny County, 1920–1937', *The Federator*, 13 (1938), 69; Gordon, *Pitied But Not Entitled*, 189.

37. Ralph Carr Fletcher and Katherine A. Biehl, 'Source of Income of Mothers' Assistance Fund Families', *The Federator* 12 (1937), 208.

38. WB Box 6. Susan Ware, *Partner and I: Molly Dewson, Feminism, and New Deal Politics* (New Haven, 1987). Chapter 12 maintains that women played a key role in New Deal social welfare legislation.

39. Argersinger, *Toward a New Deal*, 72. FERA release 7369, 'Women on Relief and Their Employment', WB Box 68, National Archives.

40. FERA release 5439.

41. WPA Research Bulletin, Series IV, no. 2 (Washington, DC, April 1937).

42. Federal Works Agency, *Report on the Progress of the WPA Program*, 30 June 1941, 51.

43. Federal Works Agency, *Final Report on the WPA Program*, 1935–1943 (Washington, DC, 1947), 45.

44. Lois Scharf, *To Work and to Wed. Female Employment, Feminism, and the Great Depression* (Westport, Conn., 1980), 124.

45. Benham, *The Woman Wage Earner*, 48; WPA Research Bulletin, Series IV, no. 2 (Washington, DC, April 1937); Argersinger, *Towards a New Deal*, 73.

46. Josephine Erkens, 'Housekeeper Service Program of the Conference of Catholic Charities', *The Federator*, 12 (1937), 64–72; Thelma Harris, *Safeguarding Motherless Children: Problems Involved in Placement of House-keepers in Motherless Homes* (New York Child Welfare League of America, 1939).

47. Erkens, 'Housekeeper Service Program', 68. See Greenberg, *Or Does It Explode?* 165–6 for a similar programme in New York City.

48. Ralph Carr Fletcher and Katharine A. Biehl, 'Occupancy of Children's Institutions in Allegheny County, 1931–1937', *The Federator* 13 (1938), 100; M. Luella Sauer, 'St Joseph's Orphanage', *The Federator* 13 (1938), 227.

49. Harris, *Safeguarding Motherless Children*, 4.

50. Edwin E. Witte, *The Development of the Social Security Act* (Madison, 1963), 163; Gordon, *Pitied But Not Entitled*, 264–72.

51. Mimi Abramovitz, *Regulating the Lives of Women. Social Welfare Policy from Colonial Times to the Present* (Boston, 1989), 156.

52. US House, *Hearings Relative to the Social Security Act Amendments of 1939*, vol. 2, Statement of Dr Abraham Epstein, 1012.

53. Witte, *The Development of the Social Security Act*, 161. ADC made a separate provision for mothers or other guardians in 1950. Alice Kessler-Harris, 'Designing Women and Old Fools: The Construction of the Social Security Amendments of 1939', in Kerber et al., *US History as Women's History*, 88.

54. US House, Committee on Ways and Means, *Hearings Relative to the Economic Security Act*, 590, 600, 796, 976–7.

55. 'Map of Approved Plans for Social Security', 8 December 1936, CB Box 546; Winifred Bell, *Aid to Dependent Children* (New York, 1965), 28–9; Gunnar Myrdal, *An American Dilemma: The Negro Problem and Modern Democracy* (New York, 1944), 359.

56. US House, *Hearings Relative to the Social Security Act Amendments of 1939*, vol. 1, 14.

57. Abramovitz, *Regulating the Lives of Women*, 317.

58. Fall River, Aid to Dependent Children Register, 15 September 1937 and 15 December 1939. Fall River City Directories, 1920–39.

59. Testimony of A. J. Altmeyer, US House, *Hearings Relative to the Social Security Act Amendments of 1939*, vol. 3, 2199.

60. Testimony of Marion B. Folsom, US House, *Hearings Relative to the Social Security Act Amendments of 1939*, vol. 2, 1134.

61. Testimony of Dr J. Douglas Brown, US House, *Hearings Relative to the Social Security Act Amendments of 1939*, vol. 2, 1221.

62. Patricia Huckle, *Tish Sommers, Activist, and the Founding of the Older Women's League* (Knoxville, 1991), 148–9.
63. Testimony of A. J. Altmeyer, US House, *Hearings Relative to the Social Security Act Amendments of 1939*, vol. 3, 2164, 2299.
64. Frances E. Kobrin, 'The Fall in Household Size and the Rise of the Primary Individual in the United States', *Demography*, 13 (1976), 127–38; Helena Znaniecki Lopata, *Widowhood in an American City* (Cambridge, Mass., 1973), 33–4.

7

Fat of the Land: The Left and the Ladies

Clara Juncker

The tantalizing blend of sex and revolution that has become the legacy of the 'Old Left' continues to intrigue its heirs, regardless, it seems, of political and professional affiliations. The history of the 'Lyrical Left', as John Patrick Diggins refers to American radicalism of the early twentieth century, is well documented in works such as Diggins' own *The Rise and Fall of the American Left* (1992), Robert Cohen's *When the Old Left Was Young: Student Radicals and America's First Mass Student Movement, 1929–1941* (1993) and Marian Morton's *Emma Goldman and the American Left: Nowhere at Home* (1992), which comprise some recent additions to an established corpus dominated by Daniel Aaron's *Writers on the Left* (1961). The history of American women also continues to command much scholarly attention, with William H. Chafe's classic *The Paradox of Change: American Women in the Twentieth Century* (1991), Melvin Dubofsky and Stephen Burnwood's collection *Women and Minorities under the Great Depression* (1990) and Susan Ware's *Beyond Suffrage: Women and the New Deal* (1981) representing three distinguished examples. However, with the conspicuous exceptions of Mari Jo Buhle in *Women and American Socialism 1870–1920* (1981) and Barbara Foley in 'Women and the Left in the 1930s' (1990),[1] historians fail to explore fully the connections between the 'Lyrical Left' and the 'Ladies'. Not enough attention has been paid to the ways in which dissenting intellectuals chose to represent women in their writings, especially in magazines like the *Masses* and the *New Masses*, and how they reveal the social and sexual perceptions of American radicals in the early twentieth century. Indeed, from the Prostitute via the Conventional Wife to the Militant, left-wing writers' addiction to feminine types served not only their satirical diagnosis of American society but also more personal, unconscious needs.

Focusing their narrative energy particularly on the 'Prostitute', the left-wing writers of the *Masses* group wrote about this daughter of the poor within a context of heated discussions about the 'fallen woman' as a social phenomenon during the first decades of the twentieth century. The rapidly expanding urban centres nourished a proliferation of vice that disturbed many Americans, who embarked on a vice crusade. Firmly believing that society could be reformed and controlled, and intent on preserving the nation's human resources, Progressive Americans directed their campaign against two fundamentals of Victorian morality, the conspiracy of silence and the double standard. The resulting nationwide exposé of prostitution made hysterical Americans believe that no woman was safe from the evil snares of procurers.[2]

In the pages of radical magazines like the *Masses*, the conspiracy of silence turned into a conspiracy of debate. The socialist contributors maintained the Marxist view that prostitution resulted from capitalist sexploitation luring young proletarian women into the only unskilled profession offering regular employment and reasonable pay.[3] One Art Young cartoon in the *Masses* depicted a forlorn woman's hat floating in a sea of prostitution, while a menacing dog labelled 'Communist Greed' patrolled the naked shore; in the background, smoking chimneys suggested the urban setting. Louis Untermeyer's poem 'Any City', published in the *Masses* in July 1913, described the cold-footed streetwalker with tear-jerking empathy. The plain, weary girl is 'man's hunger and prey – /His lust and its hideous cure', surrounded by 'The evil, the squalor, the scars;/The street with its pitiless eyes,/The night with its pitiless stars'.[4]

But to the bohemian *Masses* writers, the freedom-loving prostitute also represented an antidote to bourgeois morality and convention. In John Reed's 'A Daughter of the Revolution', the author concludes about the luxury-loving Marcelle that she was twisted not by vice, but by 'the intolerable degradation of the human spirit by the masters of the earth, the terrible punishment of those who thirst for liberty'.[5] Marcelle is the product of a revolutionary father who wanted freedom for men but not for women. All *Masses* portrayals of the 'Prostitute' as type tended to romanticize the scarlet-lipped, white-cheeked women of the night. A report from a meeting between a vice-crusader and the local San Francisco prostitutes in January 1917 presents the fifty attending women as eloquent, proud and socially aware, while James Henle's 'Nobody's Sister' portrays a warm-hearted and generous Marjorie.[6]

New Masses presentations of the 'Prostitute' type retained all strains but the *Masses'* idealizations. In Valentine Konin's 'Love and Life' (1928) and Meridel LeSueur's 'Women on the Breadlines' (1932), women such as Grace and Ellen enter into the ancient profession to escape from toil and starvation; V. F. Calverton's 'Sex and Economics' (1927) relates the prostitute to his criticism of 'the family as a permanent institution'. In the anonymously submitted 'One Is Not Made of Wood: The True Story of a Life', the promiscuous aunt who earns her money by entertaining male customers outside the lumpen proletariat family's tent unknowingly becomes the author's role-model in terms of providing an alternative to the patriarchally dominated family unit.[7]

In the *New Masses*, as well as in the 'Old', the 'Prostitute' shared mental and journalistic space with her relative, the 'Liberated Modern'. In their jubilant emphasis on paganism, living for the moment, female equality and self-expression, the pre-war Greenwich Villagers invented a new type of femininity that destroyed traditional lines between respectable and fallen women. With sexual liberation as the means of overthrowing bourgeois society, bohemians saw the body as a temple of love and puritanism as the great enemy. Women experienced the same drives and passions as men and, as Malcolm Cowley notes in *Exile's Return*, 'should have the same pay, the same working conditions, the same opportunity for drinking, smoking, taking or dismissing lovers'.[8] The exuberant, radical atmosphere and the sexual and intellectual excitement of this 'Innocent Rebellion'[9] exploded with the new poetry, the Armory Show, Freud, Bergson, New Moralists like Havelock Ellis and Edward Carpenter, and in the pages of the *Masses*, where liberated women's poems articulated a frank and erotic female sexuality, as in Gladys Oak's 'Climax':

> I had
> thought that I could sleep
> After I had kissed his mouth
> With its sharply haunting corners
> And its red.
>
> But now that he has kissed me
> A stir is in my blood,
> And I want to be awake
> Instead.[10]

Significantly, a drawing of Isadora Duncan, the epitome of liberated womanhood for many pre- and post-war intellectuals, accompanies Valentine Konin's 'Love and Life' article in the *New Masses*.[11] The full-bodied Isadora's veiled nudity simultaneously parallels and dismisses Konin's discussion of working-class prostitutes, while the dancer's closed eyes and backwards-thrust head creates an individualized creative and sexual space. The following year, in 1929, Mike Gold wrote in 'The Loves of Isadora' that her sensuous restoration of dance had revolutionized bourgeois art forms such as ballet. Isadora Duncan's liberation of the female body from patriarchal and commercial bondage accordingly constituted a significant political development. Gold claimed that 'she denied the rights of private property in dance'.[12]

Yet, at the close of the 1920s, Isadora's artistic rebellion was almost respectable. 'Love and Ping-Pong are the two most popular indoor occupations of America today', Gold noted wryly. In his analysis, the border between radical and middle-class sexual/political territory was vanishing. 'Love is respectable now. Businessmen come to Greenwich Village on pilgrimages and drink of the many fountains of Love. Congressmen mention it in speeches, and the President of a Bank recently admitted to a reporter that he had read a book on Love.'[13] Hence, though Isadora embodies the 'Liberated Modern' type of both the *Masses* and the *New Masses*, her militancy ultimately fails Gold's political examination: 'She was a Red, but not a real revolutionist. It was all emotion with her, glorious and erratic.'[14]

New Masses moderns nonetheless represented themselves in Isadora fashion. In 'Having a Baby' (1929), Dorothy Day finds inspiration in a pregnant young Greek, who at the doctor's 'posed herself easily by the door, her head held high, her coat flung open, her full figure most graciously exposed'. Back home that afternoon, Day puts on ivory beads and powders her nose: 'I could not walk lightly and freely, but it was easy to strut.'[15] On her way to the hospital, she puffs on a cigarette and clutches a girlfriend, a husband nowhere in sight. And after her daughter's birth, Day believes that the baby's 'play instinct is highly developed'.[16]

However, as the participants in the 'revolution in manners and morals' came of age, a new generation was faced with the problems of economic survival in the early Depression years. In 'Women and the New Masses' (1936), Rebecca Pitts credits the magazine with having ended her jazz-age 'drifting and lack of clarity'. She describes an International Labor Defense conference in 1932 as 'the most important single event' of her life.[17]

The anonymous writer of 'One Is Not Made of Wood' moves from a celebration of free love to a more problematic view of sex and freedom:

> I know that my life was my own to live as I wished; emotionally, I felt a rotter of the worst sort ... I wonder how many women, with the roots of their emotional life in American puritanism, have really in their own hearts freed themselves.[18]

Under the title 'Good-bye Bohemia', Nancy Evans declared in *Scribner's* that 'bohemianism and defiance are outmoded' and that the Greenwich Villagers, who triggered the sexual revolution in the years before the World War I, by 1931 were leading lives 'as regular as they are expensive, and as respectable as they are hardworking'. New women, Evans found, were turning into traditional wives.[19]

A target of compassion and contempt, the 'Conventional Woman' had long been a well-known feminine type to intellectual observers. The Greenwich Village feminist Henrietta Rodman explained in an interview of 1915 the conceit and the slave mentality of such women as the result of their sheltered existence in socially isolated homes. Protected or excluded from 'the economic struggle', they are 'kept from developing an appreciation and understanding of life as it is, from developing a broad social consciousness'.[20] Edmund Wilson speculated about his fictionalized John Dos Passos figure in *I Thought of Daisy* (1929) that 'he regarded women as the most dangerous representations of those forces of conservatism and inertia against which his whole life was a protest'.[21] Rebecca Pitts argued in her *New Masses* article of 1935, 'Women and Communism', that the social pressure towards a 'normal' life forces women into a fierce competition for husbands, 'to play by means of sex-allurement, dress, and personal charm upon male ego-sexuality'. As Pitts states with regret, 'woman under capitalism' is 'warped and twisted (by this over-emphasis upon sex) into a creature who really is inferior to man. Vain, spiteful, personal, petty: so often these epithets are well deserved'.[22]

Although Pitts in her analysis of women and communism linked the oppression of women to the capitalist system, radical political parties were reluctant to include 'the woman question' in their platforms. On the contrary, they tended to share the dominant view of female inferiority and backwardness.[23] The view that women were a threat, rather than an asset, to revolutionary activity also dominated the *New Masses*, where the 'Conventional Woman' type came to embody the privileged but vacuous class enemy. In a campaign for new readers, a subscription advertisement from 1927 portrayed the average housewife as almost incurably mindless. The message deserves quoting in full:

DEVELOP YOUR PERSONALITY

Her best friend
Wouldn't tell her
– and there isn't much a
best friend wouldn't tell.

For years she had been reading all the news unfit to print, the Saturday Evening Pest and Sloppy Stories. All her reading matter, her ideas, her thoughts, had been concocted in a capitalist sewer, strained through a bourgeois filter, and then half-baked in a progressive oven.

In consequence she had developed a fearful case of
MENTAL HALITOSIS
THEN A REAL FRIEND
told her the truth and backed it up with a copy of the
NEW MASSES

and a lively breeze of fresh air swept through her brain and fresh-
ened up her whole mental apparatus.

She is getting better. She is sitting up and taking notice. Specialists tell
her that with care and a monthly dose of NEW MASSES she will someday
be able to think for herself. And the entire treatment, for a whole year,
cost her only $2.00.

Subscribe NOW![24]

New Masses articles flesh out the stereotype.[25] The affluent Fifth Avenue
lady wishing to have Esther Fradkin repair an antique embroidery is
blind to the class divisions separating herself from her employee and
insists that 'the suffragette movement gave to all of us women the same
rights as man'. Met with Fradkin's insistence on 'one productive working class' to come about through a revolution, the lady dismisses the
author with the term 'Bolshevik' and leaves her place of work for more
luxurious turf. Again equating suffragettes with class privileges and
conventionality, Martha Foley reports from the National Woman's
Party meeting in 1926: 'The ladies of the world, soft in their silks,
perfumed, smiling and chatting, met in Paris in June. They convened,
resolved, committeed, receptioned, tead – *charming trip, wasn't it?* –
and adjourned.'[26] In 'Paint the Revolution', published in the *New Masses*
the following year, John Dos Passos opposes Mexican wall paintings
to the 'little landscapes' of New York art galleries, a 'snobmarket'
frequented by 'a lot of male and female old women chattering round
an exhibition'.[27] As a sort of climax to its equation of femininity and
consumerist corruption, the *New Masses* published the heiress Barbara
Hutton's affidavits to the surrogate court of Suffolk county.

A series of cartoons visualized the 'Conventional Woman' for the
New Masses readership. A 1932 drawing has one woman say to a friend,
'The trouble with communists is that they destroy the home!' while,
in a 1934 cartoon, a complaining wife exclaims to her newspaper-read-
ing husband, 'I must find an outlet, I think I will join the Socialist
Party'. On the same page a bejewelled, lowcut lady is accompanied by
the caption 'the fat of the land'.[28]

While the labour movement and various American observers remained blind to the political potential of the working-class woman,
other intellectuals received her with open arms. Young writers were
attracted to the exotic foreignness of New York's East Side population,
which became a vehicle for attacks upon repressed and conventional
Anglo-Saxon culture. As Henry May explains in *The End of American
Innocence*, 'a set of new stock characters was being added to American
fiction, including the beautiful young garment worker hungry for life'.[29]
Mike Gold's 1920s' poem, 'The Girl by the River' thus romanticized

the working woman as the beautiful, heroic victim of capitalist evil: 'Bosses who drove her, foremen who hated her .../O America, O you who used her, forget your money-lust now, she dreams of the river'.[30] Similarly, in Elsa Allen's 'Heaven Does Not Protect the Working Girl' (1929), burlesque dancers with beautiful but tired bodies are fragmented and consumed by the privileged male gaze, the young women representing simultaneously workers on an assembly line and its product.[31]

Other *New Masses* texts present a wider scope of working women's lives. Possibly motivated by what Arthur M. Schlesinger Jr. defines as 'the progressive intellectual's sense of guilt over living pleasantly by his skills instead of unpleasantly by his hands',[32] Meridel LeSueur situates herself among women in a domestic employment bureau, a feminine microcosm of Depression America. Here, Bernice has at thirty-five lost all her furniture and all her dreams, as well as more basic sustenance: 'She is hungry. Her great flesh has begun to hang in folds. She has been living on crackers.' An older woman waiting in the same domestic employment bureau is simply 'a living spokesman for the futility of labor. She is a warning. Her hands are scarred with labor. Her body is a great puckered scar'.[33] In a similar gesture of commitment to society's underdogs, the *New Masses* of April 1931 devoted a reader's column to a letter 'From a Working Woman', in which one Agnes Wells describes the long hours, sickening conditions and poor pay of her class of 'maltreated workers': 'And so we slave away hoping for a change to come.'[34] Here, Wells articulates the main rationale for *New Masses* ideologists' preoccupation with the proletariat: the hope for a working-class revolution.

In its satirical diagnoses of post-war America, the Left expressed disillusionment with capitalist America in the 'Militant', a feminine type characteristic of the Depression. In his autobiographical novel *Moon-Calf* (1920), the undisciplined Floyd Dell had earlier confessed to the 'antiseptic effect' of Comrade Emily and the idea of a 'comradely caress':

> Love, he felt – in spite of an effort to confine it within the sphere of his Socialist theories – was something not comradely in the least. He had an unhappy prevision of himself as falling in love – really falling in love – with some worthless little hussy who would not understand, who would not even want to understand, the Marxian theory of value.[35]

A decade later, Dell's Bohemian romanticism had been outdistanced by unwavering radicalism. In 'The Fetish of Being Outside', Meridel LeSueur not only defines herself according to the militant feminine type; she represents her descent into the proletariat as an alluring, orgasmic rebirth into fulfilment and creativity:

> It is difficult because you are stepping into a dark chaotic passional world of another class, the proletariat, which is still perhaps uncon-scious of itself like a great body sleeping, stirring, strange and outside the calculated, expedient class of the bourgeoisie … The creative artist will create no new forms of art or literature for that new hour cut out of that darkness unless he is willing to go all the way, with full belief, into that darkness.[36]

In 'Women and Communism' Rebecca Pitts stated more explicitly the underlying assumptions of LeSueur's revolutionary ardour: 'Only Com-munism … offers woman … the right to a freer, more natural sex happiness.'[37]

Whereas reformed middle-class rebels were welcomed into the com-munist ranks and the *New Masses* columns, the revolutionary heroine was preferably of proletarian origin. The anonymous author of 'One Is Not Made of Wood' described at great length her past as 'a child worker in one of the Rockefeller coal mining towns of southern Co-lorado' and casually announced her political conviction to the *New Masses* readership: 'I was, of course, a revolutionary Socialist. Only a fool could be anything else after having lived my life.'[38] A stray letter found in Oklahoma city by 'a Communist Organizer in the Southwest' was given a whole page in a 1931 issue of the *New Masses*, where it was headlined 'From a Communist Daughter (To Her Father, an Oklahoma Pioneer)'. The emotional impact of the daughter's plea for understanding and support surpassed the most eloquent Party pamphlet:

> If you really understood what the Communist Party stands for, you would not be so opposed to me … On the contrary, I am convinced that you would join us and help us all with your energy to carry out our work.[39]

Similarly, Ann Barton's articles on militant working-class women bore witness to the communists' eagerness to discover and direct revolution-ary potential and radical role models. In 'Women of Maltby' (1933), Barton detected a new militant note in meek miners' wives:

> The "backward" women of the anthracite, now as before polish their stoves to a stage where they shine like glass. But their talk is of other things. Although they would not name it that, it is of class struggle, of meetings, of demands. The women are preparing to play a decisive role in the developing struggles in the anthracite. Hunger has taught

them to question. Militant organization gives them the answer to their questions.[40]

Barton's 'Revolt of the Housewives' (1935) reported that over 10,000 New York housewives had 'left off their washing and ironing, their scrubbing and cleaning ... to join together in the mass action of a picket line. They were swept into militant activity by the issue of exorbitant meat prices'.[41] In 'The Women's Fight Against War' (1934), Barton paid special attention to the 'grey-haired, vigorous 73-year-old "Mother Bloor,"' whose 'activities against capitalism and its off-shoots of misery and war have won her a unique place in the regard and affection of tens and thousands of militant workers and farmers'.[42] A Hugert Gellert cartoon in the *New Masses* provided a humorous supplement to the magazine's presentation of female revolutionary ardor: a picketing girl is arrested and accused of 'assault and battery' against a police officer double her size.[43]

Russian women attracted particular attention among American radicals, because, as Pitts concluded in 'Women and Communism', 'the Soviet Union gives embryonic hints of the future: hints of a rich growth in personality, and socialist virtues – courage, tenacity, self-subordination – which ennoble the new woman as well as the new man'.[44] In 1936 the *New Masses* ran an advertisement for a debate entitled 'Are Women Happier in the USSR?'[45] Ann Barton emphasized in her coverage of the International Women's Congress Against War and Fascism that 'the Russian women are the most remarkable women of the congress, beautiful, with the vigor, dignity and poise that can only exist in women of the only liberated country of the entire world'.[46]

Whether Russian or American, the radical heroines of the 1930s represented the dream of the *New Masses* editors and readers to replace capitalism with communism. At the same time, however, the 'Militant' expressed, like the other feminine types of the 'Old' and *New Masses*, a range of possibly unconscious needs and creeds characteristic of the American Left before and after World War I.

The preference among radical intellectuals for representing their social visions in feminine figures originated, of course, in their fascination with the subject of love, sex and happiness. Floyd Dell's articles in the *Masses*, for example, explored a social alternative in which free love might blossom, and represented what he saw as the two competing forces of his world as woman and the machine. In the pages of the *New Masses*, committed Marxists struggled to define the 'proletarian, revolutionary attitude towards sex'.[47] V. F. Calverton attacked those revolutionists who failed to acknowledge the relationship 'between forms of family life and modes of production ... and become ardent defenders of the family as a permanent institution'. The many radicals 'who have passes into a kind of masculine menopause and ... think sex is unimportant and unperturbing as a problem', or, worse, 'believe that sex is an individual and not a social affair met with equal disapproval.[48] With her sexualized body, woman suited the intentions of American radicals busily trashing Victorian/bourgeois moral codes. The feminine typology of their political discourse helped the 'Lyrical Left' fight Dell's machine or, in the post-war scenario, to restore the machine to its proletarian operatives. In short, the types of American womanhood inspired in left-wing writers a vigorous desire essential to their cause.

At the same time, the feminine types themselves created a distance to individual women that comforted several writers. In 'Women and the New Masses', Rebecca Pitts thus uses the 'Conventional Woman' type to back-off from an earlier persona and more convincingly embrace a new radicalism. In the case of male writers, however, the long range served more complicated needs. In Edmund Wilson's *I Thought of Daisy*, the Dos Passos figure 'was rather afraid of women and seemed never to fall in love'. Instead of involving himself with the emancipated Village women he met at parties, Dos Passos resorted, in Wilson's view, to fantasy and type: 'I believe that he was always hoping for some straight, dark, spare, realistic girl revolutionist, who would be to him a comrade and a partner.'[49] In Mike Gold's review of Isadora Duncan's 'My Life', an unspoken sexual anxiety surfaces: 'The future is a black one for males. The day will come when the human female will devour the male in the Moment of Love, exactly like a female spider or locust.'[50] As this passage indicates, the representation of women as types allowed not only for masculine aloofness but also for verbal warfare. While the feminine type enabled male writers to retreat from flesh-and-blood women, it simultaneously embodied the (political) castration fears buried in their prose.

The feminization of American life in the early twentieth century contributed, no doubt, to the narrative technique of radical intellectuals. Christopher Lasch mentions in *The New Radicalism in America* the complaints around the turn of the century that social intercourse had been 'womanized'.[51] The successful garment strikes, the suffrage movement, the sexual revolution and the growing number of women in the workforce intensified the change in the social, economic and political roles of American women. As Doris E. Fleischman observes in *America as Americans See It* (1932), women are 'decorators, insurance agents. They are retail dealers, undertakers, actresses, architects, sculptors, authors, editors, essayists, metallurgists, professors, inventors, lawyers, judges, physicians, trained nurses, aeronauts, social service workers, dentists, theatre ushers, manicurists, bookkeepers and financiers'. Though Fleischman concedes that 'far fewer women reach commanding positions proportionally than men do',[52] her list suggests the increased visibility of women that was apparent also to intellectuals of the American Left. In representing ideological/political alternatives, contemporary writers accordingly employed the figures that conspicuously embodied social change: American women.

The feminine types moreover helped the political pedagogy of radical intellectuals. In order to reach an audience, they visualized social ideas in feminine types, who each represented a set of problems and beliefs essential to American society. Dos Passos' *New Masses* article, 'Paint the Revolution', discusses the strategy: 'The Revolution ... had to be explained to the people. The people couldn't read. So the only thing to do was paint it up on a wall.'[53] Though Dos Passos' own country did not face an illiteracy rate of Mexican proportions, his 'Grosz Comes to America' nonetheless argues for a 'painting visual' approach to writing: 'In the last twenty-five years a change has come over the visual habits of Americans ... From being a wordminded people we are becoming an eyeminded people.'[54] The satirical typology of American left-wing prose thus served as authorial projections of social beliefs and, perhaps, helped 'eyeminded' Americans re-imagine their world.

Ironically, the feminine types of the Left represented what Americans could not see or, as Dos Passos chose to put it, 'what we're not looking for'.[55] Since women had long been the muted other to masculine selves, and since the changes in women's lives were as yet embryonic, the feminine equalled, so to speak, the unknown. As a sort of hidden, explosive force, woman embodied the 'veins of lava' and 'unexpected places' that revolutionary writers, in Dos Passos' view, ought to tap and explore. The feminine types, in a sense, belonged to and articulated a no-man's land outside social and symbolic structures, a marginal space obviously appealing to the American Left.

Yet fascination mingled with fear in radical intellectuals' preoccupation with the feminine. Because of woman's affiliation with disorder, she inspired at the same time a certain anxiety and attempt at control. The many lists and enumerations of 'Women: Types and Movements' might therefore originate in an authorial wish to establish command. 'What are American women?' Fleischman asks, and with a list of 'school teachers, coal miners, poets, factory mechanics, boiler menders, social workers, flappers'[56] – and more – seeks to name, and thus to order, disorder.

In their description of American female types, left-wing intellectuals thus recorded accurately the contemporary social scene as well as their private and political idiosyncracies. In a little known 'Introductory Note', prepared for the Modern Library edition of *The 42nd Parallel* (1937), Dos Passos attempted in general terms to account for the blend of the social and the personal in studies of American life:

If several people describe the same scene, say a man and a woman sitting at a table in a room and talking, the results are sure to be very different. Through a bunch of such descriptions a number of identical stereotypes will appear which will reveal the commonplace attitudes and the common grounds of the human group the narrator belongs to. But there will also be found here and there in the accounts a mental slant that tends to break the stereotype and to give some added insight or breadth to the event and to relate it in some new or fresh way to the experience of the group.[57]

From the 'Prostitute' to the 'Militant', the American Left created a gallery of women who owe their shape to its interest in American society, their character to its various notions of womanhood, and their continued life to the commitment and energy that span the distance between intellectuals in the beginning of the twentieth century to those approaching its end.

Notes

1. Barbara Foley, 'Women and the Left in the 1930s', *American Literary History*, 2 (Spring 1990), 82–94.
2. See Egal Feldman, 'Prostitution, the Alien Woman and the Progressive Imagination, 1910–15', *American Quarterly*, 19 (Summer 1967), 192–206; Roy Lubove, 'The Progressive and the Prostitute', *Historian*, 24 (May 1962), 308–30; and John C. Burnham, 'The Progressive Era Revolution in American Attitudes Toward Sex', *Journal of American History*, 59 (March 1973), 885–908.
3. William O'Neill (ed.), *Echoes of Revolt: The Masses 1911–17* (New York, 1966), 182.
4. Art Young, *Masses*, 4 (May 1913), 10–11; O'Neill, *Echoes of Revolt*, 187.
5. O'Neill, *Echoes of Revolt*, 184.
6. 'A Strange Meeting', *Masses*, 9 (April 1917), 21, 14; James Henle, 'Nobody's Sister', *Masses*, 6 (January 1915), 10.
7. Valentine Konin, 'Love and Life', *New Masses*, 3 (March 1928), 8; Meridel LeSueur, 'Women on the Breadlines', *New Masses*, 7 (January 1932), 5–6; V. F. Calverton, 'Sex and Economics', *New Masses*, 2 (March 1927), 11–12; Anon., 'One Is Not Made of Wood', *New Masses*, 3 (August 1927), 5–7.
8. Malcolm Cowley, *Exile's Return: A Literary Odyssey of the 1920's* (New York, 1951), 60–1.
9. The term comes from Henry F. May's *The End of American Innocence: A Study of the First Years of Our Own Time* (1959, rpt. New York, 1979).
10. Quoted in Mari Jo Buhle, *Women and American Socialism 1870–1920* (Chicago, 1981), 263.
11. H. Walkowitz, *New Masses*, 3 (March 1928), 8.
12. Mike Gold, 'The Loves of Isadora', *New Masses*, 4 (March 1929), 20.

13. Ibid., 20.
14. Ibid., 21.
15. Dorothy Day, 'Having a Baby', *New Masses*, 4 (June 1928), 5.
16. Ibid., 6.
17. Rebecca Pitts, 'Women and the New Masses', *New Masses*, 19 (1 December 1932), 15.
18. 'One Is Not Made of Wood', 7.
19. Nancy Evans, 'Good-bye Bohemia', *Scribner's*, 89 (January 1931), 643.
20. George MacAdam, 'Henrietta Rodman: An Interview with a Feminist' in June Sochen (ed.), *The New Feminism in Twentieth Century America* (Lexington, Mass., 1971), 58.
21. Edmund Wilson, *I Thought of Daisy* (New York, 1929), 57.
22. Rebecca Pitts, 'Women and Communism', *New Masses*, 14 (19 February 1935), 17.
23. Buhle, *Women and American Socialism*, 180–4.
24. *New Masses*, 2 (March 1927), 2.
25. Esther Fradkin, 'The Fifth Avenue Lady', *New Masses*, 1 (July 1926), 11; Martha Foley, 'The Ladies – God Bless 'Em', *New Masses*, 1 (August 1927), 19–20; John Dos Passos, 'Paint the Revolution', *New Masses*, 2 (March 1927), 15; 'Letters from a Princess', *New Masses*, 10 (9 January 1934), 23.
26. Foley, 'The Ladies', 19.
27. Dos Passos, 'Paint the Revolution', 15.
28. 'The Trouble with Communists' *New Masses*, 8 (August 1932), 30; 'I Must Find an Outlet' *New Masses*, 10 (20 March 1934), 7; 'The Fat of the Land' *New Masses*, 10 (20 March 1934), 7.
29. May, *The End of American Innocence*, 282–3.
30. Mike Gold, 'The Girl by the River', *New Masses*, 1 (August 1926), 20.
31. Elsa Allen, 'Heaven Does Not Protect the Working Girl', *New Masses*, 4 (February 1929), 12.
32. Arthur M. Schlesinger Jr., *The Vital Center: The Politics of Freedom* (1950, rpt. London, 1970), 46.
33. LeSueur, 'Women on the Breadlines', 5, 6.
34. Agnes Wells, 'From a Working Woman', *New Masses*, 6 (April 1931), 23.
35. Floyd Dell, *Moon-Calf: A Novel* (1920, rpt. New York, n.d.), 233–4.
36. Meridel LeSueur, 'The Fetish of Being Outside', *New Masses*, 14 (26 February 1935), 23.
37. Pitts, 'Women and Communism', 18.
38. 'One Is Not Made of Wood', 5–6.
39. Anon., 'From a Communist Daughter', *New Masses*, 7 (September 1931), 16.
40. Ann Barton, 'Women of Maltby', *New Masses*, 8 (July 1933), 12.
41. Ann Barton, 'Revolt of the Housewives', *New Masses*, 15 (18 June 1935), 18–19.
42. Ann Barton, 'The Women's Fight Against War', *New Masses*, 12 (4 September 1934), 18.
43. Hugh Gellert, *New Masses*, 6 (December 1930), 5.
44. Pitts, 'Women and Communism', 18.

45. 'Are Women Happier in the USSR?' *New Masses*, 18 (7 January 1936), 22.
46. Barton, 'Women's Fight', 19.
47. Upton Sinclair, 'Revolution – Not Sex', *New Masses*, 2 (March 1927), 11.
48. Calverton, 'Sex and Economics', 11.
49. Wilson, *I Thought of Daisy*, 57.
50. Gold, 'The Loves of Isadora', 20.
51. Christopher Lasch, *The New Radicalism in America, 1889–1963* (New York, 1965), 66.
52. Doris E. Fleischman, 'Women: Types and Movements' in F. J. Ringel (ed.), *America as Americans See It* (New York, 1932), 108.
53. Dos Passos, 'Paint the Revolution', 15.
54. John Dos Passos, 'Grosz Comes to America', *Esquire*, 6 (September 1936), 105.
55. John Dos Passos, 'The New Masses I'd Like', *New Masses*, 1 (June 1926), 20.
56. Fleischman, 'Women: Types and Movements', 106.
57. John Dos Passos, *The 42nd Parallel* (New York, 1937), vii–viii.

8

Bureaucratic Dynamics and Control of the New Deal's Publicity: Struggles between Core and Periphery in the FSA's Information Division

Stuart S. Kidd

The cultural history of the United States during the 1930s has been an expanding field of enquiry during recent years and historians have identified the decade as a crucial juncture for the development of American art forms and modes of expression. America in the era of the Great Depression has been described as a period of cultural nationalism, in which creative intellectuals celebrated the United States, its history and its institutions.[1] Historians of the New Deal's art projects, in particular, have explored the relationships between culture and politics and have perceived crucial linkages between the New Deal's sponsorship of culture and the Roosevelt administration's concern to cultivate public support for its programmes. The most significant of these projects were established in 1935 under Federal One of the Works Progress Administration. Extending the earlier initiatives of the Civil Works Administration during 1933–4, they sought to provide work relief to unemployed writers, musicians, artists and workers in theatre. Other projects involving the creative arts that have attracted historical interest were less concerned with providing work relief than with producing public information about the New Deal. These include the photographic project established by the Resettlement Administration (RA) in 1935 which was continued under the Farm Security Administration (FSA) after 1937, and the experiments by the RA and the Soil Conservation Service in the use of documentary film. Like the work of the relief agencies, these projects articulated not only the New Deal's visions for America but they sought to redefine the very notion of America itself during a period of economic crisis and social instability.[2]

The principal focus of historians has been on the nature and character of cultural production sponsored by the New Deal. Their primary interest has been with the cultural texts themselves and the representational and ideological issues that emerge from them. The approach is that of cultural studies whereby form and theme intermesh, and text, authorship and context are related in a complex interplay of cultural representation and ideological development. Cultural historians have demonstrated how the plays of the Federal Theater Project, the murals of the Federal Arts Project, the guidebook series of the Federal Writers Project and the photographs produced by the FSA not only expressed the New Deal's values but did so through the development of appropriate and distinctive formal modes of expression. They buttressed the emerging New Deal order not only in their direct thematic references to social and economic justice but also, indirectly, by contributing to the development of a national culture that was democratic, accessible and participatory. Not only were the 'common man' and 'common woman' the most prominent symbols of 'art for the millions', but those New Dealers who supported the movement sought to make 'the people' central to it, not only as subjects but as consumers and patrons. The role of culture, then, is perceived as an important adjunct of the New Deal's political economy, for it promoted a consensus behind the new liberal order.[3]

Preoccupied by their own broad politico-cultural research agendas and privileging the representational or auteuristic aspects of cultural production under the New Deal, historians have tended to neglect or to diminish the significance of those administrators who established and operated the various cultural programmes. While administrators of the New Deal's major social and economic agencies have received extensive biographical treatment, the bureaucratic elite of the New Deal's cultural programmes have received far less attention. When administrators such as Henry Alsberg of the Federal Writers Project, Holger Cahill of the Federal Art Project or Hallie Flanagan of the Federal Theater Project assume prominence in the histories of the agencies, they are effectively treated as ciphers or catalysts for work of 'merit' or of 'social significance'.[4] Rarely are they treated as administrators whose work intersected with other bureaucratic aspects of the New Deal and whose actions were conditioned by imperatives other than missionary, cultural idealism. However, if biographical interpretation of these individuals could maintain a distance from the aesthetic and creative aspects of the agencies which they headed – if output was regarded as 'publicity' rather than 'art' – reconstructions of their experiences as administrators may yield insights about the New Deal's relationships with its cultural programmes that are not merely representational. They may provide insights about the nature of the New Deal order, the federal system within which agencies operated and the scope for creative administration within them.[5]

Conventionally, historians of the New Deal's art and publicity projects have not addressed the issues of administration and federalism, although each of the New Deal's arts and communications agencies was obliged to develop bureaucratic structures and to work within broader, decentralized frameworks. The neglect is especially apparent in the history of the RA/FSA's photography project. Historians have been preoccupied with the images of America revealed by the 80,000 prints and 270,000 negatives accumulated by its Historical Section between 1935 and 1943. One way or another, the role of the man who organized the enterprise, Roy Stryker, has been obscured by interpretations of the aesthetic or political significance of the photographs themselves. Stryker has been variously described as a facilitator of great art and as an enemy of the artist; as a 'press agent of the underprivileged' and as a factotum of the New Deal, who reconciled the American people to modernisation by proclaiming a proud but spent heritage.[6] Stryker may have been any of these things, but if we disassociate him from the aesthetics of the photographs, he becomes a more mundane and familiar figure: an embattled administrator who struggled for departmental autonomy within a federated organizational structure.

Stryker was not a New Deal apparatchik, neither was he a liberal visionary, for his political convictions were too confused. Personal ambition and professional idealism were more powerful motivating forces and Stryker sought to satisfy both by transforming the Historical Section from an institutionally-dependent publicity department into a semi-autonomous research unit. Stryker needed to be adept at bureaucratic politics because his ambitions provoked considerable opposition. In common with other Washington-based New Dealers he won his bureaucratic spurs through conflicts with regional officials within his agency who held different views on the control and deployment of information resources.

Roy Stryker was forty-one years old when he entered government service in 1934. Since 1922 he had been employed as an economics tutor at Columbia University. By his own admission he was unable to become 'the proper kind' of economist. He had a talent for description rather than analysis and he developed a niche for himself in visual information, illustrating economic issues and institutions through photographs, graphs and charts and by organizing field trips for student groups. Stryker compensated for his lack of academic credentials at postgraduate level by pioneering a pedagogy.[7] By 1935, an Associate Professor of Economics with little prospect of advancement, Stryker craved for the scope and recognition that he believed his talent deserved.

It was through Rexford Tugwell's patronage that Stryker was brought to Washington, initially as a specialist in visual information within the Department of Agriculture and, after July 1935, as head of the Historical Section within the RA's Information Division. However, government service never displaced his fundamental respect for academe. As late as the autumn of 1937 he harboured ambitions to return to Columbia, and once he came to accept that he could not hope for a post of equivalent status, worked to transform the Historical Section from a political service agency into an organizational form resembling a university research unit. He was often irritated by the 'damned newspapermen' in the Information Division, who strictly defined their roles in instrumental terms and did not share his own enthusiasm for the compilation of a documentary record *per se*. Stryker was committed to the development of an empirical visual anthropology and he referred to his photographers as 'historians of the present' or 'investigators who use the camera as a record mechanism'. He contrasted the social scientific documentary method with the work of 'pictorialists' who evaded reality by embellishing it, and photo-journalists who distorted actuality by dramatizing it. Ideally, the documentary photographer would have a detailed knowledge of their subject area because the quality of the documentary image depended, ultimately, not on technical competence, the photographer's 'eye' or imagination, but on a judicious assessment of its contents. Stryker wrote that 'the job is to know enough about the subject matter, to find its significance in itself, and in relation to its surroundings, its time, and its function'.[8] The academic working practices that Stryker encouraged were reinforced by the institutional contacts that he developed. After 1938, once the Historical Section was secure, he directed much of its work towards collaborative academic enterprises with individual scholars, educational institutions and university presses.

However, while Stryker may have had the soul of an academic, his talents were those of a politician and if he was driven by a sense of some 'higher purpose' it only served to sharpen his political acumen. Stryker was obliged to adapt to agencies whose futures were often problematic or uncertain. The issue of organizational survival was felt keenly throughout both the RA and the FSA due to the controversial nature of their programmes and the persistent criticism they attracted from many quarters. The Information Division itself was marginalized within both administrations. Because its directors were not assigned the grade of assistant administrator, the Division had no automatic right to be represented at high-level staff policy meetings.[9] For Stryker these concerns were magnified in his own parlous institutional sphere. At the outset the very status of his unit was unclear to colleagues and it was suggested that the Historical Section's title be changed to clarify its functions.[10] Even more serious were budgetary constraints during the first six months of Stryker's tenure which limited the amount of field work he could assign to his photographers and which restricted his laboratory's film-processing capacity.[11] While the Section's funding temporarily improved in the spring of 1936, under the Resettlement Administration Stryker could not expect that an adequate operational budget would be maintained or even that his operation was secure. From the beginning he felt obliged to struggle for status and funding in a wider context of institutional vulnerability and instability.

The Historical Section was one of five sub-sections of the Information Division. In 1937 a staff writer described the Historical Section's administrative status in the following terms:

> On an organisational chart of the Department of Agriculture, it can be found only with a magnifying glass, tucked away in the middle of a page where its official rank is indicated by its equality with that of a management section consisting of two stenographers whose duty is to keep the writers of Farm Security efficiently supplied with pencils and paper clips.[12]

Stryker's team of photographers, laboratory technicians, picture editors, clerks and stenographers never exceeded twenty-eight in number and fell to nine after the spending cuts of 1937.[13] During its early years Stryker was convinced that the Section was dispensable because the RA/FSA was primarily 'an action program' and his own photographic programme was 'extraneous', 'unusual' and 'peripheral'. The Historical Section was chronically liable to budget cuts and susceptible to other political pressures. As an administrator Stryker was obliged to respond both to his superiors in the Information Division and to field workers in the Regions. Central headquarters required the development of a resource base that would serve as an effective public relations instrument and as an educational medium for field workers and clients. The RA/FSA's field officials wanted the photographic project to reflect their own contributions to resettlement and rehabilitation programmes. The photographer, Jack Delano, recalled that neither side had any sympathy with work that did not support directly the programmes of the parent agency: 'Roy was constantly having problems maintaining [a] much broader concept of what [we] should be doing'.[14]

The Regions came to assume a position of central importance for Stryker, not only as subjects for his photographers but as bureaucratic entities whose interests often appeared to be at variance with his own. Stryker believed that Tugwell had originally intended that the Section's principal function was to serve regional personnel by providing material that would illustrate their programmes and educate their clients. These were the terms in which the administrator couched his request for an appropriation to finance a motion picture on land misuse to be produced by the Information Division and which became *The Plow that Broke the Plains*. 'The primary object of the motion picture is to help the

Resettlement Administration and its employees to visualize and understand better the problems confronting them', Tugwell wrote to the Comptroller General in July 1935. During the same month Stryker would have gleaned from staff conferences that the Information Division's principal functions were to coordinate information between central headquarters and the Regions and to provide support services for the RA's field staff. Indeed, one of his first specified tasks was to help 'dress up' the quarters of the regional officers with 'striking photos', maps and charts. It was this 'service function' that Stryker chose to prioritise in the Section's entry for the RA's *First Annual Report*, an emphasis that was justified at the time because its workload was biased towards the Division and the Regions rather than the general media. At the end of 1936 intra-agency services exceeded those extended to newspapers and magazines by a ratio of 10:1.[15]

Stryker's construction of the Section's role obliged him to foster harmonious, cooperative relations with field organizations. However, his attitude to the Regions was governed by complex and contradictory impulses. While he appreciated their importance for the Section, he was determined to develop a greater autonomy and a broader scope for the Historical Section beyond its regional obligations. In particular, he was determined to establish sovereignty over visual information within the Information Division.

Of all the Regions with which Stryker had to deal, those of the South were amongst the most demanding. Their officers were often practical men, steeped in the culture of their region and contemptuous of the liberal idealism that they believed to prevail in central headquarters. The recollections of George C. Stoney, an Associate Information Adviser appointed to Region V in 1940, suggest that caution and circumspection pervaded the hierarchies of the regional offices. Rehabilitation supervisors formed the junior, operational echelons. Many of them, from landowning families and college-educated, entered government service without much enthusiasm, regarding employment with the RA/FSA as a poor substitute for farm ownership and management, a career in business, or an appointment to a state or county agricultural organization. Moreover, the agency's clientele aroused an ingrained class prejudice that limited their ability to relate to the problems of the constituencies that the RA and FSA sought to assist. While Stoney was surprised by the number who rapidly became 'true believers', he noted how, given the local nature of their work, they tended to maintain a public reserve and did not compound their challenges to the South's political economy by digressing from its social conventions. The information advisers, many of whom were drawn from journalism, were particularly sensitive about public relations. They appreciated that cultivating local opinion was as important as shaping a national mood. 'We all knew that we were attached to an organization and an undertaking that was not approved by southern middle-class people, particularly in the small towns and agricultural centers', Stoney reflected. Much of his own time was spent cultivating the editors of county weeklies, writing model news stories for regional circulation and securing local radio publicity for the FSA's work. Effective public relations in the South required that advisers not only refrain from loose, progressive talk around the court-house but that they convince the rural elites – the planters, merchants, feed-mill owners, equipment retailers and local bankers – of the desirability of the FSA's programmes.[16]

The realism of the supervisors and information advisers mirrored the attitudes and approaches of their superiors. At the level of director, T. Roy Reid, the Director of Region VI that covered the states of Arkansas, Louisiana, and Mississippi, epitomized the tendency to affect the RA/FSA's progressive agenda of socio-economic reform without challenging the South's dominant culture. He had previously worked for the Extension Service in Arkansas, becoming Chief of the state service in 1928. Reid regarded himself as a practical rather than an ideological agricultural reformer. He rejected the thesis that the South's agricultural problems entailed social and economic exploitation. For Reid, both the landowner and the farm worker were 'victims of a system' that had deprived the majority of the South's farmers of the opportunity to gain a stake in society through land ownership, to the detriment of the region as a whole. He was unsympathetic to radical agitation that produced 'bitterness without any progress'. The Southern Tenant Farmers' Union described Reid as a reactionary rather than a New Dealer.[17]

Region VI conformed to the South's social norms, as Constance Daniel, an FSA race adviser, discovered in 1941. Out of a total of over 1,500 employees only eighteen were African-Americans – eight rural rehabilitation supervisors, ten home management supervisors but no clerical personnel. Daniel's findings confirmed the reason for the poor response of African-Americans to the Region's rural rehabilitation and tenant purchase programmes. Reid's strong convictions encouraged a tough-minded localism, an impatience with the constraints imposed by central bureaucracy, and resentment of intrusive progressives from Washington. Ben Shahn, one of the first photographers to be hired by Stryker, recalled his arrival at the headquarters of Region VI in 1935: 'In Little Rock I presented my credentials to our regional director. He said, "What the hell are you coming down here for making more trouble for us"'.[18]

Stryker's inexperience and the fledgling Historical Section's weakness in the autumn of 1935 prompted Region VI and other southern Regions to recommend that more freedom and financial support be given to them to conduct photographic activity at the expense of its centralised direction in Washington. During an RA Staff Conference of October 1935, Lewis C. Gray of Region IV requested that cameras be provided to field staff to enable them to do their own photographic work rather than have to rely upon specialists from Washington. Two months later, at the Conference of Assistant Administrators and Regional Directors, delegates further proposed that photographic sections be established in all Regional Information Departments.[19] This new demand was introduced by Oscar E. Jones, Information Adviser for Region VI, and one of the most determined and troublesome regional officers for Roy Stryker.

Jones attempted a bureaucratic coup at the regional level. His aims were to secure greater autonomy for his own operations and to make the publicity for his own Region more effective. He claimed that the Historical Section lacked the resources to meet regional needs and that its approach to photography was not ideal for regional publicity. Jones was especially critical of 'typical' pictures of high technical quality and with pretensions to artistic excellence. He argued that the Regions' principal outlets were mainly newspapers which were 'inclined to ignore artistic value in most cases'. Editors required 'spot' photographs, specific visual material, local and current, to accompany news items and features. 'Typical pictures from Washington, regardless of how complete your morgue will be, will be of little help in supplying this need', Jones advised Stryker.[20] Despite central headquarters' refusal to support decentralization, Jones expanded his own photography programme. Region VI purchased a processor to develop its own negatives, attempted to impress both Stryker and FSA Administrator, Will Alexander, with examples of its work and used its Annual Report to advance claims for information resources at the expense of central headquarters. The culmination of Region VI's campaign for greater independence from Washington occurred in 1938 when the Information Division reformulated the Historical Section's relations with the Regions. During the earliest days of the Resettlement Administration, Rexford Tugwell had warned of the dangers of 'setting up little kingdoms in the field'.[21] The tendencies of regional bureaucracies for self-publicity, autonomy, and aggrandizement of their functions were real threats to Stryker from the beginning.

However, regional information offices were not merely engaged in empire-building. They appear to have been genuinely beleaguered. Their effectiveness was judged, in part, by the number of press releases they secured. Washington headquarters compiled digests of press releases from the various regions and, after March 1936, required weekly reports from regional offices. The information office of Region VI claimed over 5,000 newspaper clippings for a ten-month period ending in December 1936 and estimated double the number since its inception. In addition, regional personnel prepared and distributed pamphlets and circulars, organized exhibit material for local fairs, conducted radio interviews, built up a photographic file and processed film for information advisers in other regions. Such a high volume of work was accomplished despite shortages of staff and periodic cutbacks. Although the information office of Region VI had a staff of four people in September 1935, it would appear that they were reduced to one Regional Adviser and one clerk in the summer of 1937.[22] For regional information advisers, administrative assertiveness was necessary for both success and survival.

Equally, Stryker was determined that regional information officers would not usurp the Historical Section's role within the Information Division. Professionalism was the standard that Stryker raised to counter regional aspirations to control visual information. He cultivated an *élan* amongst his own photographers that was often manifested in a disdain for regional officers. Their correspondence to base is littered with references to the handicaps of working alongside regional officers in the field. Marion Post Wolcott was the most outspoken about her contacts with regional officers and the manner in which they hindered her work. She was often infuriated by the number of 'idiots' and 'dopes' she encountered in the regional offices. Post Wolcott resented the time wasted in the arrangements and administration involved in her contacts with field officers and was irritated by the predictable and uninspiring assignments they organized for her. Her commentary on one visit to a southern project reveals a range of grievances: 'I got the coop. Veterinary giving them his little act, sticking capsules in and out of mules, mares and what have you – He was all dressed up looking like he was going to a Sat. nite dance, and wanted to know how soon Dr Alexander would see pictures!'[23] Often contributing to the friction generated by the interaction of creative artists and functionaries was the photographers' liberal self-righteousness and their contempt for provincials.

It was accepted that in all circumstances photographers' first loyalty was to the Historical Section and not to the Regions, and only one photographer took a major stand on the side of a Region against Stryker. Dorothea Lange had worked for the Emergency Relief Administration in California before joining the Historical Section and retained close and supportive links with state agencies dealing with the problems of migrant labour. Unlike her colleagues within Stryker's unit, she appreciated the value of publicity to the RA's regional offices and other governmental agencies in California. She was aware that state officials were obliged to recycle 'stale' and 'too-familiar' material, which reduced its political impact in California. 'Have we been remiss?' she asked Stryker in 1937. 'Haven't we neglected to give the Regional Office the support it needs?' Lange offered to supply regional agencies directly with unreleased negatives. Her attitude was that social and economic problems were more important than procedural or bureaucratic considerations. Stryker appears to have been embarrassed by Lange's magnanimity but was determined that her material on migrants should be reserved for prestigious national outlets. Incanting the titles of *Life*, *Look*, and the *New York Times*, Stryker advised Lange: 'Please keep definitely in mind ... the fact that we must put our best feet forward to these publications.' The impulse to draw attention to the Section's work through a national publicity scoop was a stronger force for Stryker than the selfless, political good-sense that underlay Lange's entreaties.[24]

While Stryker sought to cultivate the *esprit* of his own staff he worked to undercut the pretensions of his counterparts in the Regions. He was openly critical of negatives he received from regional offices. O. E. Jones had described his assistant, M. C. Blackman, as having 'considerable experience in newspaper photography' and Stryker grasped the opportunity to put him in his place. In 1936 he gave Blackman a basic lesson in documentary photographic strategy, advising him to develop 'an eye for the dramatic' and to avoid lining 'the family up with papa, mama, and the children in descending order'. 'Pictures of this type are of little value to anyone', Stryker pontificated. When the persistent Jones sent two prints for Stryker's technical advice in 1938 he was even more cutting. Stryker described them as overexposed, blurred, clumsily developed and flawed in composition. 'I am afraid you fellows too often take the attitude that the pictures are good enough for small town pictures', Stryker wrote. 'The danger of this lies in the fact that it isn't a very great stimulant to improve one's photography.' In July 1936 Eudora Welty, who was to become one of the South's major writers, sent a portfolio of her photographic work to Washington in an unsuccessful application to the Resettlement Administration for a post in its photographic unit. Welty was sponsored by T. Roy Reid and O. E. Jones of Region VI, an association that may not have aided her cause.[25]

The struggle for control over visual information also manifested itself in disputes over the schedules of the Historical Section's photographers when on assignment in the Regions. Stryker was determined to prevent his photographers from being commandeered for project work of a limited regional interest.[26] He also sought to ensure that full credit lines were given to the Historical Section when regional officers placed photographs from the Washington file in local newspapers and magazines.[27] As an issue, accreditation not only enhanced the Historical Section's prestige within the Information Division but increased its relative authority over the Regions with regard to visual information. Stryker was successful in mobilising the authority of his superiors to give force to his demands. From the outset they were sympathetically disposed to the Historical Section's claims for special status. The requests of regional officers during 1935 and 1936 for greater flexibility in visual information were resisted by Assistant Administrator, C. B. Baldwin and the Information Division's first Director, John Franklin Carter. Baldwin claimed that the work was 'highly specialized' and required 'highly experienced' staff, while Carter contended that 'so many people who think that they know how to take photographs, do not, and that is the truth of the matter'.[28] However, Stryker also benefited from fears in headquarters about regional ambitions. The Historical Section may have been intended to serve the Regions, but it was also regarded as an instrument of central authority over them.

At first sight, the Information Division's reformulation of its visual information policy in 1938 appears a victory for the Regions, and especially for those in the South. Its new Director, John Fischer, instructed regional advisers to do all their own photographic work of a 'regional nature', to maintain their own files and to provide prints of their best photographs for the Historical Section's own file. Region VI was designated as a film-processing centre for regional offices when Stryker's laboratory was unable to cope with demand and the Historical Section was directed to concentrate on the production and publication of material of a national interest.[29]

If the policy constituted a victory for Region VI, it was a victory that Stryker readily conceded. Indeed, it appears that he played a conscious but covert role in precipitating the policy review through his incessant complaints about the Historical Section's workload. Stryker had every reason to be jubilant at the outcome and the opportunity to reduce his obligations to the Regions. By 1938 the future of the Historical Section was more secure than at any other previous time. Not only had its work been acclaimed in the media but Stryker had begun to develop a new set of clients in Washington by performing contract assignments for other agencies. By 1941 these included the Public Health Service, the Indian Bureau, the Social Security Board and the Bureau of the Budget. The Section also designed exhibitions for its clients, composed publicity layouts, made up slide films and processed film. It worked closely with the Savings Bond Division of the Treasury Department on Defense Bond drives, with the State Department in preparing exhibitions to be sent abroad, and it accepted special commissions such as the preparation of photographic exhibits for the Rockefeller Committee on Cultural Relations with Latin American

States. This work not only increased the Historical Section's visibility in Washington but, because it was remunerated, strengthened its position within the Information Division.

It would appear that as the Section received more external contracts and the louder Stryker protested, the more commissions he received, the more sympathy for his plight he extracted from his superiors and the more resources he gained in compensation. In 1938 Stryker estimated that work for external agencies generated 3,000 prints each month and over-strained the laboratory staff as well as the field photographers.[30] In 1939 he acquired new, custom-designed laboratory facilities. Whatever grounds existed for his complaints about the Section's work for other agencies, he exploited the issue to draw attention to the quality of his Section's service, expand its scope, and increase its autonomy in relation to the Regions.

The Section's enhanced status and strengthened resource-base also permitted Stryker to become involved in other areas of activity that were more congenial to his own interests. When asked at the end of 1938 whether he considered his work complete, Stryker replied that 'we have not even scratched the surface'. The United States was in the process of constant change and photographs needed to be updated 'to keep in step with progress'. Stryker was alluding to his ambition to transform the Historical Section from a publicity unit into an archive for 'American social history'. This entailed a broader compass for the Section's work in which the file was augmented to reflect agriculture's problems as part of a wider, interrelated whole, and in which the small town and the city would feature prominently. It also coincided with Stryker's involvement with Howard W. Odum's proposal for a 'Sub-regional Laboratory for Social Research and Planning' in which thirteen piedmont counties of North Carolina and Virginia would be studied in depth. Between 1939 and 1941 three of Stryker's photographers worked at various times on the project. One of them, Jack Delano, who joined the Section in 1940, construed the Historical Section's status in terms of Stryker's ambitions for it. He did not regard it as a public relations organization for the FSA, but as an autonomous operation whose function was to develop a visual record of the times that would convey a 'historical sense' of the period.[31]

However, Stryker lacked the political security to divest his responsibilities to the Regions voluntarily. Rather than achieve independence from them, he sought to redefine their relationship on his own terms. After the announcement of the new policy in 1938 he was able to direct photographers to do regional project work by dint of his favour. In December 1938 he asserted his new authority towards the Regions as he arranged Marion Post Wolcott's itinerary for a southern tour. While he was prepared to allow Region IV to use her services for

project work, he insisted she should not get 'too deeply lost in Resettlement families'. Stryker could hardly contain his pride or restrain his
vocabulary when he advised the Director, George Mitchell, that he
wanted Post Wolcott to do 'extra-curricular' work of the sort that
made possible books such as *Land of the Free* and *Forty Acres and Steel
Mules*.[32]

Ironically, the policy of 1938 that granted the Regions greater licence
to conduct their own photographic programmes placed too great a
strain on the time and resources of some of them. By the end of 1940
some Regions had become 'overwhelmed' with photographic work and
others had 'abused' their autonomy by spending recklessly on film.
These developments presented an opportunity for Stryker to increase
his staff. He proposed adding an experienced photographer to his team
whose work would be exclusively concentrated in the Regions under
the Historical Section's control.[33] Stryker continued to use the Regions
to his bureaucratic advantage. The proposal to streamline his services
to them would have increased the Section's staff quota and allowed
his current photographers to concentrate on the work that Stryker
regarded as more prestigious.

Stryker could not sever the umbilical chord with the Regions because
it was not in his interest as an administrator to do so. To a degree
he achieved his objectives for greater autonomy by the end of 1940
when the Section could claim to be generating as much work directly
for the media as it was for the Regions and the Information Division.
During the year it had distributed almost 17,000 prints to editors and
publishers, slightly more than it provided the agency. However, in
1941, when he defined the role of chief of the Historical Section for
the Department of Agriculture, he highlighted and elaborated the
services provided to the Regions.[34] Despite the status his unit had
acquired, through his own bureaucratic efforts as much as the quality
of his photographers' work, Stryker continued to justify the role of
the Historical Section in terms of the operational effectiveness of the
Roosevelt state and its contribution to the advancement of the material
well-being of Americans.

Such institutional concerns were central to Stryker's experience of
administration in two of the New Deal's agricultural rehabilitation
agencies. Whether his bureaucratic manoeuvres were means to an end
of establishing and legitimizing documentary photography as an official
form of record or whether they were ends in themselves and that, in
his own small sphere, Stryker was engaged in empire maintenance and
aggrandizement, his administrative experience sheds as much light on
the nature and character of the New Deal order as it does on the
photographic project itself. The photographs of the RA/FSA have
come to symbolise the very spirit of the New Deal and the idealism

and liberal purpose of its social and economic programmes. The institutional context out of which they emerged may also be said to typify other characteristics of the New Deal: the scope it provided for creative administration, the conflicts between core and periphery in the development of its programmes, the vested interests established within its agencies, and the necessary compromises between idealism and practical reality which New Deal administrators were obliged to make. The vast collection of RA/FSA images deposited in the Library of Congress in 1944 is widely regarded as a monument to Stryker's documentary method and vision. It does not diminish Stryker to suggest that it is also testimony to both his bureaucractic ambition and his political finesse within the emerging institutional order of the New Deal in pursuit of personal objectives beyond the New Deal.

Notes

1. Charles C. Alexander, *Here the Country Lies: Nationalism and the Arts in Twentieth Century America* (Bloomington, 1980), 5, 6; David P. Peeler, *Hope Among Us Yet: Social Criticism and Social Solace in Depression America* (Athens, Georgia, 1987); Charles R. Hearn, *The American Dream and the Great Depression* (Westport, Connecticut and London, 1977); Alfred H. Jones, 'The Search for a Usable American Past in the New Deal Era', *American Quarterly*, 23 (December 1971), 710–24.

2. Important studies of the New Deal arts projects include Richard D. McKinzie, *The New Deal for Artists* (Princeton, 1973); John O'Connor, *'Free, Adult, Uncensored': The Living History of the Federal Theatre Project* (London, 1980); Monty Noam Penkower, *The Federal Writers' Project: A Study in Government Patronage of the Arts* (Urbana, 1977). For the New Deal's use of film, see James C. Curtis, *Mind's Eye, Mind's Truth: FSA Photography Reconsidered* (Philadelphia, 1989); Nicholas Natanson, *The Black Image in the New Deal: The Politics of FSA Photography*, (Knoxville, 1992); Robert L. Snyder, *Pare Lorentz and the Documentary Film* (Norman, OK, 1968); William L. Alexander, *Film on the Left: American Documentary Film from 1931 to 1942* (Princeton, 1981).

3. See, in particular, Jane De Hart Mathews, 'Arts and the People: The New Deal Quest for a Cultural Democracy', *Journal of American History*, 62 (September 1975), 316–39; Warren Susman, *Culture as History: The Transformation of American Society in the Twentieth Century* (New York, 1984), 9–10; Stuart Kidd, 'Redefining the New Deal: Some Thoughts on the Political and Cultural Perspectives of Revisionism', *Journal of American Studies*, 22 (December 1988), 389–415.

4. See, for example, Jerre Mangione, *The Dream and the Deal. The Federal Writers Project, 1935–1943* (New York, 1972); Belisario R. Contreras, *Tradition and Innovation in New Deal Art* (Cranbury, NJ; London; and Mississauga, Ontario, 1983); Malcolm Goldstein, *The Political Stage.*

American Drama and Theater of the Great Depression (New York, 1974), 241–92.

5. The only substantial study of the New Deal arts projects which emphasizes the bureaucratic dimension is W. F. McDonald, *Federal Relief Administration and the Arts* (Columbus, 1969).

6. The range of interpretations is represented in F. Jack Hurley, *Portrait of a Decade: Roy Stryker and the Development of Documentary Photography in the Thirties* (Baton Rouge, 1972); William Stott, *Documentary Expression and Thirties America* (New York, 1973); Alan Trachtenberg, *Reading American Photographs: Images as History, Mathew Brady to Walker Evans* (New York, 1989), 231–85; Maren Stange, *Symbols of Ideal Life: Social Documentary Photography in America, 1890–1950* (New York, 1989), 89–131.

7. Roy Stryker draft autobiography, *c.* 1940, microfilm NDA 8, Roy E. Stryker Papers, Archives of American Art, Washington DC.

8. Roy E. Stryker, 'Documentary Photography', in *The Complete Photographer*, 4 (no. 21, 10 April 1942), 1364–74, and 'The FSA Collection of Photographs' in Roy Emerson Stryker and Nancy Wood, *In This Proud Land: America, 1935–1943 as Seen in the FSA Photographs* (London, 1974), 8; Memorandum for Donald P. Stephens from Stryker, 4 November 1939, microfilm FSA/WDC 1, 90, Stryker Papers, AAA.

9. John F. Carter to Rexford G. Tugwell, 1 December 1935, Records of the Farmers Home Administration, RG 96, Series 2, Box 84 (Cincinnati Office, 1935–42), National Archives.

10. Max J. Wasserman to C. B. Baldwin, Minutes of the meeting held 5 October 1935, regarding Budget Estimates, 7 October 1935, RG 96, Series 1, Box 3 (Administrator's Correspondence), NA.

11. Stryker to Dean S. Jennings, 2, 3, 5 October, 6 December 1935; Stryker to George Gercke, 4 October 1935; Stryker to William L. Lowry, 26 March and n.d. 1936; Stryker to Ralph G. Bray, 10 October 1935; Stryker to Flora G. Orr, 29 October 1935; Stryker to Garland F. Smith, 26 October 1935; Stryker to O. E. Jones, 28 October, 4 November 1935; 31 March 1936; Stryker to John Caufield, 1 April 1936, microfilm Reel 1, FSA-OWI Textual Records, Library of Congress.

12. 'Paper prepared by Mark Adams', n.d., microfilm NDA 4, Stryker Papers, AAA.

13. A selection of employment records and budget estimates for the Historical Section during the years 1935 to 1941 is to be found in microfilm FSA/WDC 1, Stryker Papers, AAA.

14. Interview of Roy Emerson Stryker conducted by Richard K. Doud, 13 and 14 June 1964, microfilm; interview with Jack and Irene Delano conducted by Richard K. Doud, 12 June 1965, microfilm, Oral History Collections, AAA.

15. Interview of Roy Emerson Stryker conducted by Richard K. Doud, 17 October 1963, microfilm, Oral History Collections, AAA; Administrator to Comptroller General, 23 July 1935, Box 32; Minutes, Resettlement Administration Staff Conference, 26 July 1935, Box 4; memo from A. A. Mercey, 'Re: Regional Conference', 25 July 1935, RG 96 Series 1, Box 28, NA; US Resettlement Administation, *First Annual Report* (Washington,

DC, 1936), 97; Monthly Reports, 1937–8, microfilm Reel 4, FSA-OWI Textual Records, LC.

16. George C. Stoney to Stuart Kidd, 27 October 1992, letter in author's possession.

17. T. Roy Reid, 'An Arkansan Offers Remedy for Tenant Evils', *The Press-Scimitar*, Memphis, Tennessee, 3 July 1936; H. L. Mitchell to Rexford G. Tugwell, 29 March 1936, RG 96, Series 1, Box 12, NA.

18. Constance M. Daniel to George S. Mitchell, 'Memorandum re: Personnel Developments in Regions V and VI', 2 January 1942; Giles A. Hubert to C. B. Baldwin, 30 July 1941, RG 96 Series 2, Box 106, NA; Shahn quoted in Hank O'Neal (ed.), *A Vision Shared: A Classic Portrait of America and Its People, 1935–1943* (New York, 1976), 32.

19. Minutes, Resettlement Administration Conference, 9 October 1935; M. E. Gilfond to Grace E. Falke, 31 January 1936; minutes, meeting of Administrator, Assistant Administrators and Regional Directors, 1 February 1936, RG 96 Series 1, Box 4, NA.

20. O. E. Jones to Stryker, 25 October 1935; 2 April 1936, microfilm Reel 1, FSA-OWI Textual Records, LC.

21. Falke to Carter, 'Mr Tugwell's statment at the staff conference on July 26, 1935', 2 August 1935, RG 96, Series 1, Box 3, NA.

22. Annual Report of Region VI, 1935–6, Box 38; Division of Information, 'Regional Press Analysis', 23 September 1935, Box 28; C. B. Baldwin to all Regional Directors, 16 July 1937, RG 96, Series 1, Box 3, NA.

23. Post to Clara Dean Wakeham, 23 December 1938; Post to Stryker, 5 July 1939, 19 June 1940, microfilm NDA 30, Stryker Papers, AAA.

24. Lange to Stryker, 18 February, 12 March 1937; Stryker to Lange, 17 March 1937, microfilm NDA 30, Stryker Papers, AAA.

25. Stryker to M. C. Blackman, 31 December 1935; Falke to T. Roy Reid, Attention, O. E. Jones, 21 July 1936; Stryker to Jones, 18 May 1938, microfilm Reel 1, FSA-OWI Textual Records, LC; Stuart Kidd, 'Eudora Welty's Unsuccessful Application to Become a Resettlement Administration Photographer', *Eudora Welty Newsletter*, 16 (no. 2, Summer 1992), 6–8.

26. Stryker to William L. Lowry, n.d.; Stryker to Frederick R. Soule, 26 March 1936, microfilm Reel 1, FSA-OWI Textual Records, LC.

27. Gilfond to Mitchell, 11 June 1937, microfilm Reel 1, FSA-OWI Textual Records, LC.

28. Minutes, RA Staff Conference, 9 October 1935; minutes, RA: meeting of Administrator, Assistant Administrators, and Regional Directors, 1 February 1936, RG 96, Series 1, Box 4, NA.

29. 'Special Memo on Photography. To: All Regional Information Advisers. From: John Fischer', 4 May 1938, microfilm Reel 1, FSA-OWI Textual Records, LC.

30. Memorandum to John Fischer from Roy Stryker; Subject: Additional Staff, 7 June 1938, microfilm FSA/WDC 1, Stryker Papers, AAA.

31. *Washington Post*, 27 December 1938; Stryker to Harry Carman, 2 March 1939, microfilm NDA 8, Stryker Papers, AAA; Delano/Doud interview, 12 June 1965, microfilm, Oral History Collections, AAA.

32. Stryker to Mitchell, 3 December 1938, microfilm Reel 1, FSA-OWI Textual Records, LC.

33. Jack H. Bryan to George Stoney, 13 March 1941, Bryan to William H. Dent, 18 September 1940, Dent to Bryan, 7 October 1940, Box 142; 'Memorandum for Mr Roy Stryker' from Fischer, 12 December 1940; 'Memorandum to Mr R. G. Cole, Procedure Division' from Fischer, 14 December 1940, RG 96, Series 2, Box 146, NA; 'General Bulletin', 22 May 1941, microfilm, NDA 25, Stryker Papers, AAA.

34. Unsigned memorandum, 10 December 1940, 'Monthly Reports, 1940', microfilm Reel 4, FSA-OWI Textual Records, LC; report submitted by Stryker to the Personnel Division, 1941, microfilm NDA 8, Stryker Papers, AAA.

9

Whatever Happened to Roosevelt's New Generation of Southerners?

Anthony J. Badger

In 1934 Carl Elliott borrowed $25 from a grocer in Vina and travelled to Tuscaloosa to study at the University of Alabama. Thrown out by the curmudgeonly President, George Denny, Elliott surreptitiously managed to register, slept under a truck the first night, and then managed to squat in the university boiler house. Eventually he became Denny's house boy. Two years later, Elliott was president of the student body. Senator Hugo Black, on the look-out for progressive political talent, arranged for him to meet the President in Washington. Elliott never forgot that private meeting with 'the man who was, and also remains, a political god for me – Franklin D. Roosevelt.' Returning home, Elliott started a law practice in Jasper. Faced with acute distress amongst the farmers and miners, he invoked an ancient Alabama statute and halted a train, commandeered its coal and potatoes and distributed them to the needy. In 1948 Elliott was elected to Congress. For sixteen years he was part of the most liberal congressional delegation in the South, joining his House colleagues Robert Jones, Kenneth Roberts and Albert Rains, and Alabama's senators, Lister Hill and John Sparkman. During that time, back home, Big Jim Folsom served two terms in the Governor's mansion as a champion of the common man and foe of the Big Mules of Birmingham and planters of the black belt.

Increasingly targeted by segregationist forces, Elliott was finally squeezed out of Congress in the at-large congressional election of 1964 which followed re-districting. Hoping to check Alabama's slide into dictatorship and racial isolation, Elliott challenged the Wallace forces again in the 1966 gubernatorial election. Elliott's final defeat left him devastated financially. Ostracized in Jasper, Elliott lost his home and his health and eked out a miserable existence in the very years that Alabama finally made the adjustments to racial change and economic progress that Elliott had devoted his career to securing.[1]

Carl Elliott and his colleagues in the Alabama delegation were precisely the sort of southerners that Roosevelt had in mind when he counselled patience to Norman Thomas in 1936. FDR attempted to defuse the socialist leader's concern about the plight of southern share-croppers by assuring him that he knew the South and there was arising a 'new generation of leaders' in the region.[2]

The history of conservatism in the post-war South and the region's often violent resistance to racial change makes it tempting to dismiss Roosevelt's optimism as characteristic wishful thinking. The main thrust of New Deal historiography has been to stress the role of southern conservatism from the late 1930s onwards. Southerners were the key figures in the conservative bi-partisan coalition that checked New Deal reform aspirations after 1936. Roosevelt was unable to 'purge' those conservatives in the primary elections of 1938. During the war, southern congressmen took the lead in dismantling emergency New Deal agencies and blocking plans for the extension of the welfare state. After the war, hostility to the Truman administration's civil rights stance led to the Dixecrat states' rights' revolt of 1948. In examining local southern politics in the late 1930s, I myself have argued that there was a 'lack of the electoral raw material in the South to sustain an ideologically clearly defined liberal party'.[3]

Southern politicians had enthusiastically supported the New Deal throughout 1936 because, whatever their ideological doubts about federal power and federal spending, they were acutely aware that their constituents were desperate for the jobs, credit and rising farm income that New Deal relief and recovery programmes brought them. But, whereas constituency pressure before 1936 demanded support for the New Deal, after 1936 that pressure counselled caution. To the rural elites who had been so grateful for assistance in the economic emergency of the Depression, the non-emergency agenda of the New Deal seemed geared to northern and urban needs. The rural, small town elites who dominated so much of southern politics saw traditional patterns of paternalism, deference and dependence threatened: welfare programmes and union organization seemed to undermine employer control in the workplace; welfare and rural poverty programmes challenged the customary dominance of landlords and merchants over tenants and sharecroppers.[4]

The failure of the purge in 1938 seemed to confirm that the New Deal had not liberalized the South. The race issue had been used by conservative opponents from the start of the New Deal to whip up popular support for their opposition to Roosevelt's economic policies. As late as 1936, for example, when Eugene Talmadge race-baited Richard Russell, the tactic did not seem to work. Yet in 1938 it did. In 1936 men like Russell could effectively argue that the race issue was settled: in 1938 southerners, their sectional sensibilities aroused by the non-emergency New Deal, were fearful of federal intervention by a government responsive to newly Democratic black voters in the northern cities. What the failure of the purge suggested was that the New Deal had alarmed political elites by threatening traditional patterns of dependency in the region, but could not make good the threat because it had left the structure of southern politics untouched: it had failed to extend the electorate. Most potential lower-income supporters of the New Deal were effectively disfranchised. The restricted electorate, which eliminated the likelihood of sustained constituency pressure for social welfare or labour legislation, seemed to set very precise limits to the potential liberalization of the Democratic Party. Roger Biles in *The South and the New Deal* concluded: 'The small band of New Deal liberals in the South constituted a tiny minority ... Overshadowed by their more powerful conservative colleagues, these highly vulnerable New Dealers generally survived on the political scene for only a short time.' A politician who did not compromise like the unapologetic radical Maury Maverick in San Antonio would be red-baited to defeat. Even a cautious moderate who did compromise and try prudently to avoid the race issue like Luther Patrick in Birmingham would also be eventually beaten. As the saying went 'as thin as the liberalism of a Texas congressman'. The war, of course, gave southern conservatives in Congress the excuse to eliminate New Deal reform programmes on the grounds that they were hampering the war effort. Alan Brinkley in his brilliant study of New Deal liberalism in the late 1930s and during the war fails to find or mention any southern liberals.[5]

Two excellent recent books have painted a very different picture. They have drawn attention to the alternative radical strategy of modernizing the South from the bottom up: extending the benefits of the New Deal to lower-income southerners and protecting their civil rights at the same time. These southern New Dealers aimed to solve the nation's number one economic problem through federal underpinning of living standards and by sustaining the basic civil liberties of both African-Americans and union organizers.

Patricia Sullivan, in *Days of Hope: Race and Democracy in the New Deal Era* (1996), has systematically delineated a coalition in the South of New Deal liberals, labour organizers, Communist Party workers and black activists who espoused on, on the one hand, a national New Deal policy for creating mass-purchasing power in the region, and, on the other, a local strategy of organizing at the community level. Identifying this radical moment, she writes:

For a time, southerners had reached across racial boundaries to advance political and economic democracy in the region, with the support of the federal government and a strong national labor movement ... The central lesson was the power of segregation to undermine all efforts to establish a healthy democracy in the region.

If progressives in the South were to be a force for change, they required the moral, political, and financial support of democratically minded people throughout the region ... They [the activists] created legal precedents, experimented with new political forms, and organized round issues of social and economic justice. Such eclectic and improvisational efforts collectively expanded the possibilities of democracy in a racially fractured civic landscape.

Sullivan's work is particularly valuable in four respects. First, she shows how Charles Houston and Thurgood Marshall took the National Association for the Advancement of Colored People 'home' to the South in the 1930s, criss-crossing the region seeking plaintiffs to sustain a litigative strategy to challenge, or at least equalise segregated facilities. They also encouraged the formation of local NAACP branches and exhorted community leaders to register to vote. Second, Sullivan demonstrates that, despite the inaction of the New Deal in many areas of civil rights, southern African-American leaders saw the potential for federal government action in the South: for if the federal government could solve the region's economic problems in the way it did in the 1930s, then the government might intervene to solve the region's racial problems. Third, Sullivan became the first historian to show how African-Americans launched voter registration drives in the 1940s through campaigns that were not academic exercises to secure civil rights for the small number of middle-class blacks, but real responses to community grievances about police brutality or egregious discrimination.[6]

Finally, Sullivan identifies an opportunity for this New Deal alliance after *Smith* v. *Allwright* in 1944. Black-voter registration drives were underwritten by the Congress of Industrial Organizations' Political Action Committee and became part of an effort to secure the election of liberal southern candidates in the 1946 elections. Sullivan places this southern liberal upsurge in the context of a national struggle, epitomized by Henry Wallace, to secure the extension of the New Deal in the face of southern Democratic obstructionism. Bob Korstad and Nelson Lichtenstein identify a lost opportunity in the alliance of left-led unions and black workers in some southern cities. Adam Fairclough, directly complementing Sullivan's work on voter registration, has shown that in Louisiana revitalized NAACP activity was not merely a litigative middle-class strategy, but was crucially linked to voter registration, community organization against police brutality, and local labour radicalism. He concludes that the 1940s in Louisiana was the first act in the two-act play that constitutes the modern civil rights movement. Historians, he argues, have slighted 'the scope of popular involvement during the 1940s and early 1950s ... in much of Louisiana and much of the South, voter registration was tantamount to direct action'.[7]

John Egerton in *Speak Now Against the Day: The Generation Before the Civil Rights Movement in the South* (1994) takes as his starting point the fact that the 1930s was a remarkable decade of self-criticism in the South. 'It seems fair to say', he writes, 'that self-examination of the region was more advanced and more extensive than ever before.' Coupled with the changes unleashed by the New Deal and the war, this critical spirit created an opportunity for change that Egerton believes was spurned:

> One of the things I have come to see in retrospect is how favorable the conditions were for substantive social change in the four or five years right after World War II. It appears to have been the last and best time – perhaps the only time – when the South might have moved boldly and decisively to heal itself, to fix its own social wagon voluntarily. But it didn't act, and the moment passed, and all that has happened in the tumultuous days since ... has followed from that inability to seize the time and do the right thing, not simply because it was right, but because it was also in our own best interest.

Though the Birmingham conference of 1938 which founded the Southern Conference for Human Welfare was Egerton's centrepiece, his account largely features a mix of intellectuals, academics, writers, newspapermen, and black and white radicals. Politicians, for whom Egerton had little respect, find little room in his 627 pages, as 'they were conspicuously absent from the ranks of the critics and the reformers'. Trying to think of senators or congressmen or governors who were advocates of or spokesmen for reform, Egerton found that 'Hugo Black is just about the only one who springs to mind ... in the Deep South ... progressive or moderate or even mildly conservative congressmen were as scarce as hen's teeth'. In the Senate, he saw a 'depressingly familiar picture of negative leadership' matched by the House of Representatives which was equally 'as devoid of southern statesmen, a few honest plodders notwithstanding'.[8]

There was, however, a new generation of New Deal southern politicians as well. Just as in the North issue-oriented politicians came to replace patronage-oriented politicians in the Democratic party, so in the South, younger politicians ideologically committed to New Deal economic goals came to replace patronage-hungry congressmen who had only supported FDR in the economic emergency of the 1930s. This new generation of white, usually younger, politicians in the South were actually elected to office drawing on the support of an alliance of lower-income whites, organized labour, veterans, women and the small, but slowly increasing African-American electorate. They espoused economically liberal and racially moderate policies. They constituted a significant part of the South's representation in Congress. They contributed to what Ira Katznelson, Kim Geiger and Daniel Kryder (following in the footsteps of V. O. Key Jr.) have recently identified on the basis of roll call analyses: a party-based liberal coalition of non-southern and southern Democrats on welfare state, fiscal, regulatory and planning issues.[9]

In Alabama Lister Hill moved from the House to the Senate in 1937, Sparkman followed him in 1946. Albert Rains was elected in 1944, Robert Jones in 1946 and Carl Elliott in 1948. In Tennessee, Albert Gore Sr. was elected to the House from Tennessee in 1936, Estes Kefauver in 1940, J. Percy Priest in 1942. Kefauver and Gore would, in 1948 and 1952 respectively, go the Senate. In Arkansas Clyde Ellis was elected from the Fourth District in 1938. J. William Fulbright took over from him four years later and James Trimble would succeed Fulbright when he was elected to the Senate in 1944. Former New Deal official Brooks Hays was elected from Little Rock in 1942. In Texas, Albert Thomas was elected in 1936, Lyndon Johnson in 1937 and Lindley Beckworth in 1938. North Carolina produced Charles Deane in 1946 and even Mississippi elected Frank Smith from the heart of the Delta in 1950. Katznelson concluded they 'supported much of the party's social democratic agenda with a level of enthusiasm appropriate to a poor region with a heritage of opposition to big business and a history of support for regulation and redistribution'. Meanwhile in the state houses, Folsom in 1946 was followed by Sid McMath from Arkansas, Kerr Scott from North Carolina and Earl Long from Louisiana in 1948 – all of them elected excoriating the political establishments and entrenched economic interests in their respective states.[10]

The success of these issue-oriented politicians was founded on a number of factors whose importance has only recently, and sometimes partially, been acknowledged. These include infrastructure politics; a common-man, popular appeal; the relative prosperity of southern states and their new-found ability to match New Deal spending; the wartime success of southern labour; and the impact of the war on white southerners – both those who stayed at home and those who served in the armed forces.

New Deal programmes built up the region's infrastructure. Relief and public works programmes rescued the South's education system. The Works Progress Administration and Public Works Administration built roads and airports, developed ports and funded the capital projects in southern cities that in the North a generation earlier had been funded by private enterprise. Tennessee Valley Authority-inspired cheap power made possible industrial development. Federal spending in World War II dramatically quickened the pace of change: the billions of dollars on defence contracts and training facilities kick-started the region into self-sustaining economic growth for the first time. New jobs absorbed the rural surplus population; high prices, new urban markets and electrification enabled southern farmers to mechanize and diversify.[11]

John Sparkman described himself as a 'TVA liberal'. What southern New Dealers learnt from infrastructure politics was that the federal government through an agency like the TVA could regenerate an entire region and they drew from the New Deal experience the lesson that the South could not prosper on its own. Federal government assistance was to be the answer to the region's problems of education, hospital construction, medical research, vaccination provision, electrification, and the provision of rural library services and telephones.[12]

Jordan Schwarz has shown how some southern politicians saw particular personal, political, and regional opportunities arising from New Deal policies, policies that would not only bring much-needed assistance to deprived areas but would foster the dynamic economic growth that would create the Sunbelt. TVA provided the cheap power to facilitate industrial development, while great water resource projects – usually neglected by historians – not only provided flood control but made available essential water for industrial locations. The Reconstruction Finance Corporation under the Houston banker, Jesse Jones, broke the eastern monopoly on credit and made capital available for thrusting regional entrepreneurs. Public works projects provided lucrative contracts for politically-connected businessmen who in turn funded helpful congressmen. Lyndon Johnson was one of those congressmen who saw the possibilities. As his backer, George Brown, head of a construction and engineering firm, recalled, 'Lyndon Johnson would take me to these meetings of the Southern congressmen and that's the way they'd be talking. That the South would get these dams and these other projects and it would come out of the other fellow's pockets'.[13]

This emphasis, and the efforts of liberal governors to attract industry and to invest in the infrastructure of roads and schools, has led them sometimes to be described as 'business progressives' or 'Whigs.' But their strategy was not simply a top-down conservative economic approach designed to attract industry at any cost. They brought welfare benefits to their constituents that had long been denied them by conservative elites. They certainly sought industry but they did so defending the rights of organized labour and fighting for substantial increases in state minimum wages. They championed cheap power, particularly through rural electrification cooperatives and the state development of water resources, another neglected area of study. These fights put them on a bitter collision course with the major utility companies like Arkansas Power and Light and the Duke Power

Company. Their policies did have a genuinely reformist, social welfare, redistributionist element.[14]

This new generation of southern candidates espoused a common-man, popular appeal. They took their electoral case directly to the people, circumventing the local county-seat elites who usually brokered their localities' votes. Lyndon Johnson's campaign for Congress in 1937, in which he reached out to voters in the tiniest and most isolated communities and completely overturned 'the leisurely pace normal in Texas elections', is well known. Robert Caro has also shown how well-financed that campaign was. Less well known, is the successful campaign for Congress the following year by Texan Lindley Beckworth. Beckworth modelled his campaign on LBJ's in terms of reaching every voter through ten speeches a day, but he did so without LBJ's money. He had $1,100 from a note signed by twenty-five of his townsfolk. His headquarters was a room in his father's house with no telephone. He had no money for newspaper advertisements and could only afford hand-painted signs. He used two cars with crude public address systems: one borrowed, and one bought on instalment. A more unlikely 'common man' candidate was the Rhodes scholar, Anglophile and former university president, J. William Fulbright. In 1942 he campaigned for the seat vacated by the rural electrification champion, Clyde Ellis, by wearing a check shirt and reaching every nook and cranny of his hilly, 175-mile-long and 50-mile-wide district. No one ran a more basic campaign than Jim Folsom for governor in Alabama in 1946. His headquarters was a payphone in a barber's shop and he made speeches at every crossroads in the state, attracting an audience with his country band, the Strawberry Pickers, and denouncing the established interests in Alabama – the Black Belt planters and the Big Mules of Birmingham.[15]

The South's relative prosperity in World War II gave southern governors the opportunity to participate in New Deal welfare programmes that required states to match federal money. In the 1930s revenue-starved southern states often could not afford to take part, but in the 1940s they could. Even Mississippi, the poorest state in the nation, could afford to join the Aid to Families with Dependent Children programmes. The 1940s witnessed the greatest advances in state welfare provision for children in Mississippi's history.[16]

The war enabled organized labour to play a greater part in the region's politics, a role obscured by the region's anti-union reputation. Wartime prosperity, the prospects of defence contracts and federal government protection under the War Labor Board enabled unions to make dramatic gains, even in bastions of the open-shop like textiles. Textile unions broke into some of the industry's most important chains and won 436 contracts over a three-year period covering 100,000 workers. Southern textile workers received eight separate pay increases between 1941 and 1946, increasing their wartime pay in percentage terms more than any other group of mass production workers. Said one union official: 'It has been in the last four years a relatively simple matter to organize plants and to get them under contract ... there can't be much wrong with a union like that.' Unions used their political power to defeat some traditional enemies. Rubber workers helped Albert Rains defeat Joe Starnes in Gadsen in 1944. Textile workers in Rome, Georgia, helped Henderson Lanham defeat Malcolm Tarver in 1946.[17]

World War II's role in stimulating African-American expectations has been amply documented. Only recently has attention been given to the war's impact on white southerners. Some white southerners, even in Mississippi, saw the connection between the nation's democratic war aims and the need for a different domestic and international order. Keith Frazier Somerville wrote a fortnightly column in the *Bolivar Commercial* aimed at the Delta county's boys serving in the armed forces. Much of it was devoted to news about their home town of Cleveland, such as births, deaths, and marriages, and news of their fellow servicemen. In the columns, however, Somerville was at pains to stress the wartime contribution of all the county's ethnic and racial groups, in particular the black participation in the war effort. In Mound Bayou, the all-black community:

> I found America dreaming again. Dreaming of the day her sons will come marching home, dreaming of better housing and hospitalization ... dreaming too of absolute fairness. And here in Bolivar County, there are many Southern white men and women, descendants of men and women who for eighty years have had their problems close to their hearts, who are dreaming with them that when our boys of all races, creeds, and color come home again to peaceful years, we may all work together to make our dreams come true.[18]

A white Alabaman, who had moved from his farm to work in the Mobile shipyards, wrote in a laboriously scrawled pencil letter to his conservative home congressman, that African-Americans should have the vote:

> After all we are taking a stand in world affairs as a nation against oppression and it looks to me as though it is high time we as southerners had better take the lead and solve that much-kicked Republican football ... it seems that the old tradition of a damn nigger has gone and must be remedied by an enlightened and liberal stand by our own party ... I am as you know not what is called a

'nigger lover'. It is just something that has come out and I think we should do it before it explodes under us.[19]

Service overseas could make the ideological imperatives of the war seem even more powerful to white southerners. David Reynolds in *Rich Relations* has documented with great clarity the way in which service in Britain broke down local and traditional attitudes among GIs. White southerners constituted one third of the nation's servicemen. Whereas the British and the Canadians determined that their soldiers should not receive privileged treatment in comparison with local civilian populations, the Americans insisted that living conditions should be good enough for the GIs to allay any possible discontent with war service. As a result, many southerners experienced a standard of living in the military that comfortably exceeded the standards they were used to in the Depression. But service abroad posed more fundamental questions. Claude Ramsey, a future Mississippi labour organizer, remembered being stationed outside Rennes where his unit of white southerners adopted a French Moroccan who had got detached from his unit:

[He] became the favorite of everybody. Everybody really liked him. I got to thinking about it. I said, 'This is a hell of a thing. We've got a black man from Morocco, French Morocco, who is the real favorite of a bunch of white guys from the South. I'm just wondering what would happen if this was going on in Mississippi.

Rowan Thomas, from Boyle, a small town near Cleveland in the Delta, wrote a nationally reviewed book describing his service round the world with his air squadron. Poverty in India prompted him to assert:

Here is another war we have got to win after this war is over: the war against misery and poverty. This world cannot long endure dazzling jewels on the perfumed body of one lady, and only sparkling tears in the eyes of the hungry millions. [The servicemen] felt we were an integral part of a world revolution ... Soldiers everywhere agreed that we can no longer exist behind our own walls; that the peoples of the earth are our neighbors, and we must live and work with them in peace and security. [They pronounced] 'If we can't help every man, woman, and child to have the simple necessities of life, then we're wasting our time and our lives.'[20]

It is not surprising, therefore, that John Stennis, before running against rabid racist John Rankin to succeed Bilbo in the Senate from

Mississippi in 1947, should make passionate speeches in favour of the United Nations. He argued that the US should be prepared to give up some of its national sovereignty to the international organization. In 1948 Frank Smith, his publicity director, joined thirty to forty veterans in the Mississippi legislature and recollected that, 'I knew either directly or indirectly that most of them were idealists who hoped to have a part in making a better day'. Smith went to Congress in 1950.[21]

Like Smith, Jim Wright in Texas identified the Depression and World War II as the formative influences on his political development. Like many returning veterans, he was anxious to challenge the old guard on his return from service overseas. At the University of Texas Law School, he reorganized the Young Democrats who in December 1945 called for anti-lynching legislation, an end to the poll tax, and the admission of black students to the Law School. In 1946 he went to the state legislature in a group of veterans who were determined to change the shape of Texas politics. Stuart Long recalled that legislature:

> As a result, the kids came home with the feeling, 'By Golly, we've saved democracy. Now let's make it work at home.' I saw this pop out in so many places. Candidates for the legislature in 1946, the ones elected in '46. I think we had 85 or 90 house seats, something like that, who were veterans, and a large number of Senators who were. There was a great injection of youth in Texas, youthful idealism, which is another name for liberalism.[22]

Across the South there were GI revolts in which returning soldiers aimed to overthrow traditional local power structures. Sid McMath came to prominence in one such revolt in Garland County, Arkansas, in 1946. McMath, who was only thirty-four, had won a silver star serving with the marines in the Pacific. Backed by other young veterans he ran for prosecuting attorney against the local boss of the gambling resort of Hot Springs, Leo P. McLaughlin. McMath labelled the boss 'his majesty Der Fuehrer of Hot Springs' and placed words from *Mein Kampf* alongside McLaughlin's in campaign advertisements. 'The voice' McMath alleged 'was the voice of Leo, but the words are the words of Hitler.' McMath in that election organized armed platoons at service stations ready to go anywhere they thought there was likely to be trouble. They cut the telephone wires to the neighbouring county so that their opponents there could not find out by how many votes the opposition was behind and therefore how many ballots would have to be stuffed in that county to create a majority.[23]

In Florida, Dante Fascell's political world was also shaped by the New Deal and World War II. As a northern migrant when he was a small boy he had fought Klan-type gangs in his Coconut Grove school. After the war he returned home determined to take a full part in political life. In Miami's version of a GI revolt – Fascell's first political campaign and 'the damnedest political fight I have ever seen' – he crusaded for the recall of the corrupt and conservative Miami City Commission. By 1947 he was president of the Miami Junior Chamber of Commerce, the Italian-American Club and the Young Democrats. He then worked to get his commanding officer elected to the state legislature. Fascell, like Jim Wright, was elected to Congress in 1954. They consciously saw themselves as a new 'revolutionary' intake in the House.[24]

This new generation of southerners was not to be the force of the future in the South. In the 1950s and 1960s the South seemed increasingly in the grip of conservative, segregationist forces and, when racial change came, it was conservative businessmen and their allies who usually brokered the South's adaptation to new realities. What went wrong for Roosevelt's acolytes? It was clear that many of the factors that paved the way for liberal success were ambiguous in their impact.

A common-man appeal capitalizing on lower-income white resentment of established economic and political forces was not the monopoly of liberal politicians. Such an appeal could also be made by rabid segregationists like Eugene Talmadge and Theodore 'The Man' Bilbo, both elected in 1946 pandering to lower-income white suspicion of outside interests and distant government and their competitive hatred of blacks. Similarly, infrastructure politics did not always have a re-distributionist, social-justice element. Such politics were equally compatible with 'business-progressive' Whig moves to encourage investment from industries attracted to the region's cheap labour and hostility to unions.[25]

The South's new relative affluence blunted the challenges of the union movement. As southern textile firms sold off company houses to their workers, and their employees pocketed higher wages, so textile workers were increasingly tied into credit commitments both for house repayments and the purchase of consumer goods that they had come to enjoy. They were reluctant to jeopardize these purchases by losing income through strike action. As long as non-union firms matched the wages paid by unionized plants, so workers wondered if strike action to secure a union contract was worthwhile. The optimism of union organizers proved to be false.[26]

The war increased racial tension and violence in the region as much as it opened the minds of southern whites and heightened African-American expectations. Whites reacted with alarm to examples of black assertiveness and mobility. The presence of so many northern black troops in military bases near small towns, who were unwilling to comply with the established etiquette of southern race relations, fuelled the fears of local whites and law-enforcement officials and stretched to breaking point overcrowded and inadequate recreational facilities and public services. In the shipyards, the presence of black workers aroused white fears of job competition. The result, as James Burran has shown, was an upsurge of lynchings, murders and assaults, often by local police, and retaliatory race riots. The violence continued after the war, aimed at returning black veterans who dared to step out of line.[27]

The political activity of returning white veterans was not always geared to promoting racial change. Jennifer Brooks's definitive study of GI revolts concluded that returning, politically active veterans espoused a 'definition of progress that was quintessentially a southern white one'. Strom Thurmond and Herman Talmadge returned from the war to campaign for progressive reform at the state level. As Talmadge recalled: 'When I came along it was after World War II, and I knew the people of Georgia had made up their minds that they wanted to see more progress in state government. So I advocated what my father would've thought was a progressive platform.' But Thurmond and Talmadge were equally determined to defend white supremacy and they appealed to wartime sentiment to do so. Talmadge asserted that the choice in 1946 would 'determine whether or not we will fight to preserve our southern traditions and heritage as we fought on ships at sea and as we fought on foreign soil'.[28]

It is now commonplace to cite the role of anti-communism in marginalizing Roosevelt's new generation of southerners. Adam Fairclough argued in his study of Louisiana that 'the Cold War had produced an ideological chilling effect that made criticism of the social order, so commonplace during the Roosevelt era, unfashionable, unpatriotic and politically dangerous'. There is no doubt that the use of the anti-communist issue played a major part in marginalizing and excluding white radicals who openly espoused the end of segregation: the Southern Conference, the Progressive Party, the left-led unions, and radical black allies such as the Civil Rights Congress in Louisiana. No one can doubt the profound impact of social and political ostracism on New Deal liberals like Aubrey Williams, Clifford and Virginia Durr, and Will Alexander. But as Michael Heale's new study of McCarthyism in the hinterland shows, opponents of racial change, for example in Georgia, did not need anti-communism to justify violent racial repression in the 1940s. It was later, during Massive Resistance, that southern anti-communism, really flourished and stifled dissent. Most of the new generation of issue-oriented liberal politicians were red-baited in the 1940s and with the notable exceptions of Frank Graham and Claude Pepper, they survived.[29]

Like John Egerton and Patrica Sullivan, I believe that the new generation of southern liberal politicians was undone by the race issue. But I believe that these politicians had rather a longer shelf-life and were not marginalized by the race issue until the mid-to-late 1950s. Even after the Brown school desegregation decision of 1954 and the backlash that provoked, liberals could still get elected in parts of the South. What defeated the southern liberal politicians was, in part, the sheer weight of the white commitment to segregation in the South revealed in Massive Resistance, but, also, as I have argued elsewhere at length, the liberals' own fatalism. Roosevelt's new generation was undone by its own commitment to gradualism in racial change and its faith that long-term economic change would gradually erode the institution of white supremacy. As Frank Smith commented: 'Large-scale economic progress was the only avenue likely to lead to a solution of the race problem in Mississippi.' When African-Americans demanded immediate, rather than gradual, change in the 1950s and the Supreme Court mandated desegregation, southern liberals were paralysed by their conviction that mass white sentiment in the South would not tolerate such imposed, dramatic change. The fatalistic liberals retreated into a resigned silence and left a political vacuum which conservative advocates of Massive Resistance gleefully filled.[30]

Nevertheless, there was life in the Roosevelt legacy even after the 1950s. Elliot Janeway recalled that:

> Ickes told me Roosevelt had said that he was frustrated about that boy, that if he hadn't gone to Harvard, that's the kind of uninhibited young man he'd like to be – that in the next generation the balance of power would shift south and west and this boy could well be the first Southern President.

The southern boy of whom Roosevelt was so enamoured was Lyndon Johnson. FDR's new generation of Southerners may have been marginalized by the dynamics of the race issue and often by their own fearful caution, but in the end it was a southern New Dealer who, in the Civil Rights Act of 1964 and Voting Rights Act of 1965, would impose immediate, federally-mandated racial change on the South.[31]

Notes

1. Carl Elliott Sr. and Michael D'Orso, *The Cost of Courage: The Journey of an American Congressman* (New York, 1992), 43–4, 54, 72–3.
2. See Frank Freidel, *FDR and the South* (Baton Rouge, 1965).

3. Anthony Badger, 'Local Politics and Party Re-Alignment in the late Thirties: The Failure of the New Deal', *Storia Nord Americana*, 6 (1989), 77.

4. Tony Badger, 'How Did the New Deal Change the South?' in Steve Ickringill (ed.), *Looking Inward, Looking Outward: From the 1930s through the 1940s* (Amsterdam, 1990), 174.

5. Badger, 'Local Politics' 77–86; Badger, 'How Did the New Deal Change the South', 174; Roger Biles, *The South and the New Deal* (Lexington, 1994), 149; Lionel Patenaude, *Texans, Politics and the New Deal* (New York, 1983), 75; Alan Brinkley, *The End of Reform: New Deal Liberalism in Recession and War* (New York, 1995).

6. Patricia Sullivan, *Days of Hope: Race and Democracy in the New Deal Era* (Chapel Hill, 1996), 69, 84–92, 141–9, 273, 275.

7. Sullivan, *Days of Hope*, 169–247; Patricia Sullivan, 'Southern Reformers, the New Deal, and the Movement's Foundation' in Armstead Robinson and Patricia Sullivan, *New Directions in Civil Rights Studies* (Charlottesville, 1991), 81–104; Robert Korstad and Nelson Lichtenstein, 'Opportunities Found and Lost: Labor, Radicals and the Early Civil Rights Movement', *Journal of American History*, LXXV (1988), 786–811; Adam Fairclough, *Race and Democracy: The Civil Rights Struggle in Louisiana, 1915–1972* (Athens, 1995), xii, xiv.

8. John Egerton, *Speak Now Against the Day: The Generation Before the Civil Rights Movement in the South* (New York, 1995), 10–11, 71,113,148, 220.

9. Ira Katznelson, Kim Geiger and Daniel Kryder, 'Limiting Liberalism: The Southern Vote in Congress', *Political Science Quarterly*, 108 (1993), 283–306.

10. Katznelson et al., 'Limiting Liberalism', 296; Numan V. Bartley and Hugh Davis Graham, *Southern Politics and the Second Reconstruction* (Baltimore, 1975), 24–50.

11. Bruce Schulman, *From Cotton Belt to Sunbelt: Federal Policy, Economic Development, and the Transformation of the South, 1938–1980* (New York, 1991), 63–111; Gavin Wright, *Old South, New South: Revolutions in the Southern Economy Since the Civil War* (New York, 1986), 239–74; Numan V. Bartley, *The New South 1945–1980: The Story of the South's Modernization* (Baton Rouge, 1995), 1–16.

12. Virginia Van der Veer Hamilton, *Lister Hill: Statesman from the South* (Chapel Hill, 1987), 70–86.

13. Jordan A. Schwarz, *The New Dealers: Power Politics in the Age of Roosevelt* (New York, 1993), 59–96, 194–245, 249–94; Robert A. Caro, *The Years of Lyndon Johnson: The Path to Power* (New York, 1982), 472.

14. Schulman, *From Cotton Belt to Sunbelt*, 127–34; Tony Badger, 'Fatalism, not Gradualism: The Crisis of Southern Liberalism, 1945–1965' in Brian Ward and Tony Badger (eds), *The Making of Martin Luther King and the Civil Rights Movement* (London, 1996), 77–8.

15. Caro, *The Path to Power*, 389–436; Billie Burdick Kemper, 'Lindley Beckworth: Grassroots Congressman' (MA thesis, Stephen F. Austin State University, 1980), 33–8 in Lindley Garrison Beckworth Papers, Barker Center for American History, University of Texas, Austin; Randall Ben-

nett Woods, *Fulbright: A Biography* (Cambridge, 1995) 65–9; George E. Sims, *The Little Man's Big Friend: James E. Folsom in Alabama Politics, 1946–1958* (Tuscaloosa, 1985) 21–39.

16. Roger D. Tate Jr., 'Easing the Burden: The Era of Depression and New Deal in Mississippi' (Ph.D. dissertation, University of Tennessee, 1978), 191, 198.

17. Timothy J. Minchin, *What Do We Need a Union For?: The TWUA in the South, 1945–1955* (Chapel Hill, 1997) 15–19; Michelle Brattain, 'Making Friends and Enemies: Textile Workers and Political Action in Post-World War II Georgia', *Journal of Southern History*, 63 (1997), 97–8, 104.

18. Judy Barrett Litoff and David C. Smith (eds), *Dear Boys: World War II Letters From a Woman Back Home* (Jackson, 1991), 90.

19. C. C. Hodge to George Andrews, 5 March 1945, Papers of George Andrews, Auburn University.

20. David Reynolds, *Rich Relations: The American Occupation of Britain, 1942–45* (New York, 1995), 54, 71–88, 148–54, 302–24, 439–45; Donald Cunnigen, 'Men and Women of Goodwill: Mississippi's White Liberals' (Ph.D. dissertation, Harvard University, 1988), 560; Rowan T. Thomas, *Born in Battle: Round the World Adventures of the 513th Bombardment Squadron* (Philadelphia, 1944), 78, 192–3, 318–20.

21. Frank E. Smith, *Congressman from Mississippi: An Autobiography* (New York, 1964), 64–92; Dennis Mitchell, 'Frank E. Smith: Mississippi Liberal', *Journal of Mississippi History*, xlviii (1986), 89–93.

22. Jim Wright, *Balance of Power: Presidents and Congress from the Era of McCarthy to the Age of Gingrich* (Atlanta, 1996), 18–30, 40; Interview with Jim Wright, 18 November 1996. Stuart Long Interview, Texas Oral History Collection, Woodson Research Center, Rice University, Houston.

23. Jim Lester, *A Man For Arkansas: Sid McMath and the Southern Reform Tradition* (Little Rock, 1976), 8–31, 52; Sidney S. McMath interview with John Egerton, 8 September 1990, Southern Historical Collection, Chapel Hill.

24. Interview with Dante Fascell, 27 February 1997; Claudia Townsend, *Dante Fascell: Democratic Representative from Florida* (Ralph Nader Congress Papers: Citizens Look at Congress, 1972), 1.

25. Schulman, *From Cotton Belt to Sunbelt*, 112–34, 321.

26. Minchin, *What Do We Need a Union For?*, 48–68, 199–209.

27. James A. Burran, 'Racial Violence in the South During World War II' (unpublished Ph.D. dissertation, University of Tennessee, 1977).

28. Jennifer Brooks, 'From Fighting Nazism to Fighting Bossism: Southern World War Two Veterans and the Assault on Southern Political Tradition' (paper delivered to the Southern Historical Association, New Orleans, November 1995. I am very grateful to Dr Brooks for permission to quote from this paper).

29. Fairclough, *Race and Democracy*, 141; Michael Heale, *McCarthy's Americans: Red Scare Politics in State and Nation, 1935–1965* (London, 1998), 273–6.

30. Badger, 'Fatalism, not Gradualism', 67–95; Tony Badger, 'The Constraints of Southern Liberalism' (paper delivered at the Southern Intellectual History Circle, Birmingham, 1997); Tony Badger, 'Souther-

ners who did not sign the Southern Manifesto' (paper delivered at the Organization of American Historians, San Francisco, April 1997).

31. Caro, *The Path to Power*, 449.

10

FDR, the Depression and Europe, 1932–6

Patricia Clavin

In his inaugural lecture as Professor of American Studies at Keele University in 1973, David Adams described Roosevelt's foreign policy towards Europe during the first term as President as one that was 'coherent in its objectives, consistent in its general thrust and sustained in the determination with which he sought to give it implementation'. He underscored this contention in an examination of the origins of the 'Atlantic First' strategy, which later was to become the corner-stone of Roosevelt's involvement in European affairs. Adams linked Roosevelt's commitment in disarmament negotiations to a policy of parallel action designed to align America 'with western democratic nations in the pursuit of peace through the restrain of aggression'.[1]

At the time, this view challenged many critical appraisals of Roosevelt's foreign policy by European historians. Now scholars are in broad agreement that Roosevelt did take an active interest in foreign relations from the outset of his presidency, although dispute remains over the impact of domestic constraints and the extent to which the President offered clear and effective leadership on foreign policy. Much recent debate has turned on the role of internal pressures, in particular the public clamour for domestic economic recovery and the dominant isolationist sentiment of American public opinion, in confining Roosevelt's freedom to make foreign policy.[2] But it is important not to lose sight of the external constraints on Roosevelt's foreign policy. The President had to contend with negative perceptions of Europe. Special envoy Richard Washburn-Child reflected that cooperation with Europe 'just now is futile and a waste of our power', because 'Europe certainly mistrusts American ability and our experience may be said to lead us to some mistrust of [the] European ability to receive and act upon our advice'.[3]

The one aspect of Roosevelt's relations with Europe that scholars have found difficult to reconcile with the President's internationalist credentials is the history of his foreign economic policy during the First New Deal. Roosevelt's 'bombshell message' which torpedoed the World Economic Conference in the summer of 1933 is taken as the ultimate proof of Roosevelt's negation of American responsibility to the world economy – a charge from which even Robert Dallek has struggled to exonerate Roosevelt.[4] The message was seen to mark the end of Europe's short-lived expectations of future collaboration with America raised by Roosevelt's election campaign and the interregnum. The failure of international economic cooperation in the Depression has long been recognized as a major source of tension in America's diplomatic relations with Britain and France during the 1930s. The episode has taken on a new significance as recent research has also underlined the importance of international cooperation as a means to facilitate domestic and international economic recovery.

Opening with a brief survey of new scholarship on the Depression, this paper will attempt to draw the history of Roosevelt's economic foreign policy towards Europe on a broad canvas to reflect the multi-faceted economic and diplomatic dimensions. The key to understanding the failure of international economic cooperation in this period lies not in the deficiencies of American leadership, nor in the lack of viable policies, but in the lack of political will for cooperation demonstrated by all the world's leading powers. True, in Roosevelt's first term of office, forays into foreign policy were shaped strongly by the President's determination to secure a national economic revival, but so, too, were the foreign policy initiatives of Britain, France and Germany. By exploring new research of economic historians as to why the Great Depression was so severe, and the foreign economic policies of Europe's leading economic powers on international indebtedness, trade and monetary stabilization, this paper will underline the external constraints on Roosevelt's foreign policy and how, in turn, the European response to America's overtures for international cooperation to tackle protectionism only worked to sour America's appetite for further cooperation with Europe.

When it comes to apportioning 'blame' for the severity of the Depression, recent studies no longer focus exclusively on the United States' failure to act as a lender of the last resort, the central theme of Charles Kindleberger's magisterial study *The World In Depression, 1929–1939*.[5] Kindleberger and his disciples argued that the emergence of the United States as the 'world's banker' after World War I invested it with a responsibility to secure the stability of the world economy and open-trade relations. The transfer of power had profound consequences for the world economy as a whole, and the operation of the international monetary system in particular. Especially significant, was the huge growth in the volume of short-term, as opposed to long-term, credit which the exigencies of financing wartime trade demanded – a trend that continued in the 1920s with 'informal' diplomatic initiatives such as the Dawes Plan. The development made the world global capital movements, and therefore the economy as a whole, more vulnerable to monetary and economic shocks such as the decision of the

Federal Reserve Board to raise interest rates in 1929. It also made the debtor nations, which now included Britain and France, dependent on export earnings, particularly from the United States, to pay off their debts. American trade policy, too, it is argued, failed to reflect its new-found global economic responsibilities. Central to critical accounts of the United States' failure as hegemon was its adoption of the Hawley-Smoot Tariff in 1930. This tariff is castigated as the act that made it impossible for America's debtors to earn dollars to pay their debts, and triggered a flight to protectionism by governments around the world. Indeed, the failure of American economic diplomacy in the Depression has been often characterized as an absence of leadership as much as a failure of policy.

Recent research by economic historians has moved in two principal directions with important consequences for the appreciation of American and European economic foreign policy in the Depression. First, there has been considerable research into the impact of monetary policy, much of it focused around the history of the gold standard and its contribution to the origins and magnitude of the Depression. Economists and historians now argue that the character and operation of the inter-war gold exchange standard, more than any other single contributory element, both turned the 1928–9 recession into a profound depression and helped to transmit its effects around the globe.[6] Early criticisms of the inter-war gold standard focused largely on the exchange rate at which countries chose to stabilise. More recent critiques, however, have placed much greater stress on the policy regime necessary to maintain membership of the system, the so-called 'rules' of the gold standard game. These 'rules' called for confidence in the fixed exchange rate to be maintained by balanced domestic budgets, bank (interest) rates to sustain convertibility, and a positive balance of trade. This combination was inflexible and deflationary (or in modern parlance disinflationary), sensible enough in a time of plenty, but disastrous in a time of want. It was only when countries broke free from this golden strait-jacket and opted, not just for currency depreciation, but for expansive monetary policies that they found genuine respite from the ravages of depression.

As the thoughtful studies of Barry Eichengreen have made clear, the smooth functioning of the gold standard was far more dependent on international cooperation than the apparent automatism of the mechanism suggested. There is no longer an exclusive focus on America's failure to act as lender of the last resort. Instead, there is a new emphasis on the failure of the world's leading economies to undertake a strategy of coordinated devaluation (coupled with deflationary measures) to reflate the world economy. Such a strategy, which was considered and might have been favourably employed at the World

Economic Conference in 1933, was rejected by countries determined
to pursue nationally orientated policies.[7]

Although, in large part, the history of the Depression has become
a monetary history with the gold standard as a unifying theme, those
who favour monetary explanations have not had it all their own way.
The nature and extent of countries' commitment to the gold standard
emphasizes the importance of policy (not markets) to the history of
the inter-war economy and to the power of domestic political priorities
in shaping economic policy. Scholars of what has become known as
the 'historical political economy' argue that the explanation as to why
one economic policy is chosen over another lies in two overlapping
areas: the influence of historical precedent (the perception of economic
policy success or failure in the past), and the political behaviour of
conflicting interest groups or parties to secure particular economic
policies.[8]

In the wake of war and post-war inflation, the 'lessons of history'
helped to generate the political will to re-create the gold standard.
But in Europe the 'Great' War had also altered society's expectations
of government when it came to economic policy. As the war forced
the nation state to demand new sacrifices of all its citizens in the name
of loyalty, government, in return, was prompted to extend its obligations
to its people and make changes to the political system. But it proved
easier for the governments in the West to meet the demand for political
change by way of extending the franchise, than to tackle the economic
and social problems that often underpinned demands for political reform. Nevertheless, government was assigned responsibility for
maintaining a continuing level of economic activity and political legitimacy was dependent on its ability to manage the domestic economy
to the collective advantage of the electorate (or at least its participating
majority).

In Western Europe the primacy of national economic solutions over
international economic policy was underlined by the extension of political representation and the growing link between economic legitimacy
and economic success. When the tension between national and international economic obligations defied solution, as they appeared to after
1929, then national remedies inevitably took priority. Moreover, in
contrast to the political and economic order created in the West after
World War II, with its focus on international institutions and American
determination to ensure that its allies adopted economic and monetary
policies compatible with its own, the settlement after World War I
failed to give any real consideration to how the principles of economic
interdependence might be protected in times of global recession or
during instances of national hardship. Keynes was but the first in a
long line of critics to condemn the post-war settlement's failure to

include provisions for 'economic rehabilitation ... to adjust the systems of the old world and the new'.[9]

A further consequence of the financial repercussions of World War I and the subsequent peace settlements was the complex network of international indebtedness that bound together the fate of victor and vanquished. Nowhere is the complex interaction between political and economic priorities on both a national and international level better illustrated than in the area of reparations, war debts and commercial debts. The bane of international relations in the inter-war period (and of its students ever since), these payments opened up important issues of competition, cooperation and perception in America's economic relations with Europe. The evolution of European policy on war debts and reparations also had important consequences for Roosevelt's relations with Europe in the Depression.

It is now clear that reparations did the greatest harm during the first years of the Weimar Republic. The death throes of the Wilhelmine Reich in World War I left an horrendous financial legacy which combined with reparations to weaken the political will to bring the burgeoning inflationary crisis under control until 1923. Once the Dawes Plan was in place, of course, Germany received far more by way of commercial loans from the United States than it paid in reparations in the 1920s and, subsequently, international indebtedness became more of a political than economic problem. As one British Treasury official put it, the problem was 'how to persuade our own people to pay the taxation involved'.[10] This is not the place to explore the imbroglio of German-American debt relations. However, Germany's decision to pursue a vigorous foreign policy for the abandonment of reparation payments in 1930 set in train a series of developments that were to have important implications for American relations with Europe in the Depression.

The spectacular series of banking crises that swept across Europe like a bush fire in the late spring and summer of 1931 triggered the only international initiative to deal with the economic crisis, the debt moratorium of June 1931. This initiative by President Herbert Hoover postponed all payments of inter-governmental debts, reparations and debt relief, both principal and interest, for a year. Most important from the perspective of America's future diplomatic relations with Europe was the mistaken interpretation placed on it by the British government, which believed that the White House had finally recognized the inter-connection between reparations and war debts. This interpretation, reinforced by repeated American urging that the banking collapse was a 'patently European crisis', was also shaped by talks between Hoover and the French Prime Minister, Pierre Laval in October 1931. The American administration had appeared to endorse the notion that Europe should resolve reparations before turning to the United States for a talks about war debts and demanded the 'initiative on this matter should be taken early by the European powers'.[11] Britain's determination to see the end of reparations in the expectation that the United States would then reciprocate by absolving its former allies of their war debts laid a false trail that was to lead British and French policy on debts into direct confrontation with the United States.

Although both Britain and the United States believed that they were not responsible for the German financial crisis, they were persuaded that removing the burden of reparations would be of great benefit to the German economy. The calculation was motivated by political and economic considerations. Firstly, international economic cooperation on the 'German Question' seemed to be one of the few remaining routes to international cooperation. By concentrating its diplomatic efforts on Germany, the British government, like that of the United States, was able to side-step any detailed reflection of the implications of its own economic nationalism on the global economic and diplomatic crisis. Hammering on about the need for reparation and war debt revision was appealing to the European powers because it offered an accessible medium for translating the dire economic crisis into terms that politicians and their electorates could understand. Second, the extension of American commercial credits under the Dawes and Young Plan loans and British short-term credits extended during the financial crisis in the summer of 1931 had tied the major powers, and more specifically the interest of powerful financiers, to Germany's economic and political future. This was especially true of Britain which experienced a drain on its gold reserves, culminating in a sterling crisis which forced the pound from the gold standard. After 1931, the debt crisis and the convertibility crisis were linked in the minds of British policy-makers, a conviction shared by their counterparts in Central Europe and Latin America.[12]

Most important from the perspective of future Anglo-American relations was the fact that British concern for German financial stability was equated increasingly with its own. In August and September 1931 Weimar's creditors had agreed voluntarily to freeze their credits inside Germany in the 'Standstill Agreements'. The agreements had important consequences for the future course of the German domestic economy, enabling it to sustain its foreign trade and, in theory, to borrow more on existing credit lines. The agreements also liberated Germany from the 'rules' of gold standard membership, offering increased independence to formulate economic and monetary policy which official circles in Germany soon exploited to facilitate rearmament. The Standstill Agreements also had important consequences for future diplomatic relations between Britain and the United States. Accepted at first by

British and American financiers as a short-term necessity, the agreements were to become a long-term hardship. They were renewed in January and again in June 1932 when an agreement was signed for a further twelve-month period.

In the months after the Hoover Moratorium and the Standstill Agreements were secured, both Britain and the United States grew increasingly anxious to safeguard their frozen (commercial) credits inside Germany, but their policies differed in important respects. While American economic foreign policy succumbed to paralysis in the face of the domestic crisis, the new National Government in Britain, invigorated by electoral success and the apparent success of its move to protectionism and a loosening of monetary policy, was determined to take 'a big bold lead in the world'.[13] London noted with growing alarm how many in Germany had begun to blur the distinction between commercial and political debts. Britain was very anxious to nip the trend in the bud and increasingly adopted the view that commercial credits extended by Britain to Germany would be safeguarded best by the complete abolition of political debts. In other words, both war debts and reparations should be abolished. As is well known, this conviction, coupled with fortuitous political developments in France, culminated in the effective abolition of German reparations at the Lausanne Conference in June 1932. Less well known is the fact that to secure French agreement at Lausanne, Britain and France signed a 'Gentleman's Agreement' which made French ratification of the Lausanne settlement conditional on an Anglo-French war debt agreement with the American government. In Whitehall, the Foreign Office alone feared that Britain's decision to present the incoming Democratic administration with a *fait accompli* on reparations and war debts posed a serious threat to Anglo-American relations.[14]

In order to lure the United States into war debt negotiations it did not want, the British government proposed a World Economic Conference to address the growing crisis in monetary and trading relations. Enshrined in the fifth article of the Lausanne Conference, Britain sought to exploit preparations for the World Economic Conference to secure an Anglo-French agreement on war debts. It was a risky strategy, since the issues that secured American participation in the conference (alongside that of sixty-four other countries) were the flotation of sterling and Britain's move to protectionism – the very topics Britain did not want to open up to American scrutiny. The timing of the World Economic Conference was exploited very deliberately by the British, who timetabled the preparatory meetings for the conference to coincide with the December 1932 war debt payment due to the United States, with the 12 June payment falling three days before the opening of the conference proper on 15 June 1933. Britain also manipulated the conference agenda by arguing that problems like currency depreciation, trade protectionism and widespread unemployment made an immediate reduction of war debts to the United States imperative. The stakes were raised further when France failed to make its December 1932 war payment to the United States and was judged to be in default.

In January and April 1933 Roosevelt spoke of Britain and the United States working together to improve the global economic climate. Encouraged by European rhetoric at the preparatory sessions for the World Economic Conference, he repeatedly urged their governments to widen the parameters of debt negotiations to include issues of tariff protection and disarmament. However, each nation had its own agenda and its own interests. Domestic considerations set limits on the war debt concessions FDR could offer Europe. Similarly, the British and the French put their own recovery first and so were unable to do as the new President asked. Of course, the development of the President's domestic programme made the context of international monetary and trade negotiations more complex, but the fact that the British government tenaciously clung to the primacy of a war debt over monetary or trade negotiations greatly soured Anglo-American relations. The deadlock over war debt payments worsened when British Prime Minister Ramsay MacDonald, in his presidential opening address to the World Economic Conference, called for a resolution of the issue as a priority over all other cooperative measures. In his diary, the United States Ambassador to Britain, Robert Worth Bingham, reflected the sentiment, widespread among supporters of FDR's internationalism, that MacDonald's incursion into the question of war debts was 'inexcusable and unwise', serving only to weaken further the appeal of European involvement back home.[15] The conference's first 'bombshell message' had come, not from the pen of Roosevelt, but the mouth of MacDonald. The following year the debt issue grew even more acrimonious with the passage of the Johnson Act in the United States. Much to Britain's chagrin, the Act branded her as a defaulter in the same class as the French. The Act prohibited all further loans to defaulting nations.

Much less public, but no less damaging to American relations with Western Europe, were its negotiations with Nazi Germany over the commercial debt frozen inside Germany under the Standstill Agreements. While Britain's 'cooperative' stance on reparations helped to secure assurances from the German government that its commercial credits inside Germany would be safeguarded, in May and June 1933 the Nazi government attempted to default on its commercial obligations to American bond-holders. After his meeting with the new German Finance Minister and Director of the Reichsbank, Hjalmar Schacht,

in May 1933 FDR complained 'this is terrible. I am in an awful mess
with Europe ... European statesmen are a bunch of bastards'.[16] The
reference to Europeans, as opposed to Germans, was not a slip of the
tongue. Roosevelt's anger was fuelled by reports from London and
Berlin which claimed that Schacht and his old friend at the Bank of
England, Sir Montagu Norman, had concluded a commercial debt
agreement that largely protected the investments of British bond-
holders in Germany. American annoyance at an Anglo-German
commercial debt agreement, formalized into a long-term arrangement
in 1934, was no accident. It was part of a deliberate German strategy
to sow suspicion in Anglo-American relations to forestall a united
'Anglo-Saxon' front that would threaten Nazi ambitions overseas at a
time when the Reich was still vulnerable.[17] The American conviction
that 'British banking authorities are working closely with German
authorities to develop further plans satisfactory to themselves' also
undermined Presidential support for an initiative to encourage cooperation on international trade. The administration had hoped such an
initiative would strengthen its relations with Europe in general and
Britain in particular.[18]

There is now a considerable body of scholarship detailing how the
structural changes within the American economy, coupled with the
new constellation of interest-group politics and the profound desire
to avert another Great Depression, generated policies to make fundamental reforms in international economic relations in order to restore
world trade. By 1932 many, both inside the Commerce and State
Departments and outside, began to argue that the United States should
move away from the inconsistent, 'double-edged' Open Door and
adopt a reciprocal trading policy. The State Department, in particular,
was stung by repeated European criticism that American protectionism
compromised its investments in Europe, that it had prompted Britain
and France to abandon the collection of reparations, and was forcing
countries like Germany from the international economy. The shift in
official sentiment was supported by the move of largely capital intensive
industries like banking, and the oil and electricity industries, towards
a free trade position. Once Republican supporters, they were now
increasingly drawn toward the professed low-tariff position of the
Democratic party.[19]

In the new Democratic administration Cordell Hull was the un-
doubted champion of such a strategy, intent on liberating world trade
as 'the fundamental basis of all peace'.[20] Once dismissed by scholars,
Hull's contribution to successive Roosevelt administrations has been
re-appraised to stress his long-term influence on American economic
diplomacy and Roosevelt's internationalism.[21] After his appointment
as Secretary of State in March 1933, he took every opportunity to

publicize the administration's resolve to secure congressional authority to negotiate Reciprocal Tariff Act (RTA) agreements. These called for a flat rate reduction of 10 per cent of existing barriers, a corresponding percentage enlargement of quotas, and bilateral agreements within unconditional most-favoured-nation treatment.

The State Department's competition with the talented and nationalist-orientated officials responsible for devising and implementing the New Deal is well known and certainly worked to delay Roosevelt's support for the RTA until 1934. In that year the United States concluded reciprocal agreements with countries in Central and South America, reducing the United States tariff by almost three quarters.[22] Hull's initiative had important consequences for Pan-American commerce and diplomacy which have been well documented. Less well known is the fact that Hull sought to conclude his very first reciprocal tariff act with Britain.

From December 1932 (the initiative is more typically dated from 1934 or 1936), Hull's overtures for an agreement to halt the escalation of trade barriers were directed at the British government. By January 1933, three months before he was fully installed as Secretary of State, Hull had already adopted the Republican sponsored tariff truce for the World Economic Conference and planned to use it to secure the first reciprocal tariff act with the British government. The State and Commerce Departments even harboured hopes that an Anglo-American RTA would provide the basis for initiating multilateral tariff reductions throughout the world through the operation of unconditional most-favoured-nation treatment. American hopes were supported by the conviction that British power was founded on free trade and that Britain would, with American support, return to free trade. As one American official put it, 'the idea for a bilateral trade treaty with the British' arose because 'they would probably be the easiest person [sic] to do it with ... and then see what kind of animal that would be and how wide its application would be to others'.[23] American aspirations for an agreement certainly made an impact on National Socialist Germany. From February until early June 1933 both the German Foreign and Finance Ministries repeatedly expressed a profound concern that Britain and the United States were 'very likely to sign a trade agreement in the near future' heralding a new era in Anglo-American cooperation.[24]

In hindsight the first two years of Roosevelt's presidency seem like a lost opportunity in Anglo-American economic relations. Back in 1933 the timing of Secretary Hull's tariff overture appeared particularly poor – Britain's Abnormal, General and Imperial Tariffs had only just passed into law and it remained unclear how far Hull enjoyed the support of a president apparently torn between the nationalist and internationalist elements in his government. Equally unconvincing from the British perspective was the way that the State Department skirted over the sticky question of whether congressional support for the RTA could be secured. On a more fundamental level, however, the problem was one of competition. Britain's £70 million trading deficit to the United States was a genuine obstacle to the conclusion of an Anglo-American trading agreement, as well as a source of great embarrassment; so, too, was British determination to strengthen its imperial power base and to meet protectionist promises made to its electorate.[25]

The British change of heart came in 1936 when Neville Chamberlain, then still Chancellor of the Exchequer, signalled Britain's new determination to open-trade negotiations with the United States. Politics now took precedence over economics. Chamberlain was now determined to secure an Anglo-American trade agreement to present Europe's dictators with 'the possibility of these two great powers working together'.[26] But the missed opportunity for agreement in 1933 cost Britain dear. Since 1932 inter-imperial trade had grown stronger and American farmers more vociferous in their demands for access to the British market. London's new willingness to explore the possibility of an agreement could disguise neither the incompatibility of British and American tariff structures which had grown more acute since 1933, nor the cumbersome machinery of the RTA. The agreement, finally signed on 17 November 1938, did little to liberalize Anglo-American trade, impress the German aggressors of 'Anglo-Saxon' solidarity or trigger a global move to reduce international protectionism.

Of course, the drama over the issue of monetary cooperation in 1933 also served to deflect attention away from Hull's initiative and to cast American policy in an uncooperative light. It was the clash between nationalist and international elements in the early New Deal, both in terms of policy and personalities, which pulled the rug from under Hull's feet in London. In June 1933 the presidential support needed to get the RTA legislation through Congress evaporated, and Roosevelt embarked on a (superficially) radical policy of dollar devaluation which soured the climate of international cooperation. Roosevelt's famous 'bombshell message', in which he rejected a planned temporary stabilization agreement to provide a stable monetary foundation for the talks, became the ostensible cause for the collapse of the conference and the basis for persistent European suspicions of Roosevelt's foreign policy thereafter. This is not the place to unpick the intricacies of the stabilization negotiations, although the continued notoriety of the bombshell message is surprising given the twists and turns in international economic relations since 1931 and the renewed emphasis by economists on the benefits of currency depreciation (coupled with a commensurate loosening of orthodox policies) for national and international recovery.

Various explanations for Roosevelt's strong language and diplomatic *naïveté* have been offered by historians.[27] Certainly, the President's choice of language was ill-advised. His strong condemnation of the fetishism 'of so-called international bankers' for the gold standard left his representatives in London isolated and made him easy prey for British and French politicians, who wanted resolution of the war-debts issue above everything. Moreover, on the very day that the London conference opened, the British and German press announced a new Anglo-German deal on commercial debts, renewing the standstill machinery that had sustained German imports and exports. At the same time, Schacht announced that Germany would no longer honour debts to nations who had a trading surplus with Germany, namely the United States, thereby reneging on German assurances given since 1924 that Germany would not discriminate between its debtors.

Roosevelt had other good reasons to feel frustrated by the behaviour of the Europeans. In April 1933 France, though determined to uphold the sanctity of the gold standard, rejected an American proposal for a temporary stabilization agreement to cover the forthcoming conference in the hope the Americans would offer them something better. Instead, when in May 1933 American policy took on a more radical flavour, the French were forced to revive the American proposal in the face of mounting pressure on the French franc and a weakening domestic economy. Their request was taken up by the Federal Reserve Board of New York which worked hard to revive presidential support. At the same time, however, the French Prime Minister, Edouard Daladier, and Finance Minister George Bonnet, began to insist that a new, permanent stabilization agreement should come out of the conference. This demand was made despite previous assurances to Roosevelt that the topic would be excluded from conference deliberations.[28]

Equally frustrating for the American administration was the position adopted by the British government. Roosevelt and his advisers were only too aware that, since the flotation of the dollar there was, in real terms, little difference between American and British monetary policy. Both had abandoned the gold standard (whether they elected to do so or were forced off gold is a moot point), in order to raise prices, stimulate demand and investment through the fall in interest rates and to loosen the hold of orthodox policy on their economies. It is the failure to take this strategy further, economic historians now argue, that explains the slow-down in the national economies of Britain and America by the mid-1930s. Indeed, from September 1931 until April 1933 British monetary policy was a much greater source of international division than that of the United States. With the majority of the world's countries still on gold, it was often argued that Britain should demonstrate 'responsibility' and 'leadership' by returning to the gold standard.

After April 1933 British monetary policy was much closer to that of the Democratic administration than to any of the other European powers. In public, the British government rejected speculation regarding possible Anglo-American cooperation to revive the world economy. Roosevelt's intentions on monetary policy remained unclear in the summer of 1933. In private, the British government was quietly relieved that the dollar flotation had diverted international attention away from the floating pound, but was also concerned that the depreciating dollar threatened the export advantage Britain had accrued since the flotation of sterling.[29] British monetary policy, too, was governed by the primacy of domestic recovery. Equally important was the fact that the imperial dimension to British policy, which sought to rebuild British power by 'giving sterling a new force in the world', was conceived as a means to compete with America. Roosevelt was right to suspect that Britain and, to a lesser extent France, exploited his unwillingness to cooperate on monetary matters 'deliberately to discredit us for certain clear objectives'.[30]

By exploring the relationship between different areas of policy and the diplomatic context as a whole, it is possible to conclude that, in many ways, Roosevelt's first year in office provided an opportunity to improve American relations with Europe in general and Britain in particular. With the flotation of the US dollar in April 1933, membership of the gold standard was no longer a source of tension in Anglo-American relations. Much has been made by economic historians of the failure of Britain and the United States to launch a joint initiative to reflate the world economy and break the stranglehold of gold standard orthodoxy. Interestingly, scholars who have studied the internal constraints on Roosevelt's freedom to make foreign policy as he would have wished, also now argue that the best opportunities to shape public opinion to a more internationalist outlook were squandered between 1933 and 1935.[31]

For the rest of the 1930s, policy-makers in Washington, London and Paris recognized their divergence on economic issues. Many of these differences originated in the national responses to the Depression first taken in 1931 and 1932. Yet, for the most part, differences on monetary, trade and debt policy remained unresolved for the rest of the decade and beyond. The history of Anglo-American debt negotiations, for example, cast a long shadow. In an opinion poll taken in 1945, the American public revealed its conviction that Britain was far less likely to pay back its wartime loans than either Russia or China.[32] It is important that future writings on the history of diplomatic relations between the United States, Britain and France integrate research into the history of their economic relations. Incompatible domestic recovery strategies, the short-comings of cooperative arrangements like the

Tripartite Stabilization Agreement of 1936 and studies of how each power perceived the economic policy of the other (competition/cooperation), all contribute to our understanding of the failure of international cooperation between the world's leading democracies in the face of German, Italian and Japanese aggression. We also lack a clear appreciation of how the lessons of the 1930s shaped future American economic foreign policy and a comprehensive study of Roosevelt's vision of the post-war liberal economic order. This is surprising because Roosevelt's wartime diplomacy went, in Kimball's words, 'further toward establishing the American vision of a universal political economy than Roosevelt ever got with his international peace keeping structure'.[33]

The history of the inter-war period shares some interesting parallels with the world since 1990. Now the failure of international cooperation to combat the Depression is seen much more as a failure of multilateral cooperation than of hegemonic leadership. Now, as then, no single power dominates the international economic system. The need for continued international cooperation on all policy fronts seems self evident, but so, too, are the tensions inherent in promoting international cooperation in a competitive, multilateral economic environment by governments answerable only to their national electorates. The history of Roosevelt's diplomatic relations with Europe in the 1930s still has much to teach us.

Notes

1. D. K. Adams, *FDR, The New Deal and Europe* (Keele, 1973), 4, 9.
2. Thomas Guinsburg, 'The Triumph of Isolationism', in Gordon Martel (ed.), *American Foreign Relations Reconsidered, 1890–1993* (London, 1994), 90–102.
3. Memorandum by Richard Washburn-Child, June 1934, SD550. S1/1399, Records of the State Department, National Archives II, Washington DC.
4. Robert Dallek, *Franklin D. Roosevelt and American Foreign Policy, 1929–1945* (Oxford, 1979), 41–58.
5. Charles P. Kindleberger, *The World in Depression, 1929–1939* (Harmondsworth, 1979).
6. Barry Eichengreen, *Golden Fetters: the Gold Standard and the Great Depression, 1919–1939* (Oxford, 1992); Peter Temin, *Lessons from the Great Depression* (Boston, 1989), 1–87.
7. Patricia Clavin, *The Failure of Economic Diplomacy. Britain, Germany, France and the United States, 1931–36* (London, 1995); Barry Eichengreen, 'The Origins and Nature of the Great Slump', *Economic History Review* XLVII (May, 1992), 13–39.
8. Charles Maier, *In Search of Stability: Explorations in Historical Political Economy* (Cambridge, 1987).

9. John Maynard Keynes, *The Economic Consequences of the Peace* (London, 1920), 226.

10. Chancellor of the Exchequer quoted in Stephen A. Schuker, 'Origins of American Stabilisation Policy in Europe: the Financial Dimension, 1918–1924' in Hans-Jürgen Schröder, *Confrontation and Co-operation: Germany and the United States in the Era of World War I, 1900–1924* (Oxford, 1993), 398.

11. Text of Hoover Laval communiqué, 25 October 1931, US Department of State, *Foreign Relations of the United States*, vol. 2 (1931), 252–3.

12. Harold James, 'Financial Flows Across Frontiers in the Great Depression', *Economic History Review* XLV (August, 1992), 280.

13. Record of conversation between Harrison and Mills reflecting on recent comments by Ramsay MacDonald, 17 July 1931, *Harrison Papers*, Records of the Federal Reserve Board New York, New York.

14. Runciman to Baldwin, 24 June 1932, vol. 119, *Baldwin Papers*, University Library, Cambridge.

15. Entry of 15 June 1933, *Bingham Diary*, Manuscripts Division, Library of Congress, Washington DC.

16. Entry in diary of Henry Morgenthau Jnr., 9 May 1933, *Farm Credit Diary*, Book 0, Franklin D. Roosevelt Library, Hyde Park, New York.

17. Clavin, *Failure of Economic Diplomacy*, 103–9, 138–41.

18. Communiqué from Hull to Phillips, 11 June 1933, SD 862.51/3168, Records of the State Department, National Archives II, Washington DC.

19. Thomas Ferguson, 'Industrial Conflict and the Coming of the New Deal: The Triumph of Multinational Liberalism in America', in Gary Gerstle and Steve Fraser, *The Rise and Fall of the New Deal Order, 1930–1980* (Princeton, 1989), 17–18.

20. Hull's speech to the World Economic Conference, 13 June, 1933, US Department of State, *Foreign Relations of the United States*, vol. 1 (1933), 636–40.

21. Irwin F. Gellman, *Secret Affairs: Franklin D. Roosevelt, Cordell Hull, and Sumner Welles* (Baltimore, 1995).

22. Dick Steward, *Trade and Hemisphere: The Good Neighbour Policy and Reciprocal Trade* (Columbia, 1975), 208–20.

23. Entry of 7 April 1933, *Diaries and Papers of James Warburg*, vol. 3, Butler Library, Columbia University, New York.

24. Memorandum from Neurath to Ritter, 3 April 1933, GFM 33:1231, 3177/D684107, *Records of the German Foreign Ministry*, microfilm held in Public Record Office, London.

25. Britain earned £31 million from its exports to US in 1936 while importing £114 million. Ian Drummond and Norman Hillmer, *Negotiating Freer Trade: The United Kingdom, the United States, Canada and the Free Trade Agreements of 1938* (Waterloo, 1989), 42–3.

26. Arthur W. Schatz, 'The Anglo-American Trade Agreement and Cordell Hull's Search for Peace', *Journal of American History* LVII (June, 1970), 100.

27. For a summary see Clavin, *Failure of Economic Diplomacy*, 129–38.

28. Kenneth Mouré, *Managing the Franc: Poincaré, Economic Understanding and*

Political Constraint in French Monetary Policy, 1928–1936 (Cambridge, 1991), 95; Patricia Clavin, 'The Fetishes of So-Called International Bankers: Central Bank Co-operation for the World Economic Conference, 1932–33', *Contemporary European History* I (November, 1992), 296–303.

29. Memorandum by Henry Clay, 12 May 1933, OV31/22, *Country files in Records of the Bank of England*, Bank of England, London.

30. Roosevelt to Hull, 24 June 1933, SD 550. S1/Monetary Stab./47, Records of the State Department.

31. Guinsburg, 'The Triumph of Isolation', 101.

32. Susan Brewer, *Creating the Special Relationship* (Ithaca, 1998).

33. Warren Kimball, *The Juggler: Franklin Roosevelt as Wartime Statesman* (Princeton, 1991), 189.

11

'Prevent World War III': An Historiographical Appraisal of Morgenthau's Programme for Germany

Michaela Hönicke

In several respects the controversy over the so-called Morgenthau Plan is a good starting point to have another look at governmental post-war planning for Germany and, more importantly, at the different contemporary interpretations of National Socialism that informed these plans. Isaiah Berlin, who worked at the British Embassy in Washington during the war, first used the metaphor of a 'lightning flash' to describe the impact that the intervention by Secretary of the Treasury Henry Morgenthau Jr. had on American wartime planning. Morgenthau's plans for post-war Germany served to provide a dramatic focus on the government's planning for Germany and on public attitudes towards that country.[1] Strong feelings and convictions surfaced to create one of the most passionate political storms of the war. Before the publicity arising from Morgenthau's intervention, consideration within the government bureaucracy of Germany's future had been guarded and cautious. However, no amount of restrained bureaucratic language was able to calm the tempest that was generated by Morgenthau. As soon as the debate became open and public, the divisions within the administrative agencies of government became equally apparent. These fundamental differences revolved around the question of the nature of Germany's national 'illness' and how to 'cure' the Germans of their presumed prejudices and aggressiveness.

The story of the so-called Morgenthau Plan has been one of the most fundamentally misunderstood chapters of World War II and in the history of German-American relations. This particular issue contributed to the longevity and intensity of the misperceptions and defamations that continued for so long after the war in both German and American historiography and folklore.[2]

The governmental planning process was embedded in a larger public debate and shaped by differing interpretations of National Socialism and its place in German history. Public reactions had preceded official proclamations on almost all issues regarding the Third Reich. American foreign correspondents and commentators responded early and sharply to the rise of Adolf Hitler. The persecution of the Jews of Europe and later revelations of the horrors of the Holocaust magnified the negative image of Germany. Yet even that image was diffuse and varied. At no point during the war did American views of Germany coalesce into a clearly focused image of the enemy. Instead the United States witnessed a lively, rather well-informed and often sophisticated debate, both in governmental and in public circles, on the 'nature of the enemy' and on 'what to do with Germany'.[3]

The arena for the public debate on post-war policy for defeated Germany in 1943 took place in books, articles, public meetings, radio talk shows and Hollywood movies. Behind closed doors, the State Department's Advisory Committee on Post-war Foreign Policy had also systematically deliberated various aspects of post-war policy since early 1942.[4] Similarly, the Research and Analysis Branch of the Office of Strategic Services (OSS) had been dealing with every conceivable aspects of National Socialism and American post-war policy towards Germany.[5] Yet, when Germany's defeat seemed near at hand in late summer 1944, there existed no coherent plan and no public statements on post-war treatment, except the call for unconditional surrender and for the punishment of war criminals. The Allied war leaders had repeatedly and publicly stated their intention to eradicate National Socialist ideology. However, a set of conflicting ideas about the realization of this goal had begun to emerge.

Throughout the war, observers of American public and governmental opinion had commented on the ultimate relevance of American wartime images of Germany. They were well aware that such images affected American thinking on post-war issues. In spite of Roosevelt's insistence that the war first had to be won before peace plans could seriously be considered, no one interested in a peaceful Europe assumed that military victory itself would solve the German problem. Instead, in the words of one study, 'to eradicate [Germany's] false ideologies ... was considered just as important as curtailing [its] physical ability to make war'.[6]

The variety of interpretations and representations of the Third Reich in wartime America defies easy classification. The traditional historiographical juxtaposition of undeservedly harsh wartime indictments of the German people and their culture, on the one hand, and more enlightened, moderate views that held a group of Nazi gangsters responsible for Germany's crimes, on the other, do justice neither to the reality of the Third Reich nor to the complexity of American contemporary thinking on National Socialism. A closer look at the heated debate, especially among concerned citizens, politicians and intellectuals, highlights the ideological and existential nature of the war. These discussions reveal the fundamental moral and psychological questions that underlay any explanation of the war, mass murder and genocide.

The publications, internal deliberations, speeches and memoranda produced by officials in the State and War Departments, the Office of War Information and the OSS, the White House and other government agencies shared the same substantial differences in their analysis of questions about the nature of National Socialist rule in Germany that characterized the public debate. While their responses varied, they asked the same questions. How deeply was the extremist, racist, aggressively expansionist and consciously anti-democratic and anti-Western ideology rooted in Germany's political and cultural traditions? Had German history taken a 'special path' in the late nineteenth century or even earlier? Did the Allies bear a share of responsibility for the current war? Had appeasement been a mistake or had the Versailles Treaty been too harsh? These were just some of the common queries. Most concerned Americans felt that adequate answers to these questions were a prerequisite to finding a political solution to prevent Germany from starting World War III. H. M. Kallen wrote: 'The convalescence of the bled and broken world into a healthy new one will be determined largely by how its medicine-men interpret the German national character.'[7] The zealous desire to bring Germany back to the fold of democratic, peaceful nations and to cleanse its culture and popular psyche from abnormal tendencies to subjugate and destroy others, lay at the heart of the national wartime debate of which the contribution of the Secretary of the Treasury in 1944 formed an integral part.

The debate on these issues was intensive. The German historian Bernd Greiner, who offered the first book-length German analysis of Morgenthau's intentions and efforts, opened his account with a recapitulation of the Morgenthau legend as it was portrayed in Germany. This legend, perpetuated by German school-books after the war, the media, publicists and scholars alike, originated with the official Nazi interpretation of the first reports on the Treasury's proposals. The Morgenthau legend might well be called one of Goebbels' greatest success stories. The vigour of the Nazis' lies proved to be so effective that they shaped much of the consideration given to Morgenthau's arguments for the next fifty years. Taking their cue from Goebbels' 'strength through fear' rhetoric, Germans after the war continued to feel outrage over Morgenthau's blueprint for the 'genocide' and 'annihilation' of the German people. Germans were engaging in a clear case of projection, a psychological response that grew more pronounced as the defeat grew more inevitable. Familiar with their own policy of eliminating the Jewish and Slav enemy, Germans transferred these same tendencies to the United States. It was easy to graft their own language of annihilation to an American mouthpiece. Thus the myth of the Morgenthau Plan allowed the Germans to assume their favorite post-war pose, that of a victim – in this case of 'Jewish wrath' and 'Allied barbarity'.[8]

Similar conjunctions between Morgenthau's plans for the destruction of Germany's fabric and Hitler's policies of mass annihilation occurred in the United States. In addition to sporadic anti-Semitism, a stronger identification with the Germans than with their victims became apparent in varying degrees in the American reactions to Morgenthau. Secretary of War Henry L. Stimson worried that his colleague from the Treasury was 'so biased by his Semitic grievances that he is really a very dangerous adviser to the President at this time'. He referred to the Treasury proposals as 'Semitism gone wild for vengeance'.[9] Secretary of State Cordell Hull, who had originally agreed with Morgenthau's ideas, now also called them 'blind vengeance'.[10] Norman M. Littell, Assistant Attorney General, joined the choir of administrative voices privately expressing misgivings about a Jew proposing a 'harsh' treatment of Germany, thereby inadvertently confirming the severity of the anti-Semitic climate within which everyone was operating.[11] Comparisons between the destructive occupation policy of the Nazis in Europe and Morgenthau's plans for Germany followed. Stimson saw in Morgenthau's suggestions 'just such a crime as the Germans themselves hoped to perpetrate upon their victims – it would be a crime against civilization itself'.[12]

This tendency by Americans to compare Morgenthau with the Nazis is the most disturbing feature of America's reception of Morgenthau's proposal. The Republican Senator from Indiana, Homer E. Capehart, accused Morgenthau and his supporters in February 1946 of 'burning with an all-consuming determination to wreak their vengeance' and proclaimed that their 'techniques of hate' had earned them the titles of 'American Himmlers'.[13] One wonders whether those who engaged in these rhetorical excesses ever grasped the enormity of the crimes of the 'architect of the Holocaust' and, moreover, why their sympathy was so unwaveringly rooted on the side of the Germans rather than their victims.

The media also engaged in substantial misrepresentations of the Treasury programme. Indeed the negative reaction has often been cited as the trigger for Roosevelt's retreat on the Morgenthau Plan. According to public opinion reports by the State Department, it was the 'presumed removal of all German industries' to which many commentators reacted negatively.[14] Yet complete de-industrialization had never been a proposal in any of the Treasury documents or discussions.[15] Furthermore the public storm that followed various leaks of the Plan was compounded by the presidential election campaign and provided some heavy ammunition for Roosevelt's Republican opponent, Thomas Dewey. Dewey publicly declared that Morgenthau's 'private plan for disposing of the German people after the war' would lead to more American casualties in Europe as a result of a hardened German fighting spirit.[16]

It was not only public figures and political commentators who played a role in discrediting Morgenthau. Scholars, both German and American, have refused to take him seriously. Any earnest effort to study the genesis, context and intentions of his proposals was deemed superfluous, since they were considered aberrant and ill-informed. When they were magnanimous they explained Morgenthau's 'slip' by reference to the author's Jewishness, and his understandably emotional (but in their view excessive) response by his inability to subordinate his personal feelings to rational policy-making.[17]

The controversy over the Morgenthau Plan spanned far and wide and generated its own mythology. The legend of the Plan is closely linked to the idea of what may be termed 'Vansittartism'.[18] In 1943 Lord Vansittart, former Chief Diplomatic Adviser to the British govenment, complained that his British opponents had twisted his own arguments about the nature of Germany's responsibility for the war. He claimed that his critics had misrepresented and exaggerated his views on the role of the German people by converting them into accusations of 'collective national guilt'. According to this view, Germans were inherently and unreformably aggressive, verging on the socially psychopathic.[19] This perception became known as 'Vansittartism' and rapidly became a pejorative slogan used to denounce a view with which one did not agree. A 'Vansittartist' or highly critical approach to the 'German problem', to which Morgenthau and Roosevelt among others subscribed, had specific characteristics. Vansittartists rejected the notion that there was a dichotomy between Nazi leaders and a captured, innocent and terrorized German people. The proponents of this position insisted that Hitler and the Nazis drew on popular ideology and support for their views and aims, in both foreign and racial policy. Thus, the argument ran, there was a deep-seated correspondence between National Socialist ideas and behaviour on the one hand, and popular German aspirations and fears on the other. The role that ordinary Germans played in the creation and maintenance of the Nazi regime lay at the core of the controversy over Vansittartism as well as over the Morgenthau programme that emanated from Washington.

Vansittartists voiced serious reservations about the notion of the 'other Germany' or the 'good Germans' whose existence was not denied but whose political relevance and efficacy was severely doubted. Another characteristic of Vansittartism was the belief that the excesses of

National Socialism had their roots in the cultural and political traditions that had developed since German unification. Militarism and authoritarianism stemmed from the discontent and insecurity that had surfaced throughout Germany's past. In short, it was a national characteristic and not an exceptional chapter of its history.

The metaphor of a disease was broadly used in America's wartime discourse to describe the alien ideology of National Socialism and to indicate both the repulsive nature of German society and politics as well as their curability.[20] The proponents of a harshly critical view of the Germans, such as Morgenthau and other so-called Vansittartists, also subscribed to the idea of national psychopathy which, however deeply rooted, had to be and could be cured. They utterly rejected the idea that German behaviour was inherent, the result of unalterably racially or nationally determined characteristics.

In the late 1950s the German historian Günter Moltmann warned that Morgenthau's more extreme measures should not cloud our vision of his underlying intent: securing a lasting peace, not wreaking revenge on the Germans. He rejected the claim that Morgenthau had developed a 'program of hate and revenge' as an 'unjustified simplification' and pointed to Morgenthau's book *Germany Is Our Problem* for the sincerity of the politician's peaceful intentions.[21] Indeed, both Morgenthau's diaries and his book provide ample evidence for the Secretary's belief that the Germans had to be and could be reformed.[22]

In 1976 the American historian Warren Kimball offered the first comprehensive account of the Morgenthau Plan. He emphasized that 'this plan aimed at psychological and social reform' – yet he went on to explain that Morgenthau sought to accomplish this reform 'by destroying Germany both as a state and as an industrial power'. Only when the author discussed Morgenthau's motives, did he observe that the Secretary 'was a very sensitive and humane man' who did not intend 'to starve the German people'. Instead Kimball pointed to Morgenthau's Jeffersonian belief 'that reestablished contact with the land would turn the Germans into good, honest, democratic yeomen farmers'.[23] Kimball's account was the first to open a vista on the fundamental re-education effort that Morgenthau's ideas implied.

This rehabilitation was echoed in other work and deserves closer attention. The one aspect that is always cited as the most radical feature of Morgenthau's ideas, the 'complete elimination of German industry' or, put differently, the complete agrarianization of Germany, is an unfounded exaggeration of his proposals.[24] Morgenthau favoured in varying degrees the closing of plants and the destruction of mines in the Ruhr and Saar area. But these plans applied neither to all of Germany nor to its entire industry.[25] Light industry was always excluded. In a response to Stimson's sharp criticism of the Treasury memoranda, Morgenthau responded in late September 1944 by admitting to a programme that 'would effectively black out Germany's industrial war potential'. This had always been his central intention. He went on to clarify that 'the purpose of the program is not, however, to arrest Germany's economic development but to ensure that it is channelized along lines of fruitful peacetime pursuits'.[26]

In a larger study that explores the American imagination of the cultural 'other', Georg Schmundt-Thomas has offered a stimulating interpretation of Morgenthau's strategy. He sees it as a facet of an 'agrarian nostalgia'. Morgenthau's plans for Germany, he has claimed, constituted part of a New Deal effort to remake Germany in the image of an ideal self. The defeated enemy, seen as 'a practical laboratory for [the New Dealers'] plans for industrial reorganization', thus was to become 'an object lesson in the politically redemptive power of trustbusting'.[27] The author has shown 'how the tradition of Populist protest against industrial capitalism shaped the American approach to the problem of German reconstruction'.[28]

Schmundt-Thomas' exposition elucidates two important aspects of Morgenthau's ideas that further demonstrate how the charges of revenge and destruction miss Morgenthau's intent. As shown in Greiner's account, too, Morgenthau and his 'Treasury boys' were not alone in their vision of a radically reconstructed Germany which was to be not just deprived of, but liberated from the grip of cartels and the ulcer of the reactionary elites that controlled them. Schmundt-Thomas shows how Morgenthau's ideas were rooted in a particular strand of New Deal ideology. Accordingly, the intent behind Morgenthau's programme for Germany was not a 'Carthaginian peace' amounting to destruction for its own sake. Instead it aimed at a most fundamental restructuring of the material foundations of German society in order to accomplish Germany's democratization and thereby re-education.

Both Greiner and Schmundt-Thomas place Morgenthau's partial de-industrialization scheme for post-war Germany in the context of an American tradition of trust-busting and Jeffersonian democracy. But Schmundt-Thomas sees in Morgenthau's rhetoric of 'industrial discontent' only an 'imaginary return ... to the mythical origins of the erstwhile agrarian American republic'.[29] From this perspective he fails to understand that the anti-cartel ideology had actual consequences for American policy towards the Third Reich long before August 1944 and subsequently continued to shape American occupation policy.[30] This story, and Morgenthau's role in it, has been told in greater detail by Greiner who summarized the Roosevelt administration's economic warfare against German cartels – 'legally the most comprehensive anti-trust campaign in American history'.[31] Even more specific is Greiner's account of the efforts after the war to break up German cartels. The campaign against cartels was undertaken on the express assumption that they had underpinned the cooperation between German industry and the military, thus enabling Hitler to prepare for war and his ruthless occupation policy and genocide. Greiner has demonstrated that the Treasury Department generated a network of ideas that specifically linked Germany's financial and industrial structure to its totalitarian policies.[32]

A common assumption in interpreting the meaning of the Treasury programme has been to present it as unique – and uniquely harsh – within the American context. Yet from the very beginning historians have also noted that all the Treasury measures formed an integral part of the Allied discussions of post-war aims for the preceding two years. They included the dismemberment plans, the summary executions of the main war criminals, demilitarization and re-education. Morgenthau's claim to originality thus lay in his drastic proposals for economic regulation. Yet recent historiography has identified the larger context in which American liberals, particularly on the Left, framed the issue of the role played by Germany's heavy industry and its cartels. For them Germany's 'total war' effort flowed from these conditions. Morgenthau had hardly been alone in his conclusion that 'the sword of Mars is forged in Vulcan's smithy'. Other liberals shared his view that economic policy had been an important tool in Germany's aggression and that any effective security measure had to take this into consideration.[33]

The German historian Wilfried Mausbach has offered the most recent and comprehensive study on the evolution of American economic post-war planning for Germany from the late stages of the war through the early occupation period, that is from Morgenthau's intervention to the emergence of the Marshall Plan. Mausbach's work shows that the Treasury initiative had not been the temporary aberration in administrative planning that historians have previously deplored.[34] The author is the first to demonstrate convincingly that the Morgenthau programme arose from a broader context of ideas that emphasized the linkage between international security and a fundamental restructuring of the German economy. The Treasury proposals caused a dramatic shift in America's conceptualization of reparations policy. Morgenthau argued vehemently against conventional reparations which, he believed, served as a guarantee for Germany's uncurbed economic reconstruction and resurgence.[35] He urged instead 'restitution' to Germany's devastated neighbours and victims through a transfer of dismantled German plants. This process would at the same time accomplish a substantial portion of his de-industrialization scheme.[36]

Mausbach shows how Morgenthau's intervention marked the beginning of an intricate process of negotiations between different

government departments. This bargaining process resulted in a coherent economic policy programme for Germany by the spring of 1945.
Morgenthau did not prevail with his original, radical plans of completely
eliminating Germany's heavy industry. But, Mausbach argues, Roosevelt clearly favoured the idea of a radical restructuring of Germany's
economy. Thus Morgenthau's original and lasting contribution to post-
war policies in economic terms was the instrumentalization of the
reparations policy for security purposes. The fundamental change that
Morgenthau had initiated with his proposals survived subsequent US
reparations and occupation policy.[37]

As a historian who had to work from published sources, Moltmann
regretted that there had not been an 'official publication of the text'
submitted by Morgenthau. This comment highlighted another common
misunderstanding about Morgenthau's initiative. As there was no one
single Morgenthau Plan, it followed that there could be no official
version of it. Even Moltmann noted that the Quebec memorandum,
signed on 15 September 1944 by Roosevelt and Winston Churchill,
was only a pale copy of the earlier Treasury proposals. It was both
more drastic in its formulation – it was the only text that contained
the formula of a 'country primarily agricultural and pastoral in its
character' – and less comprehensive than the original Treasury sub-
missions.[38] The fact that no plan that Morgenthau submitted ever
became official policy at any point is as important to emphasize as the
fact that the Secretary himself never intended it to be more than a
proposal for the cabinet and the President. Thus he refused to be
swayed by his staff's objections to some of his more radical ideas and
counselled them: 'Let someone else water it down.' From the internal
deliberations within the Treasury it becomes clear that Morgenthau
fully grasped the fact that he was at various points submitting a programme with maximum measures. He fully intended that those
measures would undergo changes and compromises in the process of
administrative decision-making.[39]

Morgenthau knew what he was doing and his strategy has been too
often misunderstood. John Snell, for example, agrees with much of
the memoir and secondary literature and has censored Morgenthau
for overstepping his competence when he intervened and derailed the
'experts'' post-war planning for Germany, just to bring it into line
with the less enlightened temper of the times.[40] Snell's argument ignores
the substantial preceding activity of the Treasury with respect to Nazi
Germany. What is often dismissed as Morgenthau's emotional reaction
– as opposed to Stimson's sober thinking – was in fact rooted in a
decade of administrative experience in dealing with the enemy.

Bernd Greiner has provided us with the best summary thus far of
this prelude to the 1944 intervention. It began with the Treasury

joining the interdepartmental effort against Germany's cartel policy and economic warfare.[41] The Treasury's thinking was dramatically sharpened by the confirmed reports of Germany's policy of systematically murdering Europe's Jews.[42] Henry Morgenthau Jr. was the only cabinet-level member of the Roosevelt administration who grasped the news of the genocide and who actively worked towards saving refugees, overwhelmingly but not exclusively Jews, from their fate in Nazi occupied Europe. Neither his upbringing nor his social background had prepared him for taking such a determined stand as a defender of Jews. Morgenthau's son commented: 'Like most of the Jews who wielded New Deal power and had ready access to the president, my father had cautiously avoided Jewish issues.'[43] What propelled him to action was a combination of taking the news of the Holocaust seriously – a rare response among his compatriots and colleagues – and of being shocked by the incredible callousness and indifference in certain quarters of the State Department which deliberately ruined almost all chances for rescue operations.

While the thinking of the Secretaries of State and War was guided by tradition, pragmatism and practicality, Morgenthau did not feel confined by such rules of diplomatic etiquette when basic principles of humanitarianism and justice were at stake.[44] In all accounts of the administration's response to the news of the Holocaust, Morgenthau, prompted by the investigations and reports of his two assistants, Josiah E. Dubois and John Pehle, emerges as the one cabinet member who took the news seriously. He tried to move the President to do the same.[45] In the process the Secretary of the Treasury came to understand two important things. One was the fact that the nature of the German war crimes was so unbelievable that few could grasp the dimensions of the horror. Genocide on such scale was simply inconceivable. The other painful insight related to the many missed opportunities for rescuing Jews from their fate due to disregard and obstruction within the administration. The particularly shocking role of the State Department was set out in the Treasury staff 'Report to the Secretary of the Acquiescence of this Government in the Murder of the Jews' which stated that Hull's department was 'guilty not only of gross procrastination and wilful failure to act, but even of wilful attempts to prevent action from being taken to rescue Jews from Hitler'.[46] The Treasury's daunting struggle against administrative inaction would prove largely futile and by late summer 1944 only the military solution promised relief. But this experience would set an important precedent for the Secretary's effort to have his government and its Allies draw dramatic conclusions about Germany's world-wide aggression, to seek justice for its victims and to provide for adequate safeguards against its re-emergence as a military power.[47]

Closely related to Morgenthau's knowledge of the Holocaust and his post-war hopes for Germany was his department's initiative regarding the punishment of war criminals. In the early Treasury drafts for post-war Germany, Morgenthau proposed summary execution of the main war criminals. Secretary of War Stimson, on the other hand, was concerned that there was a solid and unassailable legal basis for war-crimes trials.[48] In early deliberations Stimson professed to see no chance of trying and convicting Germans responsible for 'excesses committed within Germany' which included the persecution and murder of Jews. Such a procedure would be as illegal as the attempt by 'any foreign court ... to try those who were guilty of, or condoned, lynching in our own country'.[49] This assessment corresponded with the plans of the United Nations War Crimes Commission in London, which did not provide for prosecution and punishment of persons guilty of atrocities against Jews of Axis nationality.[50] Morgenthau forcefully objected to the experts' argument that 'they had been unable to locate a "legal theory" to support the punishment of Germans for murdering Axis Jews'.[51] Pressure from the Treasury Department contributed to a reconsideration of this matter and eventually the ingenious legal construction of a 'conspiracy' charge was found which allowed for a broader indictment.

Finally, what did Morgenthau's Jewishness have to do with his views of Germany? The essential criterion for compassion with the victims of the genocide was not ethnic or religious affiliation but a particular kind of responsiveness, a readiness to believe the unbelievable.[52] Explaining Morgenthau's concern and initiative by his ethnic or religious background implies that conscience and compassion are bound to ethnic affiliation – which, fortunately, they are not. If anything, Morgenthau's Jewishness was not a motivating factor but an impediment. Leonard Dinnerstein has documented in numerous publications the prevailing atmosphere of anti-Semitism in American society of the 1930s and 1940s.[53] The predicament of many American Jews, reluctant to speak out publicly on behalf of their fellow Jews in Europe due to anti-Semitic charges of 'special interests' and 'manipulation', is omnipresent in the sources. It is also captured in Morgenthau's exasperated reaction at a particularly difficult moment in his department's rescue efforts: 'Just because I am a Jew, why shouldn't I look after the Jews, or the Catholics, or the Armenians?'[54] The issue was not that Morgenthau's reaction was personally understandable because he was a Jew; it was understandable and rational because he understood something about the German problem that others did not.

Morgenthau's sensitivities contrast to those of Secretary of War Stimson. Their respective proposals for post-war treatment of Germany were motivated by the same overriding aims: the prevention of World

War III, security against Germany and peace overall. Stimson wrote to President Roosevelt at the height of the row over the cabinet's conflicting proposals for Germany: 'Our discussions relate to a matter of method entirely, our objective is the same. It is not a question of a soft treatment of Germany or a harsh treatment of Germany.'[55] His opponent in this debate, Henry Morgenthau, concurred with his colleague's rejection of the false dichotomy of 'hard' versus 'soft' peace. However, he attributed a greater importance to the conflict over 'methods'.[56] Morgenthau was probably right in his insistence on their differences. Behind their conflicting methods emerged a significantly different image of National Socialism and the causes of the war.[57]

Morgenthau was deeply shocked when during a cabinet debate over the Treasury plans his colleague from the War Department voiced the belief that 'we can't solve the German problem except through Christianity and kindness'.[58] To Morgenthau and his staff it seemed that Stimson had not fully grasped the nature of the war the Germans were waging against the rest of the world, nor the determination with which they proceeded to carry out genocide. Indeed, Stimson had shown throughout the war a remarkable refusal to acknowledge the Nazis' deadly racism.[59] At the height of the domestic outrage over the American military deal with the fascist Admiral François Darlan in late 1942, the Secretary of War proceeded to enlighten the President regarding 'the very complex situation in North Africa concerning the race problem'. Stimson was almost scornful of Morgenthau's sensitivity. The latter's claim that it 'affected [his] soul' was dismissed in preference for a numerical calculation: namely that 'in French Africa there were twenty-five million Arabs and only three hundred fifty thousand Jews'. Stimson implied that, regardless of the discriminatory laws of the Darlan regime that threatened the lives of Jews, American concern should be with the majority in this case.[60]

Stimson belonged to that school of thought that held that Germany had temporarily been captured and led astray by a band of gangsters, but that the German people themselves were not the problem which the United States policy had to consider or to solve. His approach to Germany corresponded with the thinking that finally prevailed in the State Department. According to this view there was a fundamental difference between Nazi leaders and their henchmen on the one hand, and the masses of German people on the other. Thus Stimson stressed limited and individual culpability and was primarily concerned with Germans' responses to measures they might regard as humiliating, such as partitioning or a restructuring of their economy. In almost daily conversations and memoranda of September 1944 Stimson expressed his fear that Morgenthau's and similar proposals would 'tend through bitterness and suffering [inflicted on the Germans] to breed another war'.[61] While Morgenthau saw his programme as the only effective safeguard against future German aggression, Stimson was equally convinced that his colleague's plans 'as sure as fate will lay the seeds for another war in the next generation'.[62] The State Department and Stimson argued that for any peace settlement to be effective and successful, it should provoke 'a minimum of bitterness'.[63] Stimson agreed with the State Department that 'the assimilation of the German people into the world society of peace-loving nations' served as the 'best guaranty of security, and the least expensive'.[64] The War and State Departments were prepared to see a few clearly culpable Nazi leaders eliminated. With that exception the focus was on rehabilitation and reintegration.

Stimson saw in Morgenthau's plans a purely punitive programme to which he objected in principle. He argued that 'the penalties should be against individuals' whereas Morgenthau urged 'a destruction of the economic structure of Germany'.[65] This juxtaposition points to their different understanding of what lay at the heart of the German menace. Stimson held a number of identifiable Nazis responsible for Germany's aggression and war crimes. Morgenthau, on the other hand, saw Germany's economic structure with its cartels and its heavy industry, as the principle vehicle for German expansionism. If they were left intact Germany would eventually embark on another militarist venture.

Stimson was afraid that basic concepts of American and international law would be violated if the Treasury view prevailed. He wrote:

This country since its very beginning has maintained the fundamental belief that all men, in the long run, have the right to be free human beings and to live in the pursuit of happiness. Under the Atlantic Charter victors and vanquished alike are entitled to freedom from economic want.

Stimson wanted to apply these standards to Germany as a whole. Morgenthau wanted to make sure that they applied to Germany's victims.[66]

Morgenthau's relentless efforts to combat the German threat through economic restrictions and de-Nazification measures serve to remind that neither the outcome of the war nor the mechanism for guaranteeing against future German aggression after its military defeat were clear or certain. Today we take the ultimate achievement of the post-war efforts in pacifying Germany for granted – the wartime planners could not. Their fears and worries are not ours. It seems at times difficult for us to recall the urgency of these problems. Analysis of America's wartime debates on Germany reveals quite clearly that Morgenthau's proposals were not an aberration, were not out of line with other contemporary ideas on how to solve the German problem, and were not motivated by revenge.

A close reading of the evidence shows that there were blind spots on all sides. There is no evidence that Stimson was deeply disturbed by or even understood the Holocaust. Morgenthau, who was profoundly touched by the Shoah, did not feel obliged to grapple with the question of who bore direct responsibility for these crimes. Similarly, he did not concern himself with the incidence or extent of anti-Nazi sentiment in Germany and with evidence of surviving democratic elements in Germany.

It has been a tradition in the secondary literature on American wartime planning for Germany to criticize the absence of a coherent plan for post-war Germany by the end of the war. I would like to shift the emphasis of this argument, not to dispute the diversity, but rather to reinterpret it as something positive. The lack of fixed solutions and the multitude of interpretations and plans testify to the procedure of a democratic society and its sincere efforts to understand the problem posed by the enemy nation. This open mind also provided a chance for pragmatism to prevail over doctrine in the post-war era.

Morgenthau's voice, rising from a rare understanding of the Germans' most horrible crimes, was one of justice with regard to Germany's victims. Stimson's call for 'Christian charity', as troublesome as it was in its lack of understanding, was equally important in holding out the prospects of reconciliation with the enemy. These two positions, representative of similar ones among the American people and their government, indicate why no uniform position was possible or even desirable. They also point to the moral dilemma of doing justice to both the enemy people and their victims. This American ambiguity provided the post-war Germans with a unique opportunity to engage in both spiritual and physical reconstruction.

Notes

1. Herbert G. Nicholas (ed.), *Washington Despatches, 1941–1945: Weekly Political Reports from the British Embassy* (Chicago, 1981), 426. The following arguments are based on my research for a dissertation on American wartime interpretations of National Socialism.

2. Two recent studies provide a suitable opportunity to review the legend of the Morgentahau Plan. See Bernd Greiner, *Die Morgenthau-Legende: Zur Geschichte eines umstrittenen Plans* (Hamburg, 1995) and Wilfried Mausbach, *Zwischen Morgenthau und Marshall: Das wirtschaftspolitische Deutschlandkonzept der USA, 1944–47* (Düsseldorf, 1996).

3. Michaela Hönicke, 'Das nationalsozialistische Deutschland und die

Vereinigten Staaten von Amerika (1933–1945)' in Klaus Larres and Tor-
sten Oppelland (eds), *Deutschland und die USA im 20. Jahrhundert:
Geschichte der politischen Beziehungen* (Darmstadt, 1997), 62–94 and Hönicke, '"Know Your Enemy": American Wartime Images of Germany,
1942/43', in Ragnhild Fiebig-von Hase and Ursula Lehmkuhl (eds), *Enemy
Images in American History* (Providence, 1997), 231–78.

4. Marie-Luise Goldbach (ed.), *Dokumente zur Deutschlandpolitik*, Series 1, 2
and 4 (Frankfurt, 1986).

5. Petra Marquardt-Bigman, *Amerikanische Geheimdienstanalysen über
Deutschland, 1942–49* (Munich, 1995).

6. William Reitzel, Morton A. Kaplan and Constance G. Coblenz, *U.S.
Foreign Policy, 1945–55* (Washington, 1956), 59.

7. Horace M. Kallen in the panel discussion 'What Shall We Do With
Germany?', *Saturday Review of Literature*, 26 (29 May 1943), 4.

8. Greiner, *Legende*, 14–28.

9. Entry of 16/17 September 1944, Henry L. Stimson Diary, Yale University
Library, Reel 9, vol. 48, 82 [hereafter cited as Stimson Diary].

10. Cordell Hull, *The Memoirs of Cordell Hull*, vol. 2 (New York, 1948), 1606.
For his initial reaction to Morgenthau's plans see entry of 5 September
1944, *Stimson Diary*, 35.

11. Norman M. Littell, *My Roosevelt Years* (Seattle, 1987), 309.

12. Memorandum for the President, 15 September 1944, Stimson Diary, 84.

13. Howard Watson Ambruster, *Treason's Peace: German Dyes and American
Dupes* (New York, 1947), 387ff.

14. 'Public Attitudes on Foreign Policy: Morgenthau', 18 October 1944,
Office of Public Opinion Studies (OPOS), RG 59, Box 1, National
Archives.

15. John H. Backer, *Priming the German Economy: American Occupational
Policies, 1945–48* (Durham, NC, 1971), 16.

16. Text of Address by Governor Dewey at rally, *New York Times*, 5 November
1944.

17. John L. Gaddis, *The United States and the Origins of the Cold War* (New
York, 1972), 121; Detlef Junker, *Kampf um die Weltmacht: Die USA und
das Dritte Reich, 1933–1945* (Düsseldorf, 1988) 43ff. Klaus-Dietmar
Henke, *Die Amerikanische Besetzung Deutschlands* (Munich, 1995), 71ff.

18. See Walter Dorn, 'The Debate Over American Occupation Policy in
Germany in 1944/45', *Political Science Quarterly*, 72 (December 1957),
481–501; John L. Snell, *Wartime Origins of the East-West Dilemma over
Germany* (New Orleans, 1959), 8–13 and 75. See also Günter Moltmann,
*Amerikas Deutschlandpolitik im Zweiten Weltkrieg: Kriegs- und Friedensziele,
1941–1945* (Heidelberg, 1959), 13, 21.

19. Lord Vansittart, *Lessons of My Life* (London, 1943), 30.

20. The ambivalence of that view was best expressed in the psychological
approach to national identity that was fashionable at the time. It combined
the notion of a 'patient' to be healed with the idea of a deeply rooted
character deformation.

21. Moltmann, *Amerikas Deutschlandpolitik*, 10, 134ff.

22. Conference call, 28 August 1944, in US Senate, Committee on the

Judiciary, *Morgenthau Diary*, vol. 1 (Washington, 1967), 448, 461ff. 485 [hereafter cited as *Morgenthau Diary*]; Henry Morgenthau Jr., *Germany Is Our Problem* (New York, 1945), vol. 2, 104. See also address 'Germany and Education', 11 November 1945, Papers of Henry Morgenthau, Box 386, FDRL.

23. Warren F. Kimball, *Swords or Ploughshares? The Morgenthau Plan for Defeated Nazi Germany, 1943–46* (Philadelphia, 1976), 4, 25ff.

24. Moltmann, *Amerikas Deutschlandpolitik*, 21.

25. Mausbach, *Zwischen Morgenthau und Marshall*, 62, 75.

26. Memorandum for the President [no date], *Morgenthau Diary*, vol.1, 631ff.

27. Georg Schmundt-Thomas, 'America's Germany: National Self and Cultural Other After World War II', (Ph.D. dissertation, Northwestern University, 1992), 163.

28. Schmundt-Thomas, 'America's Germany', 165.

29. Schmundt-Thomas, 'America's Germany', 183.

30. Schmundt-Thomas, 'America's Germany', 164, 198.

31. Greiner, *Legende*, 35.

32. Greiner, *Legende*, 238–391; see also Schmundt-Thomas, 'America's Germany', 190ff. Henry Morgenthau III further helps our understanding of his father's perspective on deindustrialization plans and Jeffersonian ideology by describing his early experience as a farmer. See Henry Morgenthau III, *Mostly Morgenthaus: A Family History* (New York, 1991), 243ff.

33. Greiner, *Legende*, 32–46, 171; Mausbach, *Zwischen Morgenthau und Marshall*, 31ff., 76, 369.

34. Moltmann, *Amerikas Deutschlandpolitik*, 133; John Gimbel, *The American Occupation of Germany. Politics and the Military, 1945–1949* (Stanford, 1968), xi; Wolfgang Krieger, *General Lucius D. Clay und die amerikanische Deutschlandpolitik, 1945–49* (Stuttgart, 1987), 38ff.

35. Section 2, 'Reparations Mean A Powerful Germany', in US Department of State, *Foreign Relations of the United States: the Conference at Quebec, 1944* (Washington, DC, 1972), 131ff.

36. Mausbach, *Zwischen Morgenthau und Marshall*, 26ff and 62ff.

37. Mausbach, *Zwischen Morgenthau und Marshall*, 72, 102–9; Greiner, *Legende*, 254–334.

38. Günter Moltmann, 'Der Morgenthau-Plan als historisches Problem', *Wehrwissenschaftliche Rundschau*, 5 (1955), 15–32; Mausbach, *Zwischen Morgenthau und Marshall*, 55–66.

39. *Morgenthau Diary*, vol. 1, 448, 561, 593, 596ff.

40. Snell, *Origins*, 64.

41. Greiner, *Legende*, 31–46.

42. Greiner, *Legende*, 98–146.

43. Morgenthau III, *Mostly Morgenthaus*, xvi, xix, 152–71, 322ff.

44. Henry Morgenthau Jr., 'The Morgenthau Diaries III: How F.D.R. Fought the Axis', *Collier's*, 11 October 1947, 74, 77. Arthur M. Schlesinger Jr. was the ghost-writer of these articles.

45. Richard Breitman and Alan M. Kraut, *American Refugee Policy and European Jewry, 1933–45* (Bloomington, 1987), 182–201; David S. Wyman, *The*

Abandonment of the Jews: America and the Holocaust, 1941–1945 (New York, 1974), 178–92, 204ff., 239, 313.

46. The report was submitted 13 January 1944, by the Treasury official Josiah E. DuBois Jr. The original is reprinted in David S. Wyman (ed.), *America and the Holocaust*, vol. 8, *Showdown in Washington: State, Treasury, and Congress* (New York, 1990), 238–55.

47. Greiner, *Legende*, 145ff. and Morgenthau III, *Mostly Morgenthaus*, 335.

48. 'Suggested Post-Surrender Program for Germany' 1 and 4 September 1944, *Morgenthau Diary*, vol.1, 464 and 507. William J. Bosch, *Judgement on Nuremberg: American Attitudes toward the Major German War-Crime Trials* (Chapel Hill, 1970), 35ff.

49. Memorandum, 9 September 1944, Stimson Diary, Reel 9, vol. 48, 61; also Earl F. Ziemke, *The US Army in the Occupation of Germany* (Washington, DC, 1990), 171ff.

50. Wyman, *The Abandonment of the Jews*, 257.

51. 'Trial and Punishment of War Criminals: A Summary Statement on Treasury Department Participation in Molding the US Recommendations for Treating War Criminals' [no date], Morgenthau Papers, Box 381, FDRL. Also John Morton Blum, *From the Morgenthau Diaries*, vol. 3, *Years of War, 1941–45* (Boston, 1967), 397ff.

52. For various reactions in and outside governmental circles both in England and the United States to Jan Karski's first-hand reports from the Warsaw Ghetto and Izbica, a looting station and holding camp halfway between Lublin and the extermination camp Belzec, where Karski witnessed horrible scenes, see E. Thomas Wood and Stanislaw M. Jankowski, *Karski: How One Man Tried to Stop the Holocaust* (New York, 1994), 111–32, 187–202.

53. Leonard Dinnerstein, *Antisemitism in America* (New York, 1994), Chapter 7; also Dinnerstein, 'What Should American Jews Have Done to Rescue Their European Brethren?' *Simon Wiesenthal Center Annual* 3, (1986), 277–87. More recently Henry L. Feingold offered his insightful and complex arguments in *Bearing Witness: How America and Its Jews Responded to the Holocaust* (Syracuse, 1995).

54. Staff meeting 18 December 1943, in Wyman (ed.), *Showdown in Washington*, 99.

55. Memorandum for the President, 9 September 1944; memorandum for the President, 15 September 1944, Stimson Diary, Reel 9, vol. 48, 59, 82.

56. First draft of Chapter 2, 'The Real Issues and America's Answer' [not included in final publication of *Germany Is Our Problem*], 5 December 1944, Morgenthau Papers, Box 383.

57. Too much of the contemporary wartime simplification of a Jew acting out of personal bitterness and a more realistic and farsighted Secretary of War found its way into subsequent scholarly accounts without closer examination. See John Gillingham, 'From Morgenthau Plan to Schuman Plan: America and the Organization of Europe' in Jeffry M. Diefendorf, Axel Frohn and Hermann-Josef Rupieper (eds), *American Policy and the Reconstruction of West Germany, 1945–1955* (New York, 1993), 111–33.

58. Group Meeting, 5 September 1944, *Morgenthau Diary*, vol. 1, 527.

59. 17 November 1942, Reel 2, Morgenthau Presidential Diaries, FDRL.

60. Greiner, *Legende*, 137. Stimson's comments also included some other stock arguments of political 'realism' and moral indifference. He stated 'that the race problem there had always existed and was very complex'. Moreover, playing on fear of anti-Semitism at home, he pointed to 'the propaganda which the Axis had been putting out to the effect that if we [the Allies] occupied North Africa, we would turn it over to the Jews'. *Stimson Diary*, 27 December 1942, Reel 8, vol. 41. For Morgenthau's courageous and stubborn reactions see his diary entry of 17 November 1942, *Morgenthau Diary*, vol. 1, 330–32 and entry of 12 November 1942, Reel 2, Morgenthau Presidential Diaries, FDRL.

61. Memoranda, 9, 11, 13 and 15 September 1944, Stimson Diary, Reel 9, vol. 48, 62, 66, 70, 82–5.

62. 16 and 17 September 1944, Stimson Diary, vol. 48, 82.

63. 'The Political Reorganization of Germany, 23 September 1944', printed in Harley Notter, *Postwar Foreign Policy Preparation, 1939–1945* (Washington, 1949), 559. For the evolution of State-Department thinking on these matters see the deliberations and documents reproduced in *Dokumente zur Deutschlandpolitik*, I/2, 212ff., 424, 528, 601, 654 and I/4, 83ff., 111, 124ff., 158ff., 679.

64. US Department of State, *Foreign Relations of the United States: The Conferences at Malta and Yalta 1945* (Washington, DC, 1955), 185.

65. Memorandum of conversation with the President, 25 August 1944, *Stimson Diary*, Reel 9, vol. 48, 29.

66. Memorandum, 15 September 1944, Stimson Diary, Reel 9, vol. 48, 84. See also Treasury group meeting, 13 January 1944, reprinted in Wyman (ed.), *Showdown in Washington*, 225ff.

12

American Post-war Planning: Policy Elites and the New Deal

Leon Gordenker

Even before the United States was drawn into World War II, its political leaders instructed an obscure unit of the national bureaucracy to begin studies of how American foreign policy should be geared to the post-war world. This work, which assumed a greater urgency after the United States entered the war, passed through several upheavals and revisions. It was largely conducted outside of public view. It eventually provided the major features and indispensable details of post-war organizational structures that the President and the Congress discussed only in very general and frequently contradictory terms.

Since planning for the post-war world aimed at creating standing international institutions, the bureaucracy had the intellectual resources required to produce the draft legal documents to which governments eventually agreed. Among these were the United Nations Charter and the Bretton Woods agreements that created the World Bank and the International Monetary Fund. The mortar that held the uneven political bricks together in the post-war constructions was mixed by anonymous, highly informed officials and expert consultants who worked calmly in the midst of the high drama of the ferocious battles of war and the summit meetings of Franklin Roosevelt, Winston Churchill and Josef Stalin. As elected officials and the mass media knew little about this process until it ended, it could be characterized as an affair of an elite drawn from highly qualified specialists.[1] This essay describes this elite and its tasks. It emphasizes the elite's inspiration and use of the rapid institution-building of the New Deal as an influential model for its proposals. Moreover, a central proposition of the New Deal – that government could and should operate positively to cope with social and economic problems – was widely accepted both among those who designed and modulated policies and those who were subject to them.

Some two years before America's entry into the war in December 1941 a handful of instructed officials in the upper echelons of the Roosevelt administration began to think about the shape of the world when the fighting ended.[2] This group, largely in the foreign affairs bureaucracy, was both narrow in social catchment and small in number.

It consisted of a few men (and hardly ever a woman) who drew on the experience of Woodrow Wilson to organize world politics around the League of Nations. Its existence signified that Secretary of State Cordell Hull and some of his leading officials foresaw the need for long-term American involvement in shaping international politics and economics when the war ended. They began their work silently in a political atmosphere that remained coloured by isolationist reaction to Wilson's programme.

President Roosevelt himself gave an important public lead in thinking about the post-war world in late 1940 when he articulated the renowned Four Freedoms.[3] He had personally formulated these concepts. They were obviously consistent with the theory and practice of the New Deal. They also fitted with Hull's unbroken interest in freeing world trade from tariff barriers and other restrictions.[4] The Atlantic Charter, issued by Roosevelt and Winston Churchill that year, was largely consistent with the Four Freedoms and included vague words about international organization.[5]

Soon after the United States entered the war, Hull initiated within the Department of State a systematic, serious effort to prepare for the post-war world.[6] From the outset, discussions centered on plans for multilateral international institutions. Roosevelt gave specific approval to these efforts which after several transmutations ended with draft proposals that were amended and endorsed at the Dumbarton Oaks Conference and served as the basis for the inaugural meeting of the United Nations, convened in San Francisco in April 1945. Well before the planners reached their conclusions, Roosevelt abandoned any conventional notions of directing world politics by the victorious great powers – the Four Policemen in his formulation. Rather, he and the planners opted for multilateral, inter-governmental structures for decision-making about maintaining peace and promoting the general welfare. These structures would be based on constitutional documents that had the force of law and accorded with international legal practice.[7]

The actual post-war planning process took place largely in secret.[8] The initial discussion was centred in an Advisory Committee on Problems of Foreign Relations, located in the State Department in 1939. The Committee consisted mainly of State Department officials whose work was kept within bureau files. A fortnight after American entry into the war, Roosevelt approved the creation of a successor body, the Advisory Committee on Post-war Foreign Policy. Its instructions were broad and general. In the background were the general assumptions that the League of Nations had failed, that referring to it would immediately stir storms of opposition and that it should not be revived. Nevertheless, the planners studied it deeply and tried to draw lessons from the earlier experience.[9]

The new committee, chaired by the Secretary of State, met formally in February 1942. Directed by State Department personnel, at first it involved only senior governmental officials with roles in foreign affairs. Later it included a careful selection of members of Congress, a handful of interest groups, such as the Council on Foreign Relations, and military personnel. The committee had practically nothing to do with the actual conduct of the war except through indirect input into wartime conferences of governmental heads, such as those at Teheran and Yalta. These conferences did consider post-war plans. Because of the sheer complexity of the undertaking, Churchill and Roosevelt relied heavily on the planners in their respective bureaucracies where the issues had been refined and sharpened. Problems of international organization did not lend themselves to instinctive political answers in the way that, say, issues of territory did.

To understand how the broad lines of policy were adopted and translated into specific institutions, the manoeuvres and deliberations at the bureaucratic level must be surveyed. In the normal workings of government in the United States, this process usually gives birth early on to inter-departmental committees served by experts from within or outside the permanent bureaucracies. Post-war planning followed this pattern. The Advisory Committee on Post-war Foreign Policy promptly established six subcommittees and some of these set up further specialized groups. This expanding structure heralded the entry to the planning process of representatives of bureaucracies whose brief lay in domestic economic and social foci, not foreign relations. At the same time, military interests were represented. Some interest groups, such as the League of Nations Association and the labour movement, were also involved. With the exception of the congressional representation, none of them enjoyed public recognition. All of them occupied positions in the bureaucratic hierarchy or had political connections that gave weight to their expert counsel. It was thought vital to have no public leaks, so they were sworn to silence.

The procedures, deliberations and structures that evolved from the Advisory Committee were shaped in part by the internecine quarrels of Cordell Hull and Sumner Welles and in part by the momentum generated by the major international conferences that began in 1943. These conferences, including those held at Hot Springs, Bretton Woods, and Dumbarton Oaks, planned and created the UN Relief and Rehabilitation Administration (UNRRA), the Food and Agriculture Organization, the International Monetary Fund and the World Bank. However, the preparatory deliberations remained confined to a small, hand-picked group of experienced public servants. The State Department's planning apparatus, now called the Policy Committee and the Post-war Programs Committee, was under the leadership of the economist Leo Pasvolsky, who was Hull's *homme de confiance*. He supervized a handful of experienced diplomats drawn from the foreign service, itself an elite defined by advanced education, restricted entry and privileged knowledge. Pasvolsky did draw on other experts, around one hundred of them, but they too were drawn mainly from his own department or from the top universities.[10]

Only after the Dumbarton Oaks conversations in 1944 was an attempt made by the State Department to engage broad public attention to the specific results of these planning deliberations.[11] It was helped by the existence of organized interest groups, such as the League of Nations Association and the Commission to Study the Organization of the Peace, which hitherto had served only to provide back-channels of information and had stimulated general, rather vague discussion on the shape of the post-war world. In addition, the activities of the internationalist-minded politicians, such as Wendell Willkie and Henry Wallace, provided extra yeast for the deliberations that were eventually to envelop a broadened constituency.

The other major forum of debate on post-war institutions was the United States Senate. While it debated the matter in 1943 and 1944 it never did so in the context of specific proposals by the President or Secretary of State. Rather the impetus came from coalitions of senators who sought the adoption of overall normative recommendations. The war itself had stilled the voices of isolationist and nationalist organizations prominent in the pre-war foreign policy arenas. What was left of their public positions was still well represented in Congress, much to the chagrin of Hull and Roosevelt. The debate in Congress on resolutions setting out the broad, rather abstract principles of the desired shape of the post-war world galvanized that narrow part of the electorate that was interested in this aspect of foreign policy.[12]

Once the Dumbarton Oaks talks had finished, the State Department went public. It allowed its personnel to conduct off-the-record talks with interested groups and began what can be justifiably called a propaganda campaign. It encouraged various publications and even commissioned a film that came to be widely viewed. Its officers travelled around the country to speak about official post-war plans. Its new public relations programme was headed by a renowned New Dealer, the poet Archibald McLeish, whose New Deal credentials had been established in drafting speeches for the President. This public effort served to sharpen Congress's views. Given the efforts that had gone into the planning process, Congress yielded somewhat by leaning to the administration for leadership and guidance in the organization of post-war collective security.

A closer look at the administration's planning process makes clear both its elite nature and its New Deal approach. The formation of governmental policy necessarily rests in the hands of elites – that is, of persons who by training, experience and vocation lead polities. As most governments, most of the time, deal with domestic issues and operations, it follows that foreign policy and its application engages only a narrow segment of the policy and administering elite. Discussions involving broader, undifferentiated publics take place in legislatures, in the mass media and in various citizens' groups, including churches, vocational and business associations, and in casual meetings.

The New Deal approach characteristically favoured creating new large-scale state institutions to cope with social problems. The new agencies were reformist, experimental and modernizing, and contrasted with the more conventional approach of giving new instructions to old bureaucracies. New Deal institutions, moreover, had no detailed mandates but rather structures and processes that were expected to define further regulations and programmes in consultation with those affected. Before giving the lead on new institutions, President Roosevelt usually had access to high-grade technical advice, especially from outstanding university researchers and lawyers. Above all, the New Deal agencies were inspired by the belief that a dose of planning and direction would be needed to realize new social goals.

The shaping of the post-war planning process has to be understood in the context of the procedure of government bureaucracy. Planners have to work within defined briefs. They start with broad statements of policy, such as the Four Freedoms address by Roosevelt, or the United Nations Declaration of 1 January 1942. In these particular instances, persons with senior governmental responsibilities and their staff paid attention to the detailed implications, alternatives and applications of policy. Even though what is said in the Congress and especially the Senate influences the atmosphere in which policy is developed by the President and the bureaucracy, the usual congressional agenda hardly ever centres mainly on foreign affairs. During the war, the immediate issues related to the military effort took precedence over what necessarily could be only general statements of attitude about the post-war world. There was little meat in them for the legislative mill. At best, they only indirectly affected the atmosphere in which specific proposals were prepared.

The planners' deliberations are also shaped by their own experiences and background. In the United States, the pre-New Deal foreign policy elite characteristically came from well-to-do circles that kept strong identification with the boarding schools, top-flight private universities of the East Coast and its financial community.[13] They were protected by deference. One study has estimated there were only 1,000 Americans who had any more than superficial knowledge of the conduct of foreign affairs.[14] As the New Deal concentrated on domestic issues, many bright new recruits who did not enjoy the privileges of birth flocked to the new agencies that dealt with social reform. They left foreign affairs mainly to the existing elites. Old networks continued. Members of the foreign policy elite often had known each other since their school days. This is illustrated by the careers of such diplomats as Joseph Grew, William Bullitt, Sumner Welles, and by such top political-level officials as Dean Acheson, James Forrestal and John Foster Dulles.

The original membership of the Advisory Committee on Foreign Policy shows the expected elite accent. Hull, who was always in fragile health, in fact yielded the leadership to Welles, and later, when the agenda had been shaped, in a simmering quarrel wrested it back.[15] Welles had the background and credentials of the foreign policy elite and held views about international organization that did not essentially clash with those of Hull. Their quarrel had more to do with personal antagonism and the fact that FDR preferred to consult more closely with Welles on matters of planning. This aggravated Hull's well-known irritation with the President's cavalier manner of dealing with the State Department and its head.

Other members of the Advisory Committee on Foreign Policy who could be identified with the old foreign policy elite were Norman Davis, President of the Council on Foreign Relations, erstwhile Under Secretary of State and head of the American Red Cross; Acheson, then Assistant Secretary of State and formerly of the Treasury; Isaiah Bowman, president of Johns Hopkins University who had advised Wilson on self-determination; Hamilton Fish Armstrong, editor of *Foreign Affairs*, the influential journal of the Council on Foreign Relations; Green H. Hackworth, legal adviser of the Department of State whose office had strong connections with the few leading law schools that bothered with serious international law courses; and Anne O'Hare McCormick, the well-connected foreign affairs columnist of the *New York Times*. These people matched other members of the Advisory Committee who had less identification with the State Department hierarchy and more affinity for domestic politics and the New Deal. These included Benjamin V. Cohen, lawyer and speech writer for Roosevelt; Adolf A. Berle Jr., Assistant Secretary of State and former Columbia University law professor, who had a close affiliation with Roosevelt from early in the New Deal; Leo Pasvolsky, Hull's increasingly influential spokesman for post-war planning; and Myron Taylor, a Chicago steel executive who had been Roosevelt's special envoy to the Vatican. The last two members were Herbert Feis, the economic adviser in the State Department and Harry C. Hawkins, who dealt with commercial policy. None of them was then openly identified with any defined pattern of post-war organization. None of them had been household names in the futile efforts to connect the United States with the work of the League of Nations.

The appointees to the Advisory Committee held compatible views of how to approach the post-war world, irrespective of their individual backgrounds. The senior policy sources, whether or not they had emerged with the New Deal, harmonized with those members of the old foreign policy elite who were strongly aware of the record of the League of Nations. Moreover, their diplomatic experience necessarily involved the assumption that governments were the basis of relations among states. Thus whether or not they had reformist or experimental tendencies, they had observed and worked with large-scale, society-wide institutions. They were familiar with and tended to favour the use of government institutions in treating the economic depression of the 1930s and to accomplish social goals. Most had been staunch advocates of the New Deal and many had played a role in setting it up the New Deal, together with the broad new public law that underpinned it. Some also had direct knowledge of international law which necessarily would be relevant to post-war organization.

Those with most direct New Deal experience were mainly officials or else appointees of the President. They did not come from the electoral arena nor from popular social movements, such as the labour unions or the farmers' interest groups. They were all experienced in bureaucratic politics in Washington.

The composition of the Advisory Committee was telling. Significant sectors of public life were excluded. Initially there was no military representation. Nor was there representation for the many foreign policy interest groups that had been so active before America's entry into the war. Only insiders, particularly the Council on Foreign Relations, participated. Nobody from Congress migrated to this list.[16]

Exclusivity was the hallmark. From the beginning, all the planning exercises took place outside the public eye and in confidential sessions. If leaks from the inner sanctum did occur, they would drip, at least in the first instance, only into the safety of privileged groups who were privy to the discussions anyway. Only later would they reach a broader public.

In fact, the Advisory Committee met in plenary session only four times. By its last meeting in the spring of 1942, Hull had moved to broaden its reach. Membership of succeeding committees came to include five senators, three members of the House of Representatives, two representatives from the labour unions, three senior military officers, one representative from the Library of Congress, four representatives from wartime agencies and more officials from the Department of State. While this expansion was partly *pro forma*, the membership reflected the political practicalities of giving specific plans a chance to win general endorsement. Yet it came so late in the planning process that the new recruits were confronted with existing agreements and plans formulated by the foreign policy elite and their counterparts from departments only peripherally concerned with foreign affairs.

The real work proceeded in subcommittees until the summer of 1943 and then continued in the Informal Political Agenda Group that Hull had set up to replace the original committee. The briefs of these subcommittees were broad, covering much of the subject matter that concerns any modern government. The Informal Political Agenda, formally chaired by Hull, met seventy times before it finished the American draft for the Dumbarton Oaks Conference.[17]

The procedures of the Agenda Group and the assumptions of its membership reflected the New Deal pattern. They were pragmatic and they built on the experience of government in the 1930s. 'The emphasis', Anne-Marie Burley has commented, 'was on pragmatic solutions to concrete problems rather than on implementing any grand theoretical design.'[18] The tempo of deliberation and the sense of vision was consistent with the New Deal practice of practical improvisation. It did not aim at 'building a world order out of idealism'. Of necessity, the specialized agendas of the subcommittees required advice from more varied professional sources than those of the plenary committees. The subcommittees included officials from the departments of government, such as Agriculture, Commerce, Labor, Treasury, and some of the New Deal agencies. Whatever their backgrounds, their professional activities brought them into the network and vortex of the policy elite. Together and as individuals they had experience and expertise in constructing governmental mechanisms to cope with issues posed by the attitude of a socially-inclined government.[19]

Moreover, it was immediately apparent that planning had to be fully grounded in expert knowledge. Consequently, each subcommittee had access to experts, many of them from universities and from law and generally leaders in their fields. They were brought to Washington to serve as consultants on specific studies undertaken. Their work became an important source of specific ideas. This advisory structure was overseen by Pasvolsky and his close associate, Harley Notter, who had a strong hand in producing drafts and later wrote the valuable official chronicle of the entire effort.

A few of the advisers had exhaustively studied the work of the League of Nations and its tributaries, usually as professors of international law.[20] It is doubtful that any had been at the Versailles Conference. A handful had some role in specific geographical and interest groups or in international organizations, such as the Commission to Study the Organization of the Peace and the Carnegie

Endowment for International Peace. However, one of this group, Clark Eichelberger of the League of Nations Association, was associated as a consultant from early on. At this particular bureaucratic level, there were no representatives of broad-based popular organizations or elected officials present.

A substantial number of the experts would later figure prominently in the operation of post-war agencies and in academic research and the practice of law. One of them was Ralph Bunche, who, as UN mediator in the Israeli-Arab war in 1948, won the Nobel Peace Prize and later steered the UN peace-keeping force. Others included Grayson Kirk, a professor of international relations who became President of Columbia University, and Andrew W. Cordier, who was an influential UN under-secretary and later President of Columbia University. Among the international law authorities were Norman J. Padelford of the Massachusetts Institute of Technology and Leland M. Goodrich, then at Brown University. Several of the advisers served at the San Francisco Conference. Others represented the United States in UN organs. None of them later took on any substantial role in electoral politics or in the cabinets of future administrations.

Not all of the post-war planning was neatly centred in the specialized structures of the State Department advisory committee or its successors. Several functions were spread out between departments. The rather untidy result was consistent with Roosevelt's inclination to compart-mentalize sectoral planning as well as with his administrative style.[21] The Treasury Department and to some extent the Federal Reserve were responsible for the Bretton Woods construction, which, next to the United Nations, was perhaps the most influential international instrument of the post-war world. Planning in the Treasury Department was strikingly concentrated in the hands of Harry Dexter White, the senior official in command of post-war affairs, who negotiated directly with his British counterpart, John Maynard Keynes, in producing the drafts that the Bretton Woods Conference considered and largely approved.[22] The Commerce Department also made contributions under this topic. The Agriculture Department was heavily involved with the preparations for the Hot Springs Conference that led to the creation of the Food and Agriculture Organization. Planning for the Inter-national Civil Aviation Organization had inputs from the Commerce Department. All of this matched or exceeded the State Department's reliance on a policy elite.

Another example of post-war planning that fell outside the purview of the State Department was in the field of international social welfare. In 1944 the International Labour Organization (ILO), one of the few agencies associated with the League of Nations to which the United States had adhered, held an extraordinary assembly in Philadelphia.

Its aim was to draft a plan for social problems in the post-war world. In time of war, such a meeting clearly had to have high-level approval and participation by the United States government. Again, it was not prepared in the State Department's planning structures but rather in the Department of Labor. The outcome of the meeting could be found in the Philadelphia Declaration that set out a sweeping programme for post-war reconstruction and international approaches to economic and social problems which its quarter-century of operations had helped to anticipate. Much in this document reflected New Deal ideology and especially opinions in American organized labour. However, its lofty rhetoric on social justice disappeared with hardly a trace as the US's planning process matured. The final plans contained little on the preoccupations of the ILO. The ILO's association with the League of Nations, together with the Soviet government's opposition to its aims, was enough to bury any significant contribution.[23] In addition, the lack of continued attention by the President and the foreign policy elite to the preparations may help to explain the ineffectiveness of the Philadelphia Declaration.

The framework that constituted the advanced plans emerged in packages coordinated and bound together by Pasvolsky through several titular metamorphoses. These bundles included the suggestions and reports for the establishment of an international trade organization that eventuated in the General Agreement on Tariffs and Trade in 1948; the World Health Organization; the vitalizing of the International Telecommunications (formerly Telegraphic) Union; and a refugee organization. Here also crept in the idea of international protection of human rights, driven by the horrors of Nazi policies and the earlier experience of protection of minorities under the League of Nations. These components were to be brought together by coordinating recommendations from a future United Nations organ, which eventually took shape in the UN Charter as the Economic and Social Council.[24]

The parallels with the New Deal strategies and constructions are too striking to be pushed aside. The New Deal attempted to mitigate the scars of Depression through the intervention of state agencies with specific ameliorative briefs. They included the establishment of new financial agencies that supplemented or replaced banks in areas where banks could not or would not function; new regulatory agencies to deal with labour relations; a commission to supervise telecommunications; a host of new institutions, such as the Farm Security Administration and the Rural Electrification Administration to help beleaguered farmers and promote development; and the massive experiment in regional planning in the Tennessee Valley Authority. The post-war plans, like those of the New Deal, were driven by the general assumption that coping with social problems and maintaining a fair society required the attention of government.

On the international plane, this global New Deal would assist with tempering social conflicts. This could best be done by creating specialized organs to treat defined subject areas in the improvizing fashion that the New Deal agencies did. Peace would be underpinned by a social harmony that was to be promoted by new subject-specific institutions. Lessons would be learned from the mistakes of the past in the wake of World War I in the same way that the New Deal tried to learn from the presumed errors of social policy in the 1920s.

Yet the planning process remained removed from the public eye. Two aspects in particular confined it to elite circles. First of all, Hull, Roosevelt and Welles intended to contain it within the administration, presumably until it was advanced enough for politicians and the communications media to savour it. The addition of congressmen to advisory committees only well after the agenda was set gives support to this view. Secondly, the subject matter itself was difficult to bring into public discussion. It was unconnected with the progress of the war. It was full of technical issues and concepts that usually received little attention outside of specialist publics. These included seeking consent of sovereigns to treaties in place of legislative decisions and certain administrative rules, understood only by experts in the field. Moreover, when plans matured to the point where draft agreements could be presented, the language was much coloured by international legal usage that was considered inaccessible to people not professionally trained in law and thus susceptible to misinterpretation.

The confinement of planning processes to experts within government bureaucracy shaped the pattern of international life after 1945. The flooding institutionalization of international relations that followed the war may have signalled two important long-term developments. First, the nature of international relations took on entirely or partly new regularities and form. The depth and scope of operation of such institutions as the World Bank or the Office of the UN High Commissioner for Refugees, which was partly anticipated by the United Nations Relief and Rehabilitation Association, greatly surpass the modest constructions created after World War I.[25] Such operations could not have emerged if there had been no mechanisms for providing institutional structures to the conduct of international relations.

Second, this institutionalization may have facilitated the enormous expansion in trans-national relations of the post-war world. This includes trans-national industrial and commercial enterprises and instant electronic communications in a time of unprecedented migration and population growth. It also includes the overlapping networks of non-governmental organizations that monitor, shape and operate many trans-national ventures. To a considerable degree, the planning for institutions after the war hurried along this growth. This, too, would have fitted with the modernizing assumptions and aims of the New Deal.

Too many leading historical studies of the period concentrate on organization to maintain international peace and security and neglect these other areas. Several reasons underlie this emphasis. Most important is the context in which the designing of the post-war order took place. The planning effort was made during the most destructive conflict of modern history. The war came less than thirty years after the end of World War I – a time lag that was painfully short. Memories were sharp. The first priority was to avoid future bloodshed and so the architects of international organizations concentrated on peace-keeping. On the surface this concentration seemed to be a reworking of old ideas. However, historical treatment has neglected the experience that the planners had gained from the New Deal order and the way such experience was grafted on to all aspects of international organization.

Reorganizing after wars was not new; it had been woven into the fabric of diplomacy since at least 1648 when the Congress of Westphalia met. Precedents and experience accumulated over years of diplomatic practice and were particularly sharpened in the nineteenth century when several landmark conferences were held to settle European wars and carve out colonial empires. Diplomats refined their bargaining techniques. Everybody involved knew the broad outlines: winners got rewards in territory and other privileges, such as maintaining military superiority over losers. Large states did not disappear and when smaller units did, it was to serve the victors and protect their security. After wars, generally speaking, governments had control of defined territories and the people within those borders. Outside interference was largely restricted. All of this was set out in dignified legal language in treaties that had benefited from three centuries of increasingly sophisticated jurisprudence. Such legal tradition was deeply embedded in the minds of the foreign affairs elite.

Diplomatic practice also included several attempts to set up permanent organizations to maintain peace. This was the intention of the Holy Alliance arranged in the Congress of Vienna. It was the aim of the Hague Conferences. It was at the heart of the League of Nations. In all of these constructions, the ultimate control was the military ability of members to respond to breakdowns of commitments to find pacific settlements of disputes.

The post-war planning that preoccupied the leaders of the United States and Britain slid neatly into these traditions. Both Roosevelt and Churchill were nationalists and resisted any proposed reductions in national autonomy. They knew that any division of conquered or liberated territory would cause controversy among them. However, they could agree to the establishment of a permanent organization that would limit the use of force by others but left open their own capacity to make independent decisions.[26] They were content to leave to the planners the design of institutions that would give such aims concrete form. It was scarcely surprising, then, that post-war institutional designs that emanated from the elite group of planners were modelled on the New Deal.

The most novel elements of the post-war framework pertained to the long-term future of colonies, the social benefits to be expected from government and the protection of human rights. These were distantly but pregnantly referred to in Roosevelt's Four Freedoms speech. The President's interest in revising the colonial system had roots in his experience in Woodrow Wilson's government but also drew on the older diplomatic practice of sharing out vanquished territory after wars. American war aims, then, included a significant reformist content. That content was elaborated in the bureaucratic planning and accorded with the style and method of the New Deal. It was home territory for the policy elite that was involved in the process.

The treatment of this planning process in most general texts on American foreign policy understandably has emphasized the diplomatic context.[27] It emphasizes the dramatic circumstances of wartime, the interplay of personal leadership and the geopolitical calculus. It concentrates on the abstractions in which leaders phrase their intentions. It traces the ebb and flow of bargaining by heads of government and senior ministers but rarely dips into the complexity of the political process beyond the well publicized congressional and other public debates. It overlooks the multiple organizational actors and the interplay of their expert knowledge. It uses broad and often undefined and allusive concepts, such as idealism and realism, to point up the areas of conflict. It does not draw on the experience and reference of the planners who laid the groundwork.

The formation of American policy takes place, according to these interpretations, in conflicts between isolationists and interventionists, internationalists and nationalists, realists and idealists and realpolitik and utopias. Authors draw upon convenient evidence of changing military fortunes, possession of territory, spheres of influence, and published statements and agreements. They also sometimes add some colourful, spicy titbits about the appearance of the participants, their health, the places of meetings and even their sexual foibles.[28]

This personal and conventional approach to understanding the post-war planning results in a good story and reinforces an outlook that emphasizes the role of great leaders. However, it ignores important elements in an elaborate political process that includes crucial contributions by government bureaucracies. It falls well short of elucidating the way in which the New Deal experience affected post-war planning and how it tended to offset the traditional, not to say atavistic, tendencies of the foreign offices, the military apparatuses and the political top drawer. It does not draw on studies of bureaucracies and seldom illuminates on the mechanisms and functions of their structures and organizations. It leaves aside the detailed conceptual explorations of realism, idealism, institutions, regimes and multilateralism that political scientists and philosophers have conducted in recent years.[29]

Above all, usually such accounts simply fail to trace or explain items on the post-war agenda that grew from unelaborated phrases to great chapters of international cooperation. One of these is human rights, which had a cue in the Four Freedoms address and connected directly with colonial issues. Another is the persistent utility of international law both as outcome and method in post-war planning.[30]

Finally, the entire subject of creating structures for economic and social cooperation needs further study.[31] One of the principal underlying ideas in planning for the United Nations was surely the use of that organization for helping to set out principles for broad economic policy. (The Organization for Economic Cooperation and Development (OECD) has followed this model for the highly developed countries.) The term 'full employment', which still carries poignant ideological baggage, even made its way through the various planning disputes into the final UN Charter.[32] All of this accords with New Deal thinking and the popularity in the United States of a government that actively develops programmes to cope with social issues.

More scholarly attention has been devoted to the World Bank and International Monetary Fund.[33] These two operating agencies were intended by the planners to be only part of a broad system that resembled other bureaus of the New Deal in dealing with pressing problems. They were not intended merely as tactical devices for executing pro-capitalist American geopolitical aims. In any case, their prominence makes clear that post-war planning in the economic and social areas has had important unintended effects.

The institutions that emerged at war's end still exist. Some, like the United Nations, are embattled, while others, such as the Bretton Woods agencies, flourish. Whatever their fate, their survival over half a century is a testimony to the policy elite that successfully employed its experience in improving institutions to carry out the aims of the New Deal in the international arena. These adaptations of the New Deal still inform international organizations and still influence societies in every part of the world. By adopting a more comprehensive perspective about the wartime planning process, historians could help to explain why and how this particular institutional model captured popular imagination and governmental policies in the creation of a more structured world order after 1945.

Notes

1. By elite I mean persons who have a superior position in ordering society. The term has no special value implications. The specialists comprising this elite who did most of the post-war planning were neither elected nor appointed directly by elected officials. The small list of elected officials that was informed comprised specialists on foreign affairs issues, rather than generally acknowledged opinion leaders.

2. The official, very informative history of bureaucratic effort is US Department of State, Publication 3580, *Postwar Foreign Policy Preparation 1939–45* (Washington DC, 1950). Its author is Harley Notter, who participated in much of the planning work. Additional detail can be found in Ruth B. Russell with Jeanette E. Matter, *A History of the United Nations Charter: the Role of the United States 1940–1945* (Washington DC, 1958). Russell had access to the State Department archives. See Robert A. Divine, *Second Chance: The Triumph of Internationalism in American During World War II* (New York, 1967) for a detailed historical account that emphasizes the interplay of congressional and public opinion with that of the President and his entourage on the broad lines of a post-war order.

3. Specifically, freedom of speech and religion and freedom from want and fear. Roosevelt said in the President's annual message to Congress, 6 January 1941, that their application would result from victory over the dictators. Earlier Roosevelt had unsuccessfully tried to stimulate American support for international cooperation against the influence of the European dictators. This resulted in his famous speech in October 1937 in which he proposed a quarantine of the aggressors. See Robert Dallek, *Franklin D. Roosevelt and American Foreign Policy* (New York, 1979), 142–50.

4. Hull had been interested in trade policy from the beginning of his career in the House of Representatives in 1906 and had always opposed high tariffs. See Cordell Hull, *The Memoirs of Cordell Hull*, 2 vols (New York, 1948), vol. 1, 124, 352–77.

5. They were in fact vaguer than Winston Churchill's original proposition. See Dallek, *Franklin D. Roosevelt and American Foreign Policy*, 281–4.

6. Hull, *Memoirs*, vol. 2, 1631–3.

7. The best working definition of multilateralism can be found in John Gerard Ruggie, *Winning the Peace: America and World Order in the New Era* (New York, 1996), 20 He writes: 'In its pure form, a multilateral world order would embody rules of conduct that are commonly applicable to all countries, as opposed to discriminating among them based on situational exigencies or particularistic preferences.' For details of the

evolution of Roosevelt's ideas on international organization see Warren Kimball, *The Juggler: Franklin Roosevelt as Wartime Statesman* (Princeton, 1991), 103–5 and Chapter 5.

8. Roosevelt strongly desired this secrecy. It fitted with his self-proclaimed role as 'juggler' in politics. Kimball, *The Juggler*, 9, 14, 102.

9. George Schild, *Bretton Woods and Dumbarton Oaks: American Economic and Political Postwar Planning in the Summer of 1944* (New York, 1995), 57–8.

10. Notter, *Postwar Foreign Policy Preparation*, 208–13.

11. For details of this process, see Robert C. Hildebrand, *Dumbarton Oaks: the Origins of the United Nations and the Search for Postwar Security* (Chapel Hill, NC, 1990). Hildebrand concentrates on plans to maintain peace and security and mainly ignores the rest of the agenda of the Dumbarton Oaks conversations. See also Notter, *Postwar Foreign Policy Preparation*, 301–38.

12. See Divine, *Second Chance*, 65–8, 103–5.

13. See David Fromkin, *In the Time of the Americans* (New York, 1995). Fromkin repeatedly cites the social backgrounds of the changing American leadership from Wilson to the present.

14. Townsend Hoopes and David Brinkley, *FDR and the Creation of the U.N.* (New Haven, 1997), 44. In this example the authors engage in hyperbole.

15. Details of the long worsening of relations and the eventual use of allegations of homosexuality against Welles are given in Fromkin, *In the Time of the Americans* and Irwin F. Gellman, *Secret Affairs: Franklin Roosevelt, Cordell Hull, and Sumner Welles* (Baltimore, 1995). Hull and Welles did not differ on the crucial foreign policy point that the post-war world would need international institutions. They both supported the planning effort.

16. An exception was the presence of Clark M. Eichelberger, who was long associated with organisations to promote American membership of the League of Nations. His name is listed by Notter as one of the experts.

17. Schild, *Bretton Woods and Dumbarton Oaks*, 59.

18. Anne-Marie Burley, 'Regulating the World: Multilateralism, International Law and the Projection of the New Deal Regulatory State' in John Gerard Ruggie, *Multilateralism Matters: the Theory and Praxis of an Institutional Form* (New York, 1993), 135.

19. This construction was vast indeed and whether or not it achieved its goals, neither the agencies nor the results could be regarded as negligible. See William E. Leuchtenberg, *The FDR Years: On Roosevelt and His Legacy* (New York, 1995), 237–82. For a treatment of the changing perception of the New Dealers, many of whom were engaged by the end of the war in international affairs, see Alan Brinkley, 'The Idea of the State' in Steve Fraser and Gary Gerstle, *The Rise and Fall of the New Deal Order, 1930–1980* (Princeton, 1989), 85–121.

20. Their names are listed in Notter, *Postwar Foreign Policy Preparation*, appendices 22 and 23.

21. Schild, *Bretton Woods and Dumbarton Oaks*, 106. Kimball noted that Roosevelt 'often simply muddled through, sweeping obstacles under the rug in the hope that they would go away in time'. See Kimball, *The Juggler*, 8.

22. See Dean Acheson, *Present at the Creation* (New York, 1969), 112–15, 122–7. Acheson shows the way the upper levels of the bureaucracy functioned. An elaborate subcommittee structure in the economic and social area, noted by Notter, does not seem to have made nearly as much impression as the counterparts in the political and security sectors. Also, Schild, *Bretton Woods and Dumbarton Oaks,* 107–8.
23. Anthony Alcock, *History of the International Labour Organisation* (London, 1971), 171–93.
24. Russell, *History of the United Nations Charter,* 777–807.
25. This organization was the largest institutional operation history up to that time and well beyond. See George Woodbridge, *UNRRA: the History of the United Nations Relief and Rehabilitation Administration,* 2 vols (New York, 1950).
26. This is the significance of the veto privilege extended to permanent members of the United Nations Security Council on matters of substance in connection with the maintenance of peace and security. A perceptive early treatment that still stands as authoritative is Inis L. Claude Jr., *Swords Into Ploughshares,* (New York, 1964), 133–46.
27. See, for example, Dallek, *Franklin D. Roosevelt and American Foreign Policy* and Divine, *Second Chance.*
28. See Gellman, *Secret Affairs.*
29. See, for example, such standard works as Robert Gilpin, *War and Change in World Politics* (Cambridge, 1981); Robert O. Keohane and Joseph S. Nye (eds), *Transnational Relations and World Politics* (Cambridge, Mass., 1972); Stephen D. Krasner (ed.), *International Regimes* (Ithaca, 1983); Hans J. Morgenthau, *Politics Among Nations* (New York, 1966); R. B. J. Walker, *Inside/Outside: International Relations as Political Theory* (New York, 1993); and Kenneth Waltz, *Theory of International Politics* (Reading, MA, 1979).
30. None of the historical accounts published since 1967 that I consulted includes either of these terms in its index.
31. Schild, *Bretton Woods and Dumbarton Oaks* is an important exception.
32. In the drafting process at San Francisco the US delegation objected to the inclusion of 'full employment' as an UN objective. See Leland M. Goodrich (ed.), *The Charter of the United Nations* (London, 1949), 372.
33. For example, Richard N. Gardner, *Sterling-Dollar Diplomacy* (New York, 1969).

13

The Clintons and the Roosevelts

William E. Leuchtenburg

Alone of the ten presidents who have succeeded Franklin Delano Roosevelt, William Jefferson Clinton has no direct memory of him. Harry Truman served as FDR's Vice-president; Dwight Eisenhower knew that it was Roosevelt who had approved his selection to head the European command; John F. Kennedy recalled dinner conversations when his father was Ambassador to the Court of St James's; and Lyndon Johnson once said that FDR was 'a daddy to me always'. Richard Nixon, Gerald Ford, and George Bush all served in World War II under Roosevelt as Commander in Chief. Jimmy Carter remembered the day that the New Deal brought rural electrification to south Georgia, and Ronald Reagan, 'a Roosevelt manqué', voted for FDR all four times.[1] Bill Clinton, though, was not born until 1946, a year after Roosevelt's death.

As a consequence, when Clinton campaigned for the presidency in 1992, FDR seemed a remote figure – to him and to others of his generation. At the Democratic convention that nominated Clinton that year, one reporter wrote, 'I listened for the grand anthem of the Democratic Party, for "Happy Days Are Here Again", but instead got Fleetwood Mac'. Clinton himself, as former chairman of the Democratic Leadership Council, had identified himself with centrists who were jettisoning the New Deal legacy. When he did cite FDR during the campaign, he sometimes gave a conservative spin to his record. 'Roosevelt', he reminded a panel of *New York Times* correspondents, 'ran for President on a balanced budget'. Denying that he was a 'tax-and-spend liberal', a term long associated with Harry Hopkins, Clinton declared that he was 'a different kind of Democrat', code language for not a New Deal Democrat.[2]

Yet, as someone raised in Arkansas, he had heard many times what devastation the Great Depression had wrought and how much the New Deal had done for his state. When accused of being a closet Republican, Clinton responded, 'My grandparents ... told me that in the Depression Franklin Roosevelt ... gave people hope again by giving them ... work to do'. He added, 'My granddaddy thought when he died he was going to Roosevelt'. One journalist thought that the clue to him lay in recognizing that 'Clinton is a product of a region that was rescued by the New Deal policies that brought electricity and economic revival to rural areas, and he has always appreciated the role that government can play to improve lives'.[3]

Furthermore, Clinton had to recognize that FDR was not only a national icon, especially for liberal Democrats, but a man of international stature. In June 1992 in the midst of the presidential campaign, at the presentation of the Franklin D. Roosevelt Four Freedom Awards by the Roosevelt Study Center in Middelburg, Lord Carrington, former Secretary-General of NATO, recalled how one of FDR's addresses had inspired him as a young British army officer in World War II. 'Those who are charged with the duty of leading their nations could do worse than to reread that great speech of President Roosevelt and make it the cornerstone of their policy', he said.[4]

In response to these considerations, and also because Clinton was instinctively an activist with certain liberal impulses, he did at times identify with the Roosevelt tradition. When he spoke of a 'New Covenant', a rubric that never caught on, he observed, 'sixty years ago, Franklin Roosevelt renewed that promise with a New Deal', and he asserted, 'I want one of those great 100 days in which Congress would adopt my ... policies ... to make this country great again'. He gave out enough such intimations of what he would do once in office to permit a *New York Times* writer to say, 'Mr Clinton is expected in his first hundred days as President to take a muscular, Franklin Roosevelt-like approach'.[5]

Clinton had given an interesting twist to these forecasts when, at a National Press Club breakfast even before he had formally announced his candidacy, he said, after fielding a question about his wife: 'Two for the price of one. Buy one, get one free. If I get elected president, it will be an unprecedented partnership, far more than Franklin Roosevelt and Eleanor.' In an interview with David Frost, Hillary Clinton dismissed her husband's analogy as 'very nice hyperbole', but, a critic later noted, Bill Clinton had undeniably left the impression 'that he intended the first couple to share the perks of the boardroom as well as the pleasures of the bedroom'.[6]

At Clinton's inauguration in 1993, I was on the CBS television team at the same time that I was in the final moments of getting to press a revision of my book *In the Shadow of FDR*, with a new subtitle *From Harry Truman to Bill Clinton*, and I was hoping that Clinton would oblige me with a pertinent quote. When the advance copy of his inaugural address arrived that morning, I was delighted to see that he had. Clinton that day quoted only two people: St Paul and Franklin D. Roosevelt. Drawing on FDR's 1932 Ogelthorpe address, he urged: 'Let us resolve to make our government a place for what Franklin Roosevelt called "bold, persistent experimentation"'.[7]

In his first year in office, Clinton, by a series of actions, including recommendations for a jobs programme and an ambitious health-care initiative (both of which Congress scuttled), persuaded a number of correspondents that he was, in fact, walking in FDR's footsteps. In late February of 1993, David Gergen, who would later join the White House staff, wrote that Clinton had 'come down decisively in favor of a new age of liberal rule, picking up where Franklin Roosevelt and Lyndon Johnson left off'. In December a Chicago *Tribune* correspondent reported from Washington, 'it sometimes seems that people here think Franklin Roosevelt has come to life as Bill Clinton with another New Deal', and on a television programme early in 1994, a Washington *Post* writer exclaimed: 'Look, you know what we're watching? This is Rooseveltilian ... This is Franklin Roosevelt. This is a new New Deal.' [8]

Clinton encouraged this impression when, only four weeks after he was sworn in, he went to FDR's ancestral home at Hyde Park to speak at a school that had been built by the Works Progress Administration and that Roosevelt had dedicated. However, the continuity was more theatrical than substantive. As he 'sought to evoke the personal spirit and political presence of his predecessor', wrote Thomas Friedman in the *New York Times*, 'the President seemed to be searching for a way to persuade Americans that they could trust the Government to work for their common good'. In short, the homage Clinton paid to FDR was ritualistic. He was manipulating his homage to Roosevelt for programmatic ends. [9]

In his address at Hyde Park's Haviland Middle School, Clinton revealed how tangential was his relationship to the emphases of the New Deal. During the recent campaign, he said, he had been 'absolutely enthralled' by Geoffrey Ward's *First Class Temperament*. 'What moved me most', he explained, 'was the way President Roosevelt came to grips with the fact of his polio and learned to live with it and learned to triumph over it and learned to use it to make himself stronger inside and not to be defeated by it'. It is significant that Ward's outstanding biography stops short of the presidency. It was not the New Deal but FDR's struggle with paralysis that stimulated in Clinton interest in Roosevelt.

In the core of his speech, the President advocated some new advances and deplored trying 'to cramp the role of government', but his main theme was the need to curb 'a horrendous government deficit'. He bragged that he had cut the budget in every department, including, he acknowledged, 'programs that help a lot of good people but that I don't think we can afford at the present level anymore'. Once again, he quoted FDR on the need for bold experimentation, but this time he insisted, 'if it doesn't work, you quit'. With regard to government, he stated, 'We're very good at starting things and absolutely terrible at stopping them'. In sum, even in a speech at Hyde Park, the lesson he drew from Roosevelt was not to expand government but to diminish it. FDR remained a vague figure for him.[10]

When he arrived at the Roosevelt estate, however, he had an un-anticipated emotional experience. As David Shribman of the Boston *Globe* has perceptively noted, 'Clinton came to Roosevelt relatively late, and when he went to Hyde Park ... it was as if he were seeing Roosevelt for the very first time'. When he entered the foyer of Roosevelt's home, reported Sidney Blumenthal in a memorable piece for the *New Yorker*, 'he was transfixed, his eyes wide, his jaw slack'. Unable to get enough of Rooseveltiana, he blurted out, 'I just love this'. On walking into FDR's dressing room, he asked, 'Those are still his clothes?' Blumenthal commented: 'Putting it in the present tense framed the question oddly. Would Roosevelt return to find his things undisturbed?' Aides tugged at him to remind him he was running late, but Clinton seemed mesmerized. When he came to FDR's desk, 'Clinton viewed it from all angles', Blumenthal wrote. 'He was measuring himself'. As he prepared to leave, Clinton said 'I belong here'.[11]

Clinton's visit to Hyde Park in February 1993 did not end his association with FDR. In September he signed the National and Community Service Trust Act of 1993 with a pen belonging to FDR. Clinton had phoned the Roosevelt Library at Hyde Park to borrow the pen because it was, conceivably, one Roosevelt had used to sign the legislation creating the Civilian Conservation Corps, which Clinton regarded as the father of his National Service Corps. And so captivated was the President by his 1993 visit to FDR's home that two years later he took Boris Yeltsin to Hyde Park as if on a pilgrimage to a shrine.[12]

Clinton discovered, though, that Roosevelt's shadow could be a burden as well as a blessing, at no time so acutely as on the hundredth day of his presidency. Like FDR's nine other successors, Clinton found himself required to give an accounting on Day 100 of his term. 'Face it', said one columnist, 'the 100 Day Syndrome is artificial hype. There are things you can do in 100 days – breed rabbits, read all of Marcel Proust, program your VCR, lose 20 pounds. "Reinventing government" isn't one of them'. Without question, gauging Clinton's first hundred days by FDR's achievements in unique circumstances was unfair, but Clinton's campaign rhetoric had invited the contrast. 'His boasts naturally elicited comparisons with the master and originator of the 100 Days, Franklin Roosevelt', one critic noted, though Clinton confronted a quite dissimilar situation: 'no Depression, no bank crisis, nothing comparable to 1933's catastrophic unemployment rate', and no 'Congress beholden to him'. So desperate was the White House to avoid a poor report card that it turned out a sleek thirty-two-page brochure with a long list of inconsequential events, including the President throwing out the first ball to start the baseball season in Balti-more.[13]

That ploy did not work. A North Carolina newspaper, in an editorial entitled 'Not Quite Another FDR', concluded, 'Clearly, Clinton has failed to deliver on his promise to give the American people "an explosive 100-day action period ... the most productive period in modern history"', and the *Wall Street Journal*, under the headline, 'After 100 days, Mount Rushmore Is Still Safe', quoted a prominent political scientist who called Clinton's record 'the worst 100 days since Warren G. Harding by any reasonable standard'.[14]

Clinton responded to these harsh verdicts defensively. In a magazine interview he pointed out that his illustrious predecessor had enjoyed two advantages over him: Roosevelt had not had to take office until March and the massive unemployment had made the country more receptive. All along, Clinton apparently drew comfort from the thought not of FDR triumphant but of FDR beleaguered. When James Mac-Gregor Burns, author of *Roosevelt: The Lion and the Fox*, spoke to Clinton in the fall of 1992, he had found him 'just as interested in FDR's frustrated leadership during his gridlocked second term as in the famous "100 days"'. Two years later the President, in the midst of a conversation about FDR's influence, said, with an air of some satisfaction, 'Well, Roosevelt had his enemies too'.[15]

Nothing about his visit to Hyde Park made him any more inclined to pursue New Deal policies. While taking enough liberal stands, especially on government regulation and taxation, to persuade some commentators that he was FDR's heir, Clinton for the most part moved in a centrist, even conservative, direction. In the summer of 1993 Kevin Phillips wrote: 'The extent to which Clinton has abandoned old Demo-cratic victory formulas must have Franklin D. Roosevelt rolling over in his grave. FDR ... has now seen fellow Democrat Clinton emerge as a kind of Roosevelt-in-reverse.' If Clinton's first visit to Hyde Park was affecting, it was not transmuting.[16]

Yet if Clinton's policies dismayed liberals, they left conservatives apoplectic. Right-wing commentators filled the air waves with abuse of the President, especially on gender issues, ranging from his solici-tousness toward gays in the armed services to his appointment of his wife to head a national task force on health insurance. Clinton com-plained:

What they said about Franklin and Eleanor Roosevelt would curl the back of your hair. But it was never subject to mass distribution, and certainly highly personal attacks never found their way from the right wing back into the mainstream media.

The veteran Washington correspondent Elizabeth Drew pointed out:

> Clinton saw himself as a descendant of FDR, but he not only lacked a perceived emergency but was up against deep skepticism, even cynicism, about government. That may have been his most active foe. He was the first activist President in the age of cynicism.

Battered by the Right, and with little enthusiasm for him on the Left because of his departure from the Roosevelt tradition, Clinton approached the 1994 elections seriously in disarray.[17]

The mid-term elections turned out badly for the Democrats, but they had a curious denouement. Though commentators viewed the success of the Republicans, under the leadership of the arch-conservative Newt Gingrich, in winning control of Congress for the first time in forty years as a decisive repudiation of Roosevelt' policies, Gingrich, in his 'coronation speech' on his first day as Speaker, startled everyone by calling FDR 'the greatest president of the 20th century'. Gingrich confessed that when faced with a dilemma he often imagined how FDR might have acted. Like Roosevelt, he sought to be 'a transformational leader' who would do for conservatism and the Republican Party what FDR had done for liberalism and the Democrats – create a seismic change that would last a generation or more.[18]

Even before Gingrich co-opted the Democratic party's idol, Clinton had been hearing that if he truly wanted to be faithful to the spirit of FDR he could do that best by proving himself as adaptable as Roosevelt had been. Just as FDR had abandoned unworkable Old Guard approaches, so should Clinton get rid of the big government attitudes that had flopped. One writer, noting that Roosevelt in his 1932 Oglethorpe address had said that if a method 'fails, admit it frankly and try another', claimed that Clinton would be an FDR legatee if he acknowledged that welfare had failed and should be scrapped. The Democratic Leadership Council did not hesitate to say that were Franklin Roosevelt alive today, he would be opposed to the New Deal.[19]

It came as no surprise that Clinton, as former head of that organization, chose to interpret the 1994 elections as a rejection of his liberal policies, though it was far from clear that that was what had happened. (Early in 1995, Arthur Schlesinger Jr. spoke of 'the delusion that Bill Clinton has been a vigorously liberal president'.) Under the guidance of the political mercenary, Dick Morris, Clinton calculatedly turned his back on the New Deal legislators in his party and accepted many of Gingrich's basic assumptions.[20]

When, on 12 April 1995, the fiftieth anniversary of Franklin Roosevelt's death, Clinton travelled to Warm Springs, Georgia, the site of

FDR's 'Little White House', to pay tribute to the former president, he converted FDR into a New Democrat. He declared:

> If President Roosevelt were here, he would say 'Let's have a great old-fashioned debate about the role of government, and let's make it less bureaucratic ... Those people in Washington don't know everything that should be done in Warm Springs' ... He wouldn't be here defending everything he did fifty years ago ... Should we reexamine the role of Government? Of course, we should. Do we need big, centralized bureaucracies in the computer age? Often we don't.[21]

Over the course of the next year Clinton moved steadily away from the policies with which FDR was identified. In his State of the Union address in 1996 he announced, 'The era of big government is over'. That same month, the *New York Times* reported: 'He has steadily retreated to embrace his rivals' goal of balancing the budget in seven years. This has meant accepting a level of cuts in domestic spending that Mr Clinton's own advisers had repeatedly denounced as unthinkable'. Later that year, he put his name on what a high-ranking Clinton appointee who resigned in protest called 'this terrible legislation', cutting the heart out of the welfare program created in 1935, though his Secretary of Health and Human Services had handed him an analysis showing that the bill would drive more than a million children into poverty. It was a 'sad day', said the head of the American Federation of Labor, to see Clinton sign a bill that was 'anti-poor, anti-immigrants, anti-women and anti-children – unravelling the safety net Franklin Roosevelt had put in place sixty years before'.[22]

Even commentators of rather moderate views found fault with the President's acquiescence in Gingrich's designs. Clinton took pride in his success in reducing the deficit, but the irony of that success did not go unnoticed. In the fall of 1996 a writer in the *New York Times* said of the FDR Memorial as it neared completion: 'Poignantly, its gardens and waterfalls, sculptures and bas-reliefs of breadlines and impoverished farmers are being assembled just as the political wrecking ball has demolished one of FDR's social welfare pillars, the guaranteed cash subsidy for the most impoverished children.' At about the same time, a North Carolina newspaper, noting that 'Clinton's new mantra is "Let's build a bridge to the 21st century"', responded: 'Fine. But the president obviously doesn't understand the role of a bridge. It ... takes you where you're going but also from where you've been'. The writer was not impressed by Clinton's invocation of Franklin in his inaugural address. 'Franklin Roosevelt? Shhhhhh. Clinton would rather forget him'.[23]

The President ran into difficulty of a different sort when in late June 1996 the Washington *Post* created a sensation by publishing an excerpt from a forthcoming book by Bob Woodward, co-author of the Watergate exposé, revealing that, under the tutelage of a New Age pop psychologist, Hillary Clinton had been talking to Eleanor Roosevelt, dead these more than thirty years. In one sense, it was surprising that the account should have stirred up such a fuss, for Hillary Clinton had been quite open about her rapport with Eleanor Roosevelt. In 1992 she had let it be known that she kept a collection of the former First Lady's column 'My Day' at her bedside, and that she would talk to her and 'ask her the tough questions'. Engaging the spirit of the woman who had received such abuse, she had inquired, 'How did you put up with this? How did you go on day to day ... with the kind of attacks that would be hurled your way?' Only a few days before the Woodward excerpts appeared, she had written: 'I occasionally have imaginary conversations with Mrs. Roosevelt to try to figure out what she would do in my shoes. She usually responds by telling me to buck up or at least to grow skin as thick as a rhinoceros'.[24]

Woodward, though, made these interchanges much more vivid by focusing attention on Hillary's spiritual guide, Jean Houston, who in the spring of 1995 at a session in the solarium atop the White House, had instructed the First Lady to probe more deeply into her feelings towards Eleanor Roosevelt. According to Woodward, Houston said, 'You're walking down a hall ... and there's Mrs. Roosevelt ... What is your message to her?' Hillary told Eleanor, 'It's hard. Why was there such a need in people to put other people down?' Houston then suggested that Hillary pretend to be Mrs. Roosevelt and answer. Woodward wrote: '"I was misunderstood," Hillary replied, her eyes still shut, speaking as Mrs. Roosevelt. "You have to do what you think is right."' Houston also got Hillary Clinton to converse with Mahatma Gandhi, but when she went on to propose a talk with Jesus Christ, the First Lady balked. That 'would be too personal'.[25]

Critics of the Clinton administration exploited to the fullest what the press called 'Eleanor-gate' or 'Guru-gate'. Though therapists pointed out that the technique of imaginary conversations was well accepted, Houston was derided as a 'mountebank', 'the First Lady's sorceress', and a 'touchy-feely guru', while Hillary Clinton's behavior was likened to Nancy Reagan's altering her husband's flight itinerary because the moon was in Aquarius. Mrs Clinton fully understood she was engaging in an exercise, but she was made to appear to be speaking to the dead through a medium. Maureen Dowd, who dipped her pen in brine whenever she wrote of the First Family, said of 'the First Lady's mystic, mythic, psychic, just plain ick sessions in the solarium' that 'Hillary Rodham Clinton is so desperate for friends she's hanging out with the quack and the dead'. The *Los Angeles Times* alluded to 'the famous seance ... where ... Hillary Rodham Clinton chatted up Eleanor Roosevelt', while another commentator stated that Hillary 'traded her grip on reality for a chance to cavort with the ghost of Eleanor Roosevelt in the Lincoln bedroom'.[26]

The First Lady, though palpably wounded, coped with this by giving as good as she got. In October 1996, when she unveiled a statue of Eleanor Roosevelt to a gathering at Manhattan's Riverside Park, she said jocularly, 'When I last spoke with Mrs. Roosevelt, she wanted me to tell you how pleased she is by this great, great new statue'. And more than half a year later, musing on the standing figure of Eleanor Roosevelt (the first ever of a First Lady) at the newly dedicated Roosevelt Memorial not far from the White House, she jested: 'It's more convenient for me. I can just go over there and talk to her'.[27]

She had also, well before this, taken seriously the admonishment that she had misperceived the experience of Eleanor Roosevelt. 'Mrs R.' had exerted her influence behind the scenes; her one government post, in civil defence, had been a disaster, one she had made sure not to repeat. Hillary Clinton, too, after her role in the doomed health-care scheme had such bad repercussions in the Republican gains in the 1994 elections, withdrew from administration but continued, at the urging of Doris Kearns Goodwin and others, to speak out, as Mrs Roosevelt had, for the neglected.[28]

Some commentators turned 'Eleanor-gate' into an opportunity to challenge the President's claimed ideological credentials. A writer for the Madison *Capital Times* said:

> My only sadness about the whole Eleanor-and-Hillary affair is that Jean Houston ... didn't spend a little more time encouraging President Clinton to have imaginary conversations with Eleanor's husband ... Franklin Roosevelt became the greatest president of this century not by trying to reflect the Republican line, nor by currying favor with Wall Street – as too many current Democrats do. Roosevelt did not try to rival the Republicans when it came to government bashing and scapegoating of the poor ... Wouldn't it be wonderful if, in the midst of the current welfare reform debate, President Clinton were to hold a conversation with President Roosevelt?[29]

That suggestion came at a time when analysts were experiencing increasing difficulty with positioning the President along a political spectrum. 'The good news is that we may elect a Republican president this year', said a Republican consultant in 1996. 'The bad news is that it may be Bill Clinton'. Similarly, the *New Statesman* wrote that the Republicans had a secret plan for dropping Bob Dole and replacing him with a younger, more articulate nominee with an extraordinary conservative pedigree, a candidate with the core values of modern Republicanism, [including] tax cuts, reducing welfare payments, balanced budgets and deficit reduction ... There is only one catch. The near-perfect Republican candidate for 1996 is William Jefferson Clinton, who, it must be assumed, will continue to call himself a Democrat despite compelling evidence to the contrary.[30]

During the 1996 campaign Clinton made a point of saying that his policies on the deficit, crime and welfare were not 'wildly liberal measures' and were 'different from what, traditionally, people have thought of as Democratic politics'. He added: 'I know it's convenient for the Republicans to raise the flag of "Oh, these people would be so liberal if you let them, Clinton will be liberal in his second term"'. That contention, he said, 'won't fit with what I'm planning to do in my second term'. When Clinton triumphed in November, it quickly became a cliché to say that it was the first time a Democratic incumbent had been re-elected since FDR prevailed in 1936. But Clinton's victory, asserted the historian Ronald Radosh, 'scores a final defeat for the old, stalwart liberalism that for many people has long defined the essence of the Democratic Party'.[31]

The President had broken with the past, his champions said, because, given the political cards he held, he had no other choice – a not unreasonable, yet insufficient, explanation. 'Of course, this is no easy time to be a liberal', the co-editor of The American Prospect, Robert Kuttner, acknowledged. 'The market is rampant and the state constricted. The overhang of the Reagan debt adds further constraint'. Besides, Clinton confronted the ineluctable arithmetic of Republican majorities in both houses of Congress and a national temper that did not invite large-scale experimentation. Yet Clinton was in no small part responsible for that situation and, with all of the potential of his office, empowered to alter it. Kuttner wrote that Clinton 'has validated conceptions of liberty and opportunity that make it difficult to use the state in either its fiscal or regulatory incarnation ... Clinton has added to the general climate of contempt for the competence and value of government'.[32]

Clinton did still identify with Roosevelt, but now it was with Theodore more than Franklin. To be sure, he told a press conference late in April 1997 that he had read a great deal about FDR and 'sometimes I feel like I'm talking to him, instead of Hillary talking to Eleanor'. It was the notion, though, of using the White House as a 'bully pulpit', as Teddy had, that increasingly appealed to him. His press secretary explained that in the age of Franklin D. Roosevelt or

Lyndon Johnson, 'government was really the tool we used to address the country's problems'. Today, with the era of big government ended, 'the solutions to our problems are much more likely to be found in awakening a spirit of problem-solving in the American people, which the president has a major role in doing'. This meant that, instead of using the powers of the office he had sought to compel change, Clinton would preach to the private sector, a far cry from the TR who busted trusts, regulated railroads, and 'took Panama'. Clinton's sermonizing, one scholar remarked, was 'of the "I'm O.K., you're O.K." school. It is not designed to pain the powerful'. Similarly, a *New York Times* writer observed, 'Mr Clinton used his bully pulpit not to afflict the comfortable – whose campaign cash he was assiduously soliciting – but to push highly popular poll-tested ideas such as youth curfews or school uniforms.' [33]

Clinton's second term, David Broder had predicted a month before the inauguration, was 'likely to be the most conservative Democratic administration this century', and this forecast proved prescient, for by June Clinton's ambitions were being encapsulated as the 'Incredible Shrinking Agenda'. It was indicative that the President got rid of Harold Ickes's son and namesake and chose for Chief of Staff, the post Ickes sought, a venture capitalist who was a political moderate. So drastically was the White House staff reshaped that one aide said, 'We're all New Democrats now'. In his first major address after the election, appropriately enough to the Democratic Leadership Council, Clinton claimed, 'We have clearly created a new center'. Early in the spring, a writer for the Scripps Howard syndicate declared:

Bill Clinton, a '90s Democrat, has been taken over by the ghost of President Dwight Eisenhower, a '50s Republican ... Like Ike, he was good to business, and business was good to him – in the case of the Chinese, perhaps excessively so. Also like Ike, he became ever more public in his craving to play golf ... he has the soul of an elderly – and bald – Republican icon. Others note a family precedent: Hillary Clinton channels Eleanor Roosevelt, and maybe Bill Clinton was trying to channel Franklin Roosevelt and just misdialed. [34]

On 3 May 1997, the chequered relationship of Bill Clinton and Franklin Delano Roosevelt came to a climax at the dedication of the long-delayed FDR Memorial in Washington. It was a special moment for me, because twenty years earlier I had been asked to provide the quotations from Roosevelt for it, and now for the first time I was seeing them set in rough carnelian granite for ages to come. Among the speakers that morning in the brilliant sunshine at the tidal basin was FDR's god-daughter, Princess Margriet of The Netherlands, who presented two large bouquets of a new rose named for her godfather in an orange tone appropriate for the House of Orange. ('Roosevelt' in Dutch means 'field of roses'.)

The principal speaker, as was to be expected on such an occasion, was President Clinton. Not only was he there as head of state, but he and his wife had hosted a $10,000-a-plate banquet at the White House to raise funds for the memorial. Roosevelt, 'the greatest president of this great American century', Clinton told the thousands assembled there, 'electrified the nation, instilling confidence with every tilt of his head and boom of his laugh'. Commentators, however, noted the paradox of the memorial being dedicated by the man who had announced the end of the age of big government, and pointed out that, though Clinton did acknowledge FDR's faith in 'strong and unapologetic' government, he never mentioned the New Deal and foresaw that Roosevelt would be remembered more as a far-sighted statesman than as the creator of 'specific programs'. 'It's hard to visit the memorial', wrote a columnist a few weeks later, '. . . without being reminded of the hollowness of the president who dedicated it, comparing his own accomplishments to those of FDR, even as he dismantles the last remnants of the New Deal'.[35]

This series of developments suggests that the shadow of FDR, which loomed so large for so many of Clinton's predecessors, may have waned almost to oblivion. Reporting from Chicago in the late summer of 1996, the chief of a Washington press bureau related:

Just before the dinner hour Wednesday, the Democratic convention brought on an actor portraying Franklin D. Roosevelt. The FDR pretender did not look, act, talk or bear himself like Roosevelt. Outside of that, he was fine. He limped onto the stage as if he had a touch of rheumatism, rather than the polio that put Roosevelt in heavy leg braces. He proceeded blithely to talk about all the new contraptions of the late 20th century – teleprompters and the Internet. Then he put the cigarette holder back in his mouth to display plenty of teeth and limped off the stage. This is what, more or less, FDR has become to the Democratic Party – just a cartoon character like George Washington or Abraham Lincoln, who pops up at tourist venues to pretend he just emerged from a time machine. Perhaps later, department stores will hold sales in his memory.[36]

There is some reason to believe, though, that the shadow of FDR has not altogether vanished. 'Roosevelt', said a Chicago *Tribune* correspondent in 1996, 'is omnipresent during this campaign year', while *The Economist* stated: 'FDR still towers over the land like a colossus, his works largely intact and broadly popular ... The era of bigger and bigger government may truly be over. But the era of big government, FDR's creation, is alive and kicking and remarkably resilient'. When in January 1997 I spoke in the US Senate to the Democratic members about the pertinence of the New Deal to the present situation, they leaped to their feet cheering – not just older Senators like Ted Kennedy but younger ones such as Paul Wellstone of Minnesota and Carol Mosely-Braun of Illinois. There are some signs, then, that the legacy of FDR is not moribund yet, however little meaning it may have to Bill Clinton.[37]

Notes

1. William E. Leuchtenburg, *In the Shadow of FDR: From Harry Truman to Bill Clinton* (Ithaca, 1993); Sidney Blumenthal, 'Rendezvousing with Destiny,' *New Yorker*, 8 March 1993, 40.

2. Alan Lupo, 'The Silent Generation', Boston *Globe*, 25 July 1992; *New York Times*, 28 June 1992, 3 May 1992; Raleigh (NC) *News and Observer*, 26 September 1992; Thomas C. Barrow to the Editor, Boston *Globe*, 10 August 1992. For Clinton's centrism, see Roger Morris, *Partners in Power: The Clintons and Their America* (New York, 1996), 240.

3. Raleigh (NC) *News and Observer*, 24 November 1991; *Wall Street Journal*, 19 March 1992; David S. Broder, 'As Clinton Wins, Many Democrats Wince', Raleigh (NC) *News and Observer*, 9 April 1992; *New York Times*, 26 April 1992; Bob Kuttner, 'Liberalism without the Liabilities', Boston *Globe*, 16, 24 July 1992.

4. *The Roosevelt Review*, newsletter of the Roosevelt Study Center, Middelburg, The Netherlands, 1992, 3–4.

5. Boston *Globe*, 11, 16 July 1992; Ann Reilly Dowd, 'His First 100 days', *Fortune*, 126 (November 1992), 41; Raleigh (NC) *News and Observer*, 30 April 1993; Steven Greenhouse, 'Market Watch', *New York Times*, 11 October 1992.

6. George Carpozi Jr., *Clinton Confidential: The Climb to Power, The Unauthorized Biography of Bill and Hillary Clinton* (Del Mar, Calif., 1995), 307–8; David Brock, *The Seduction of Hillary Rodham* (New York, 1996), 267; Memphis *Commercial Appeal*, 6 February 1996.

7. *New York Times*, 21 January 1993.

8. *US News and World Report*, 1 March 1993, 42; Chicago *Tribune*, 4 December 1993 (courtesy of Howard Rubin); *Washington Week in Review*, 28 January 1994.

9. *New York Times*, 20 February 1993.

10. Geoffrey C. Ward, *A First Class Temperament: The Emergence of Franklin Roosevelt* (New York, 1989); *Public Papers of the Presidents of the United States: William Jefferson Clinton*, vol. 1 (Washington, DC, 1994), 137–43.

11. Boston *Globe*, 4 May 1997; Blumenthal, 'Rendezvousing with Destiny', 39–44; Julie Anne Dumont Rabinowitz, 'The Use of Condensation Symbols to Establish Presidential Leadership: Bill Clinton's Appropriation of

Franklin Delano Roosevelt' (MA essay, Department of Communication Studies, University of North Carolina at Chapel Hill, 1997), 71–80: *New York Times*, 21 February 1993; *Newsweek*, 1 March 1993, 24.

12. The Roosevelt Institute and Library, *The View from Hyde Park*, VIII (Winter 1994), n.p.; Verne W. Newton, '"Guess Who's Coming to Lunch": Two Presidents Visit the FDR Library', National Archives and Records Administration, *The Record*, 2 (January 1996), 1, 9.

13. Sandy Grady in Raleigh (NC) *News and Observer*, 30 April 1993; R. Emmett Tyrrell Jr., *Boy Clinton: The Political Biography* (Washington, DC, 1996), 246; Atlanta *Constitution*, 29 April 1993. The columnist Charles Krauthammer, noting that Clinton 'consciously invokes FDR as his model', protested: 'The problem with the analogy is that 1993 is not 1933. FDR was elected president of a broken country ... Bill Clinton begins his presidency with the economy growing at ... the highest rate in five years.' Houston *Chronicle*, 7 March 1993.

14. Durham *Herald-Sun*, 29 April 1993; Paul A. Gigot, 'Potomac Watch,' *Wall Street Journal*, 23 April 1993. See also Sam Smith, *Shadows of Hope: A Freethinker's Guide to Politics in the Time of Clinton* (Bloomington, 1994), 42–3. Even the Whitewater scandal had a Rooseveltian dimension, for one of the principals, Jim McDougal, was so ardent an admirer of FDR that he got into financial difficulty by sinking four million dollars in a hare-brained scheme to build a resort on Campobello Island, which had been the Roosevelt summer retreat in New Brunswick and now houses an FDR museum. Carpozi, *Clinton Confidential*, 196–7; John Brummett, *Highwire: From the Backroads to the Beltway – The Education of Bill Clinton* (New York, 1994), 242–9.

15. *US News and World Report*, 3 May 1993, 42; James MacGregor Burns to the editor, *Time*, 22 March 1993, 9. Clinton made the remark about 'enemies' in a conversation with me about his reading *In the Shadow of FDR* at a picnic on 10 September 1994.

16. Houston *Chronicle*, 30 August 1993 (courtesy of Howard Rubin).

17. Burmmett, *Highwire*, 283; Elizabeth Drew, *On the Edge: The Clinton Presidency* (New York, 1994), 167.

18. Gannett News Service, 16 January 1995; Allan Freedman, 'Newt and Franklin', *National Journal*, 7 January 1995, 49; Elizabeth Drew, *Showdown* (New York, 1996), 14–15.

19. Mortimer B. Zuckerman, 'Bill Clinton, Professor-Elect', *US News and World Report*, 4 January 1993, 116; Denver *Post*, 31 August 1996; Arkansas *Democrat-Gazette*, 6 March 1994. See also James P. Pinkerton, 'Can Clinton Match FDR's Pragmatism?' *Newsday*, 25 April 1996.

20. *Daily Yomiuri*, 30 January 1995. Clinton, said a national news magazine, was the architect not of the New Deal but of 'the Small Deal, an ad hoc activism that sought to meliorate problems rather than write and staff expensive programs to solve them', an approach that suited younger party members but that 'had a disappointingly Lite taste to older Democrats'. *Newsweek*, 18 November 1996, 127.

21. Cable News Network, 12 April 1995. See also Bob Woodward, *The Choice* (New York, 1996), 143.

22. William Jefferson Clinton, 'Address Before a Joint Session of the Congress on the State of the Union (23 January 1996)', *Weekly Compilation of Presidential Documents*, 29 January 1996, XXXII, 90–8; *New York Times*, 2 January 1996; Peter Edelman, 'The Worst Thing Bill Clinton Has Done', *Atlantic Monthly*, CLXXIX (1997), 58; Boston *Globe*, 27 August 1996; Olivia Goldsmith in *Time*, 18 November 1996, 43.

23. Boston *Globe*, 4 December 1996; Greensboro (NC) *News and Record*, 4 September 1996. 'The venerable principles' of the Democratic Party, wrote Richard Goodwin, one of the architects of the New Frontier and the Great Society, 'have been abandoned'. Richard Goodwin, 'Has Anybody Seen the Democratic Party?' *New York Times Magazine*, 25 August 1996, 34.

24. Washington *Times*, 26 February 1993 (courtesy of Cathleen Shrader); *New York Times*, 24 February 1993; Boston *Globe*, 24 June 1996.

25. Woodward, *The Choice*, 129–32.

26. Montgomery *Advertiser*, 26 June 1996; Durham *Herald-Sun*, 26 June 1996; Houston *Chronicle*, 2 July 1996; *New York Times*, 27 June 1996; *Los Angeles Times*, 17 October 1996; Philip Terzian, associate editor of the Providence *Journal-Bulletin*, in New Orleans *Times-Picayune*, 29 June 1996; Fresno *Bee*, 30 June 1996; Pittsburgh *Post-Gazette*, 28 June 1996.

27. *Los Angeles Times*, 25 June 1996; *Palm Beach Post*, 6 October 1996; Washington *Post*, 3 May 1997.

28. Richmond *Times-Dispatch*, 21 November 1994: *Los Angeles Times*, 17 October 1996. Joan Hoff has pointed out the ways in which the two presidential wives differed. Unlike Hillary Clinton, Eleanor Roosevelt had established an independent political base and hence her position did not derive wholly from her husband's status, and unlike the current First Lady, she was not an avowed feminist, though, Hoff added, 'Mrs. Clinton's feminism, while more apparent, is compromised by her "stand by my man" public persona and male-oriented careerism'. Joan Hoff to the Editor, 19 January 1996, in *New York Times*, 22 January 1996.

29. John Nichols in Madison *Capital Times*, 2 July 1996.

30. Washington *Post*, 21 July 1996; Gavin Esler, 'Hail Bill! Vote-Stealer Supreme', *New Statesman*, 9 August 1996, 16. Stephen Hess at the Brookings Institution said: 'I don't understand him. Most of us still would like the real Bill Clinton to stand up. He's infinitely better at campaigning than at governing ... There are a lot of parallels with Franklin Roosevelt in terms of his political agility, but FDR had stronger core values.' Fresno *Bee*, 25 August 1996.

31. Boston *Globe*, 24 September 1996; *Newsday*, 10 November 1996. Asked 'What would you want historians to say about your record in the White House?' Clinton listed among his achievements: 'ending welfare as we know it'. *Northwest Arkansas Times*, 1 November 1996.

32. Robert Kuttner, 'A Liberal Dunkirk?' *American Prospect* (November-December 1996), 8–9. 'The very phrase, New Democrat', Kuttner pointed out, 'suggested there was something fatally wrong with old Democrats'.

33. Jonathan Alter, 'Bully or Woolly?' *Newsweek*, 18 November 1996, 26; Chattanooga *Free Press*, 26 April 1997; Chicago *Tribune*, 20 January 1997; *New York Times*, 19 January 1997.

34. Boston *Globe*, 19 December 1996; Washington *Post*, 9 June 1937; Raleigh (NC) *News and Observer*, 12 December 1996; Dale McFeatters in *Rocky Mountain News*, 24 March 1997.
35. *New York Times*, 3 May 1997; Hugh Sidey, 'Truth in Memory', *Time*, 20 May 1997, 32; Fresno *Bee*, 3 May 1997; Ruth Conniff, 'The FDR Theme Park', Madison (Wis.) *Isthmus*, 23 May 1997.
36. Richmond *Times Dispatch*, 1 September 1996.
37. Chicago *Tribune*, 18 August 1996; *The Economist*, 28 September 1996, 38.

Appreciation: David Adams

Robert A. Garson

This volume is presented to honour the recent retirement of David Adams, Professor Emeritus of American Studies at Keele University, and founder and former Director of the David Bruce Centre for American Studies at Keele. All the essays had a first airing in the sixth international colloquium of the David Bruce Centre, held at the Roosevelt Study Center, Middelburg, The Netherlands, in June 1997. The colloquium, on the theme of 'The United States in Depression and War', consisted of scholars who were linked in some way or another to Adams. The participants were former departmental and professional colleagues, research students, protégés and some younger scholars, who, while not directly connected, were in some way beneficiaries of the Adams heritage. Other close associates who do not appear as authors in this volume but have worked closely with David Adams include Cornelis van Minnen, Maurizio Vaudagna and Richard Maidment.

David Adams' reputation rests on his missionary spirit as much as on his scholarship. He spent most of his professional life as a campaigner for closer links between Britain and North America and latterly between Britain and continental Europe. These endeavours earned him his well-deserved award in 1997 of the Order of the British Empire. He has served as Chair of British American Associates and Deputy Chairman of Canada United Kingdom Colloquia, an organization dedicated to the holding of major conferences on public issues and characterized by a mix of university, commerce and politics. These meetings reflected David Adams' priorities. Throughout his professional career he has always insisted that academics should not just be talking to each other but serving as conduits to the wider community.

Adams' own scholarship on the Roosevelt years covers a wide range, a range that the contributors to this current volume wish to emulate. He has written essays on Upton Sinclair, British perceptions of the US, Churchill and FDR, and neutrality in the 1930s. He has edited *British Documents on Foreign Affairs: Reports and Papers from the Foreign Office Confidential Print* for the inter-war years, running to some twenty-five volumes, and authored *America in the Twentieth Century*, a textbook that was widely used in the 1960s and 1970s. He has edited seven volumes of essays, three of them in the *European Papers in American History* series.

Professor Adams' work is distinguished by his ability to take fresh looks and ask the most simple, but most puzzling, questions. His skill is that of *agent provocateur*. His work has not been that of the traditional scholar who mines and regurgitates in monograph the minutiae revealed in archival holdings. Rather he has used his famously persuasive manner to convince readers that that they should not shy away from ordinary common sense in their readings of history. So often, he believes, the best explanations stare the scholar in the face.

His writings have certain common themes. He is a Hamiltonian. He believes that constancy, continuity and identifiable authority are essential ingredients of effective leadership – scarcely surprising perhaps from somebody who held the Chair of the American Studies department at Keele for nearly thirty years. In his view the United States did well to have FDR as President for four elected terms.

Adams' earliest work was on Roosevelt's foreign policy. His practice of diplomatic history is in many respects old-fashioned. He did not engage in the liberal/revisionist controversies of the 1960s and 1970s and would probably be bemused by a post-revisionist label. He has a natural and healthy scepticism of the truisms of some of the post-modernists with their preoccupation with structuralism, tropes and contradictory consciousness. Adams does not entertain the idea that liberal politics is inherently imperialistic nor does he believe that hegemony inevitably arises where there is knowledge. Despite his traditionalist methodology Adams does have a sophisticated appreciation of the dynamics of foreign policy. He is all too aware that it is about power, security and markets. Behaviouralism is not for him. The man or the woman makes a difference. It is the interposition of the person that makes the world what it is.

Adams' immersion in the history of the Roosevelt administration is no surprise to anybody who knows him. Roosevelt's famed charm and his relish for diversity and challenges are characteristics with which Adams identifies. He believes that effective leaders make a difference. They thrive most when they can convert diversity and competition into a creative process of decision-making. To Adams, structured and healthy disagreement is at the root of wisdom. Roosevelt's personal achievement was to combine the psychological rush he experienced in the midst of a scrap with an affability that seldom failed to disarm.

These essays serve as a *Festschrift*. The editors and all the contributors hope that they conform in some way to the Adams formula. If they churn a little and still make good sense, they are a fitting swan song.